RESTRICTED

The information given in this document is not to be communicated, either directly or indirectly, to the Press or to any person not authorized to receive it.

Pz Kw VI
(Tiger)

Military College of Science
SCHOOL OF TANK TECHNOLOGY
Chobham Lane   Chertsey

Fully-Restored Edition
with an introduction and commentary by Bruce Oliver Newsome, Ph.D.,
and higher-resolution reproductions of the original images

TANK ARCHIVES PRESS

PzKw. VI Tiger Tank: The Official Wartime Reports

Edited by Bruce Oliver Newsome, Ph.D.
www.BruceNewsome.com

Find bonus chapters and photographs at:
www.patreon.com/bruceolivernewsome

This reproduction includes copies of pages from wartime printings, with some of the original blemishes and anomalies.

Published by: Tank Archives Press, PO Box 181802, Coronado, CA 92178, United States of America

Copyright © 2020 Tank Archives Press

All rights reserved. No part of this publication may be reproduced or stored in a retrieval system or transmitted, in any form or by any means, electronic, mechanical, photocopying, recording or otherwise, without prior permission in writing from Tank Archives Press.

HIS027100	HISTORY / Military / World War II
HIS027240	HISTORY / Military / Vehicles
NHWR7	Second World War
NHWL	Modern warfare
JWMV	Military vehicles
JWKF	Military Intelligence

ISBN: 978-1-951171-04-9

Acknowledgements

The editor wishes to thank:

- Colin Alford, Canadian Armed Forces
- Rebecca Eveleigh, Ingram Content Group
- John R. Fisher, Curator, Base Borden Military Museum, Canada
- David Fletcher, Historian, Tank Museum
- Ed Francis, independent armoured vehicle historian
- Lyndsey Hardy, Lightning Source
- Jonathan Holt, Archives Assistant, Tank Museum
- Sheldon Rogers, Archives Assistant, Tank Museum
- Katie Thompson, Archives Assistant, Tank Museum
- Stuart Wheeler, Archives Manager, Tank Museum
- David Willey, Curator, Tank Museum

All photographs are courtesy of the Bundesarchiv (Germany), Tank Museum (Britain), and Bruce Oliver Newsome.

CONTENTS

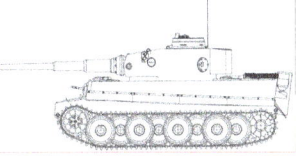

Editor's Introduction	4
What is Tiger 131?	4
How was Tiger 131 captured?	4
What happened to Tiger 131 after capture?	5
How did Tiger 131 get to Britain?	6
What happened to Tiger 131 in Britain?	6
Preliminary Report (November 1943)	7
Foreword	8
General Specification	11
General Construction	12
Armour	13
Armament	14
Ammunition Carried	15
Observation	16
Pistol Ports	16
Access Doors and Escape Hatches	17
Engine	18
Gearbox and Transmission	21
Steering	22
Final Drive	23
Brakes	23
Suspension	24
Tracks	24
Instruments and Controls	25
Electrical Equipment	25
Fire Fighting Equipment	26
Ventilation	26
Deep Wading and Submersion	26
Elevation Drawings	29
General Description (Part 1) (January 1944)	31
Foreword	32
Introduction	33
General Description	35
Exploded View (colour)	44
Sectional Drawing (colour)	45
Elevation Drawings	46
General Specification	49
Armament (Part 2, Section I) (February 1944)	55
Introduction	57
8.8 cm Gun and Mounting	58
Co-Axial Machine-Gun	63
Auxiliary Machine-Gun	64
Sights	64
Fire Control	66
Auxiliary Armament	67
Ammunition	68
Appendix: Elevation Scale	72
Fighting Arrangements (Part 2, Section II) (February)	73
Introduction	75
Fighting Chamber	76
Vision	77
Stowage (Part 2, Section III) (February 1944)	79
Introduction	81
Internal Stowage	82
External Stowage	83
Equipment Table (translation)	84
Addenda to Part 2; Gunnery Trials (November 1944)	89
Introduction	91
8.8 cm Gun and Mounting	92
Co-Axial Machine-Gun	93
Sights	93
Fire Control	93
Auxiliary Armament	94
Ammunition	94
Fighting Arrangements	96
Vision	96
Gunnery Trials	100
Stowage	104
Plans and Sections	105
Engine: General Description (Part 4, Section I) (September 1944)	113
Introduction	115
Leading Data	116
Sections	117
General Description	120
Design	120
Engine: Detailed Description (Part 4, Section II) (no date)	121
Crankcase and Cylinder Blocks	123
Engine Mounting	126
Cylinder Heads	127
Pistons	129
Connecting Rods	131
Crankshaft	132
Valves and Valve Gear	135
Timing and Auxiliary Drive Gear	139
Lubrication System	140
Sectional Drawings	141
Exploded Drawing (colour)	143
Engine Cooling System	147
Water Pump	147
Dynamo (Part 4, Section V) (April 1944)	149
Introduction	151
General Description	152
Constructional Details	153
Test Results	154
Inertia Starter (Part 4, Section VI) (March 1944)	157
Introduction	159
Principle of Operation	161
Method of Construction	163
Data	166
Automatic Fire Extinguisher (Part 9, Section I) (January 1944)	167
Introduction	169
Principal of Operation	170
Method of Construction	171
Ventilation (Part 9, Section II) (September 1944)	173
References	176
Normal Running	176
Submerged Running	178
Three-Dimensional Section (colour)	179

INTRODUCTION

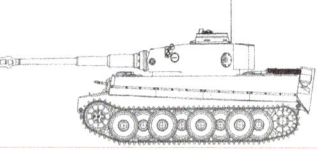

Welcome to the first new edition of the official reports on Tiger 131 since the Second World War, reconstructed after consulting all surviving copies, and fully restored with higher-resolution images than were available for the original printing. These reports reveal what the Allies knew, as they discovered it. The reports also reveal the facts to counter the propaganda and myths that have accumulated in subsequent history books.

What is Tiger 131?

Tiger 131 is the most famous tank in the world: the first of its type recovered to Britain; the most studied and photographed tank in Allied intelligence; and the only running Tiger in the world today.

The type was the product of a long programme by that name, with several projects. In fact, the programme produced two different models of tank named "Tiger." The other type was a losing bid by Ferdinand Porsche: he produced at least one pilot tank and one full-production tank in the programme, plus another 90 hulls that were converted into self-propelled guns. Both types were designated as *Panzerkampfwagen VI*, meaning "armoured fighting vehicle" or "tank," sixth model. The two types were differentiated by parenthesizing their respective design authorities/assemblers. Thus, the Porsche Tiger was abbreviated as "PzKw. VI(P)." The winning type, supplied by Henschel, was abbreviated as "PzKw. VI(H)." The War Office's section for technological intelligence (MI10) read about a Tiger in decrypted signals in September 1942, and confirmed it in January on the battlefield, but did not learn about the Porsche until about May 1943. In December 1943, MI10 reported a captured document, indicating a change of designation to "PzKw. Tiger, Model E." This explains British amendments, by hand, of the titles of their official reports, from "H" to "E" (as indicated in the table opposite). However, in May 1945, Henschel's chief research engineer told them that the "E" was used exclusively by the Weapons Office.

The particular tank brought to Britain was accepted from Henschel by the German Army in February 1943. It was immediately issued to 504th *schwere Panzer Abteilung* (Heavy Tank Battalion), which was still incomplete and in transition to Tunisia, where the Germans had intervened to forestall the Western Allied invasion in November 1942. The unit numbered the tank using a convention common to German tank units of the time: the numbers "131" refer to the 1st Company, 3rd Platoon/Troop, first tank of the platoon (normally the platoon commander's mount).

How was Tiger 131 captured?

Tiger 131 was already a battle-scarred veteran before, on 23rd April, it responded to a British attack on a close collection of eight hills, overlooking the highway to Tunis and the Medjerda River. The evidence suggests it was the only Tiger committed. For two days, it fought parts of four battalions of Churchill tanks and six battalions of infantry.

It was abandoned late in the day of 24th April, in a position from where it had commanded the road across the tallest of the hills (identified on wartime maps by its summit, in metres, as Point 174). Prior damage had left the turret traverse and gun elevation sticky and inconsistent; the final straw was surely a freak shot that buckled the roof over the driver's head and jammed the turret. The Germans likely intended to recover the tank if the hill could be recaptured, or to demolish it if recovery were impossible, but they never had another chance. British infantry occupied the summit, under artillery and air attack, until the final Allied offensive started on 6th May. Hours later, engineers arrived to recover Tiger 131.[1]

(Right) Tiger 131, as differentiated by the step welded to the nose and the filled apertures above the driver's visor, takes a track in April 1943. This is the only known German photograph of Tiger 131. It proves extensive damage from high-explosive shells: the top-most smoke discharger on the turret's left side is missing; and the cupola, upper edge of the turret, mantlet, and driver's plate are scarred, particularly to the main armament's left and in its shadow.

1. See: Bruce Oliver Newsome, The Tiger Tank and Allied Intelligence, Volume III, Tiger 131: From Africa to Europe, Coronado, California: Tank Archives Press, 2020.

Volume title	Part		Section		Author	Publisher	Date
	No.	Title	No.	Title			
	Preliminary Report No. 19: PzKw VI (Tiger)				Major A.D. Lidderdale (REME)	School of Tank Technology (part of the Military College of Science)	November 1943
Report on PzKw VI (Tiger) Model H [on most copies the "H" is crossed out by hand and replaced by "E"]	1	General Description			Major J.D. Barnes (RTR) and Mr. D.M. Pearce (STT)		January 1944
	2	Armament, Fighting Arrangements, Stowage, and Power Traverse	1	Armament	Lieutenant P.L. Gudgin (RTR)		February 1944
			2	Fighting Arrangements			February 1944
			3	Stowage	Gudgin, plus Major Shaw (RTR; DTD)		February 1944
				Addenda to Sections I, II, and III, and Report on Gunnery Trials	Major W. de L. Messenger (RTR; Experimental Wing, Gunnery School)		November 1944 (gunnery reports: 17th March; 14th April)
	4	Power Plant	1	General Description of Engine	Major J.D. Barnes (RTR), Mr. D.M. Pearce (STT), and Lieutenant G. Boyd (RAC)		September 1944
			2	Detailed Description of Engine	(none given)		(none given)
			5	Electrical Equipment (Engine): Bosch Dynamo	Major J.D. Barnes (RTR) and Mr. D.M. Pearce (STT)		April 1944
			6	Bosch Inertia Starter			March 1944
	9	Special Devices and Equipment	1	Automatic Fire Extinguisher			January 1944
			2	Ventilation	Major J.D. Barnes (RTR), Mr. D.M. Pearce, and G. Boyd (RAC)		September 1944

(Above) This table summarizes the official reports on Tiger 131 produced during the Second World War. The gaps in numbering betray reports that were planned but never produced. The dates are taken from each report's introduction, rather than the title page, which is often dated earlier. Perhaps each title page was printed with a scheduled date, before the content was delivered. Even the introductions are unreliable: in some cases, the reports were released as enclosures to communications dated a couple months later. The absence of a plan, a contents page, and page numbers adds to the uncertainty. All surviving copies, from Britain to North America, were consulted in order to make this restoration.

What happened to Tiger 131 after capture?

Tiger 131 was recovered by the workshop that was serving the same two brigades of Churchill tanks that had fought against it. This workshop was operating in the open air on a small plain a few miles south-west of the battlefield. Here it restored Tiger 131 to working order, although without proper documentation. Automotively, Tiger 131 seems to have needed little more than fluids. Turret control was partially restored by working out the burr on the turret ring. The main structural repair was a welded plug in the buckled hull roof. The damaged hatches in the turret and the missing smoke discharger were replaced with parts salvaged from other Tigers. The kinetic damage to the wheels, track guards, turret stowage bin, and centrifugal air cleaners was never repaired.

The restoration was probably scheduled around a visit on 14th May by the commander of 1st Army and some technicians from the regional commands. At the same time, an Army Film and Photographic Unit filmed Tiger 131 running around a cross-country course and posing behind cover. The film was used to train soldiers in recognition of the type, but also to propagandize its supposed flaws.

Tiger 131 spent the rest of May corralled with other captured equipment for casual inspection by personnel camped nearby or passing through. On 24th May, it was driven to Tunis for display. Its visitors there included the British Prime Minister (Winston Churchill) and the principal British civilian and military decision-makers (2nd June), and King George VI (18th June).

(Right) Churchill, Anthony Eden (Foreign Secretary, under dark hat), General Harold Alexander (18th Army Group, behind gun), Field-Marshal Alan Brooke (Chief of the Imperial General Staff, on turret, behind Alexander), and Lieutenant-General Kenneth Anderson (1st Army, next to Brooke) descend the front of Tiger 131. This photograph gives a close view of the emblems painted in late May: 1st Army's shield was painted in white, with the red cross of St. George and a sword; 25th Tank Brigade's sign consisted of two black triangles opposed vertically. The same emblems were painted on the left (nearside) rear mudguard.

How did Tiger 131 get to Britain?

Technicians had urged home authorities to get Tiger 131 to Britain since May, but it waited months for shipping, with no priority. The only advantage of this delay was that more time was available for the collection of equipment for testing in Britain. This collection was performed by Major A. Douglas Lidderdale (REME: Royal Electrical and Mechanical Engineers), who had commanded the workshop that had recovered, restored, and exhibited the tank, but was now dissolved. He also used the time to draft a report that would form the basis for the official "Preliminary Report" in this volume.

Tiger 131 was transferred between various inappropriate ports and ships until it finally left Tunisian waters on 20th September, resting atop a cargo of iron ore. After one stop in Gibraltar, on 8th October it reached the cargo's destination – Glasgow, which is as far as any British port from the tank's destination.

What happened to Tiger 131 in Britain?

The equipment reached the Department of Tank Design (DTD) at Chobham Heath in Surrey on 19th October; Tiger 131 itself, and Lidderdale, reached the School of Tank Technology (STT) at Chobham on the next day. Both were departments of the Ministry of Supply; they would now co-operate in the exploitation of Tiger 131, but in a distracted and chaotic way that lasted into 1945, still without completion.

Lidderdale authored the preliminary report in November 1943, while the tank was photographed and drawn. For the new edition, now in your hands, the originals of these beautiful and accurate images are reproduced at higher resolution than in the original wartime reports, which were printed on poor quality paper.

Unfortunately, no plan has survived for the investigation, although clearly the reporters were working to a plan, such that some part numbers and section numbers were reserved for reports that were never completed. Some reports seem to have been commissioned opportunistically: for instance, an inertia starter was the first automotive part to be reported, even though the engine, gearbox, and steering had been identified in Tunisia as most advanced.

By then, DTD and STT were preoccupied with development and trials of Allied tanks and variants in time for the invasion of North-West Europe in June 1944. This helps to explain the use of junior authors, whose affiliations were given as RTR (Royal Tank Regiment) or RAC (Royal Armoured Corps), not technical branches.

Meanwhile, Tiger 131 was again diverted for political and propagandistic purposes. On 15th November, it was carried to London for another audience with the Prime Minister and entourage, even though he had quietly travelled overseas already. Then it left on a tour of British cities as part of a campaign to raise funds for the war effort, before returning to Chobham a few days before 1944, by when its guardians were on leave. Lidderdale then started a new assignment, and never worked again on Tigers or any technical intelligence.

STT published its first internal reports in January, including some by Lieutenant Peter Gudgin. He was awaiting a course at STT, after being invalided home from Tunisia. Although he did not claim so at the time, decades later, after retirement, he claimed that Tiger 131 was the Tiger that had knocked out his tank and hospitalized him in his first battle. He amended Lidderdale's documents to re-locate the place of recovery to conform with his own battle, he re-captioned photographs, and he influenced the Tank Museum to paint out the emblems associated with its real captors, and to credit his own unit and brigade. These false attributions marred his and the Tank Museum's books on Tiger 131 (published as recently as 2011), which included some excerpts from the official reports.

Thus, a new edition of the wartime reports is long overdue: uncorrupted, uncensored, and restored to higher resolution than the original print run. These same reports and images are still consulted by the staff at the Tank Museum who keep Tiger 131 in complete and working order. I dedicate this volume to them.

RESTRICTED

The information given in this document is not to be communicated, either directly or indirectly, to the Press or to any person not authorized to receive it.

PRELIMINARY REPORT N° 19
Pz Kw VI
(Tiger)

[Editor's note: This "Preliminary Report" was numbered consecutively after 18 prior preliminary reports on other types of captured vehicle. Thus, the number "19" bears no relation to the ordinal numbers used in other reports on Tiger 131. This report is, in fact, the first of the official reports on Tiger 131.]

Military College of Science
SCHOOL OF TANK TECHNOLOGY
Chobham Lane   Chertsey

November 1943

FOREWORD

This vehicle is a well armoured tank of sound construction designed to carry an 8.8 cm. gun in a fully traversing turret. It has deep wading facilities and a limited underwater performance to a depth of approximately 15 feet. This feature is worthy of special note as it is an essential part of the basic vehicle design.

The introduction of plate interlocking in addition to the normal stepped jointing is a distinct development in German A.F.V. construction. It must, however, be remembered that hitherto no German vehicle has carried armour of greater thickness than 50 mm, whereas the bulk of the armour of the Pz. Kw. VI is of 62, 82 and 102 mm. thickness.

Against the tank's tactical advantages, derived mainly from its armament it incorporates some important disadvantages, the most outstanding being the restriction on transportation due to its width and weight, and its limited climbing ability due to the small height of the centre line of the front sprocket above the ground. A further serious disadvantage is its restricted radius of action, due to its small petrol tank capacity and heavy consumption, stated by the enemy to be 2.75 galls. per mile on normal cross-country running. Against this must be offset the feelings of the crew, who have a good sound tank, able to outrange any it has met, roomy, and with comfortable positions for all. Driving, in particular, is a pleasure, and the gunner's layout as convenient as he could wish.

[Editor's notes: These photographs were printed without captions. Both were taken in May 1943 on the plain being used by Lidderdale's workshops, south of Medjez-el-Bab. Above, Tiger 131 is facing west, so that the rising sun is lighting its left side. The top hatches are closed but the stowage bin lid is open. In the background is a Churchill tank and a scout vehicle. The furthest elevated ground on the horizon is nearly 10 miles (16 km) away. Medjez-el-Bab is hidden in the low ground just 2.5 miles (4 km) away.

Below, Tiger 131 is being driven by Lidderdale himself, on its first test run, according to a caption in his own album. The date is some day between 7th May, when he towed it in, and 14th May, when he demonstrated it to its first official audience. The location is just south of the previous photograph. Indeed, Tiger 131 is returning to the workshop area.

The image overleaf was based on a photograph taken at STT in November 1943. There, a print was painted to remove the background, accentuate the tank's features, and smooth its areas of shadow and shine, before the touched-up print was copied for printing in this idealized style. For authenticity, the image is reproduced here as printed in the original report.]

PRELIMINARY REPORT

ON

Pz.Kw. VI (MODEL 'H')

(Ex North Africa)

STT/8/2/11

EXAMINED AT CHOBHAM   D.T.D. PROJECT NO. 3016   NOVEMBER, 1943

EXAMINER: MAJOR A.D. LIDDERDALE, A.M.I.Mech.E., R.E.M.E.

GENERAL SPECIFICATION

TYPE   Pz. Kpf. Wg. VI H. Model H.1.
Tank No. 131. Chassis No. 250122. Turret No. 230639

ARMAMENT   One 8.8 cm. tank gun KwK. 36 and one 7.92 M.G. 34 co-axial in turret.
One M.G. 34 in superstructure front plate.
One 9 mm. machine carbine stowed.

ARMOUR   26 - 102 mm. (There is local thickening of the gun mantlet to 110 mm.).

WEIGHT   As received on narrow tracks: 50 tons 5 cwts.
(Less crew of five, their kit and rations, and with petrol tanks half full and half complement of ammunition).
Estimated weight in battle order is therefore: 56 tons.

MAXIMUM SPEED   No accurate figure available but 18 m.p.h. recorded.

CREW   Five - Commander: Gunner: Loader: Hull Gunner — Wireless operator: Driver.

DIMENSIONS

Length (excluding gun)	20' 8½"
" (including gun at 12 o'clock)	27' 9"
Width (overall)	12' 3"
Height	9' 4¾"
Ground Contact	12' 6"
Track Centres	9' 3½"

ENGINE   Maybach V. 12 cyl. 650 metric H.P. (642 British B.H.P.)

GEARBOX   Maybach Olvar - Preselector - hydraulically operated.

STEERING   Controlled differential - hydraulically operated by steering wheel.
For emergency steering - steering levers operate vehicle brakes independently.

DRIVE   Front sprockets.

SUSPENSION   Torsion bar. Sixteen single and four twin bogies on each side giving a total of 24 tyres.
When narrow track is fitted - eight twin and four single bogies on each side.

TRACKS   Manganese steel 4/4 lugs.

CONDITION

The general condition of the vehicle is reasonably good both structurally and mechanically.

Heavy frontal attack is in evidence at the front of the vehicle. An oblique hit which registered at 12 o'clock on the superstructure top plate has fractured the lateral weld along the centre of the plate. The round struck the turret ring joint damaging the pneumatic sealing tube and jamming the turret traverse. The blow on the top front plate also resulted in the complete disintegration of the wireless set.

There are no penetrations of the armour although the vehicle has been subjected to heavy fire, the front vertical plate and the turret front being considerably scarred. Apart from a minor defect in the starting apparatus the vehicle was in good mechanical condition when received in this country.

1. GENERAL CONSTRUCTION

Hull - the construction of the hull departs from the familiar German practice in that the front and rear superstructures are in one unit and the whole is welded to the lower hull. Interlocking stepped joints secured by welding are used in the construction of both the lower hull and superstructure. A pannier is formed over each track by the extension of the superstructure. This space is continued from the front vertical plate to the tail plate.

The top front plate covers the full width of the panniers thus providing a horizontal seating 10' 4" wide upon which the turret ring is mounted. It is this exceptional width which enables the turret ring of 6' 1" internal diameter to be fitted.

The belly of the hull is formed of one 26 mm. plate measuring 5' 11" x 15' 10$\frac{1}{4}$".

The hull is divided into four compartments. The forward compartment on the nearside accommodates the driver and his controls. A centrally disposed gearbox to the front of which the steering unit is mounted, separates the driving compartment from the offside forward compartment in which the hull gunner is seated.

The third compartment, the fighting chamber, occupies the central portion of the hull and is separated from the rear engine compartment by a bulkhead and from the forward compartments by an arched cross member. The floor of the fighting compartment is suspended from and rotates with the turret.

Turret - The turret is centrally mounted between the hull side plates with the centre of the turret ring approximately 6$\frac{1}{2}$" to the rear of the transverse centre line of the vehicle.

The vertical sides and rear are formed by the bending into horseshoe form of a single 82 mm. plate. The toe of the horseshoe forms the rear of the turret whilst the extremities at the front are tied in by two 100 mm. rectangular section bars which are dovetailed and welded to the main plate. The upper and lower edges of the sides converge towards the front in order to allow movement of the gun mantlet when the gun is elevated or depressed.

The roof of the turret consists of a single rolled plate of 26 mm. bent slightly forward of the centre line to suit the taper of the side plate at the front. The roof plate is recessed into and welded to the turret wall.

The main trunnions which are of spherical type are mounted in the turret sides and carry an external robust cast steel mantlet and the gun cradle. Removal of the complete mantlet and gun cradle can be effected by the removal of four set bolts. The mantlet projects over the side plates and affords adequate protection for the open front of the turret. The trunnions are extended outwards to form lifting lugs for the removal of the turret. A further lug is provided at the rear of the turret on the vertical centre line, thus providing correctly balanced three-point slinging.

Cupola - a circular fixed cupola is mounted in the turret roof -- the cupola has an inside diameter of 20" and is offset to the extreme nearside.

2. ARMOUR

		BASIC	EXTRA	ANGLE
A.	Cupola top	15 mm.		90°
B.	" front and sides	50 - 80 mm.		0° Cylindrical
C.	Turret top front	26 mm.		81°
D.	" " rear	26 mm.		90°
E.	" sides	82 mm.		0°
F.	" rear	82 mm.		0°
G.	" front		(local	5°
H.	Gun mantlet	100 - 110	(thick-	Moving
J.	Front vertical plate	102 mm.	(ening	10°
K.	Front glacis plate	61 mm.		80°
L.	Front nose plate	102 mm.		24°
M.	Front lower nose plate	63 mm.	(approx.)	63°
N.	Side superstructure	80 mm.		0°
	Pannier floor	26 mm.		90°
P.	Side hull plate	63 mm.		0°
Q.	Top front plate	26 mm.		90°
R.	Top rear plate	26 mm.		90°
S.	Top rear engine cover plate	26 mm.		90°
U.	Belly plate	26 mm.		90°
W.	Tail plate (upper)	82 mm.		8°

(The "Angle of Plate" given is the angle between the plate surface and the vertical, which is equal to the "Angle of Impact" for horizontal attack).

The cast front plate of the gun mantlet has a thickness of 92 mm. over the full height and breadth. Measured through the gun sight borings the thickness is 100 mm. In the centre portion where the front plate is reinforced around the gun, the thickness is increased to 200 mm. There is no spaced armour or the provision for the fitting of it. The stowage of a spare length of track on the front nose plate adds to the effectiveness of the armour at this point.

There is no face hardened armour. The thin horizontal plates, 26 mm. thick, range from 298 - 343 Brinnel and the thick vertical or near vertical plates range from 257 - 310 Brinnel. The bulk of the plate is not comparable with British standard machineable quality.

Except for the fact that the front vertical plate projects slightly above the top front plate and may afford some protection to the turret ring and the hatches on either side of the top plate, there is no splash protection for the turret ring joint. This is interesting in view of the fact that a pneumatic rubber sealing ring is fitted in this joint.

Deflector bars are fitted at either side of the driver's visor and on the glacis plate immediately in front of it.

3. ARMAMENT

One 8.8 cm. Tank Gun KwK 36)
One 7.92 mm. M.G. 34   )   Co-axial in turret.

One 7.92 mm. M.G. 34   )   In ball mounting on offside of front vertical plate.

One 9 mm. Machine Carbine.

8.8 cm. Tank Gun

The 8.8 cm. gun is approximately 17 feet in length, of which 7 feet overhangs the hull, and it is fitted with a double baffle muzzle brake. The breech, which is of the semi-automatic vertical-falling-block-type, is actuated by the lever breech mechanism at the right of it. It is electrically fired from a control incorporated in the elevating handwheel. An electrical safety device identical to that fitted in the Pz. Kw. III and IV is provided which prevents firing if the breech is not closed, the gun not fully run out, or the buffer not full. An extension to the rear of the gun carries a canvas sack for receiving the ejected cases. A recoil indicator is fixed on the left arm of the frame and shows a maximum normal working recoil of 580 mm. Buffer and recuperator are of orthodox pattern.

The unbalanced weight of the gun is counteracted by a system of levers from the mantlet to a compression cylinder located in the starboard wall of the turret, with a smaller secondary cylinder forward of it.

Sights - to the left of the gun a mounting is provided in the mantlet for the binocular sight which consist of two articulated telescopes of stationary eyepiece type. The eyepieces are offset from the telescopes to permit adjustment of interocular distance. To allow elevation and depression, the graticule box, which moves with the gun mantlet, is hinged to the body of the sight and the eyepiece end is suspended from the turret roof on a hinged link.

A hand lever causes the rotation within the sight of a circular scale, graduated both for 8.8 cm. gun and machine gun, in metres. The rotation of the figures on this scale to coincide with a fixed pointer at 12 o'clock brings about the raising or lowering of the three arrow heads, which remain level with each other whatever their position vertically in relation to the figures around the circumference of the scale. Thus for any given range the sight gives a correct adjustment of elevation for each gun without the gunner losing sight of his target, and requiring only the use of his free left hand.

Elevation - Elevation of the turret guns is by handwheel on the right of the gunner.

$$\left. \begin{array}{l} \text{Maximum Elevation} - 17° \\ \text{Maximum Depression} - 6.5° \end{array} \right\} \text{approx.}$$

On the right of the gunner is a clinometer incorporating an illuminated bubble, the graduations giving 400 mils (22.5°) elevation, and 100 mils (5.625°) depression shown in red. There are in addition, metre graduations from 0 - 8,000 metres.

Traverse - The turret may be traversed through 360° by power or hand. A hand operated lock in the form of a spring loaded plunger which engages co-incident holes in the fixed and moving members of the turret ring locks the turret at 12 o'clock, 6 o'clock or 11.30 o'clock.

The "hour" of traverse is indicated by the now familiar turret position indicator which registers on a dial on the left of the gunner and on a toothed annular ring in the cupola.

Power Traverse - The turret is rotated by engine power, through a hydraulic coupling in which is incorporated the gunner's control for direction and speed of rotation. A small universally jointed shaft driven by a gear in constant mesh with the gearbox input shaft conveys power to a shaft in the base junction. A cone clutch mounted on this shaft is controlled by a lever mounted at the rear of the gearbox on the hull gunner's side. This lever also controls the engagement of the bevel gear in this junction by means of which the power is taken up the vertical centre line of the turret, and so through another pair of bevels to the horizontal input shaft of the hydraulic coupling. A further position of the lever engages the bilge pump, (see Para.19 "Submersion Arrangements"). A hand lever on the hydraulic coupling controls the engagement of a dog clutch on the input shaft. The hydraulic coupling consists of a large cylindrical oil reservoir with filler, level and drain plugs, and containing in separate compartments two eccentric vane oil motors. The rotor on the input side is driven through the shaft and gearing described, whilst the body has horizontal motion from the fully eccentric position on one side to the fully eccentric position on the other (i.e., completely reversing the flow of oil through the assembly). This movement is controlled by a treadle operated by the gunner's foot.

The inlet and outlet flow of oil pass through separate passages in a central stationary spindle which passes through to the other compartment where it forms the centre spindle of the similar eccentric vane motor on the output side. The rotor on the output side is connected through a universally jointed shaft to the turret traverse gearbox. The body of the output motor has a similar horizontal motion giving either the fully eccentric position on one side or a position on the same side but with one half the amount of eccentricity (i.e., two speeds of rotation). This movement is controlled by a lever on the output end of the casting. An overload clutch is incorporated in the traverse gearbox.

It will be observed that all the hydraulic mechanism is carried in the turret and with the removal of the turret no disconnection is required as the vertical drive shaft incorporates a dog clutch at its upper end leaving the base junction in position on the hull floor.

Co-axial M.G. - This is a M.G. 34 mounted to the right of the 8.8 cm. gun in a cradle fixed in a bracket bolted to the rear of the mantlet. It is fired mechanically by a foot operated trigger at the gunner's right foot.

Auxiliary M.G. - The weapon is a M.G. 34 and is carried in a ball mounting with internal moving mantlet, on the offside of the front vertical plate.

The sighting of the gun is by telescope of orthodox German design. The gun is fired by hand by its own trigger.

Smoke - Six smoke candles are carried, three each side of the turret, each in a discharger cup 9 cm. diameter by 15 cm. long. The front discharger cup is pointed forward and slightly outwards, 2 and 3 are set on progressively lower elevation and progressively greater angles. They are fired electrically by three buttons in a small box set in the turret roof each side of the commander's seat.

4. **AMMUNITION CARRIED**

8.8 cm.

Two types of ammunition were found in this vehicle, APCBCHE and HE. Both have electric primers. The cartridge cases are marked "8.8 cm. Flak 18" and "8.8 cm. 39St" respectively.

A total of 92 rounds of 8.8 cm. may be stowed as follows:

Fighting Compartment

	Rounds
Stowed horizontally in 2 bins forward at each side each holding 16 rounds	64
Stowed horizontally on floor in 2 bins at each side each holding 4 rounds.	16
Stowed horizontally in bin under floor	6
Stowed in bin in pannier alongside driver	6
Total	92

7.92 mm.

Details of the quantity and disposition of S.A.A. carried will be given in a subsequent report.

5. OBSERVATION

Cupola - The commander is provided with five horizontal slits giving all round vision. The slits are equally spaced around the cupola and measure $7\frac{1}{4}$" x $\frac{5}{8}$". No shutters are provided for these visors - a sighting strip is fitted to the foremost visor.

Turret - In addition to the binocular sight the turret gunner's vision comprises a vision slit at 10 o'clock in the nearside turret wall. No external B.P flap is provided.

A similar vision slit is provided in the offside wall of the turret at approximately 2 o'clock for use by the loader.

Hull - The driver's visor which is mounted in the front vertical plate on the nearside, is of single slitted type. It has a sliding shutter, moving vertically and operated by a handwheel, easily accessible from the driver's position. In addition the driver has a fixed non-adjustable episcope mounted in his access hatch in the superstructure roof which is aimed forward at 30° to the nearside of the tank's longitudinal centre line. A strip of 15 mm. plate, of inverted channel section, welded to the hatch cover, ffords some protection to the episcope.

It is noted with interest that in this vehicle the apertures over the driver's visor for the "KFF 2" episcope have been plugged by welding.

In addition to the M.G. sight, the hull gunner is provided with a fixed episcope in the access hatch immediately above him.

The instrument is of identical pattern to that in the driver's hatch and is aimed forward at 30° to the offside of the centre line of the tank.

All vision slits are fitted with readily removable laminated glass blocks.

6. PISTOL PORTS

A pistol port is provided at 8 o'clock in the nearside turret wall. The port is formed in a heavy circular plate bolted to the turret wall. It may be opened or closed by the rotation of an internal disc with a similar slot.

A detachable sealing clamp is carried in the vehicle equipment to render this port watertight for submersion.

ACCESS DOORS AND ESCAPE HATCHES

In general the access doors and escape hatches in the vehicle appear to be well placed and of reasonable size.

Their disposition and purpose is given hereunder:

Cupola - a circular hatch with an inside diameter of $18\frac{1}{4}$" is provided for the use of the Commander and gunner. The cover is of 15 mm. plate and is hinged at approximately 2 o'clock. It is secured by three cockspur latches from the inside and may be locked from outside the vehicle by a square key operating a separate turnbuckle. A spring loaded catch is provided to retain the door in the open position. A compensating device consisting of a slotted lever, the spring loaded fulcrum of which is mounted on the cupola top and a trunnion welded to the door which retains the slotted end of the lever. The whole of this mechanism is externally mounted. A rubber sealing ring is fitted in a recess in the door.

Turret - The loader's access hatch is a rectangular opening 14" x 20" in the offside front of the turret roof. The hatch cover is hinged at its leading edge and is formed by the hot pressing of 15 mm. plate. The hatch is secured by four bolts which are placed diagonally on the door and are operated by a central lever. Sealing of the hatch for submersion is achieved by the fitting of a rubber seal and a central clamping screw which applies leverage to the securing bolts.

A catch is provided to retain the door in a slightly open position. A vertical rim formed at the sides and rear of the hatch frame affords some protection when the door is thus adjusted.

Complete closure of the door is delayed by the fitting of an enclosed compression spring on the turret roof - The spring is compressed when a plunger is engaged by an arm mounted on the door.

A circular escape hatch of $15\frac{1}{2}$" diameter is provided at the offside rear of the turret. The hatch cover of 82 mm. plate is hinged at 6 o'clock and secured by a heavy vertical bar and two hand screws.

Superstructure - A circular hatch of 19" diameter is fitted in each side of the superstructure top plate forward of the turret. These are for use by the driver and hull gunner. The hatch covers are hinged at their outside edges and their closure is retarded by similar compensating mechanism to that on the cupola hatch, but mounted internally.

A spring loaded catch is fitted to retain the doors in a half-open position. The doors are secured by three bolts operated from a central lever. Three independent clamps are carried in the vehicle equipment for sealing the doors for submersion.

A fixed episcope is mounted in each of these hatches (See para. 5 "Observation").

Access to the engine compartment is provided by a rectangular door in the rear engine cover plate measuring 3' 8" x 3' 6". The door is hinged to the rear and is secured by four heavy turnbuckle latches operated by a square key. There are in addition six screw clamps for sealing the door for submersion. These are operated by a key with an internal square. A rubber seal is inset in the frame in which the door is seated. An air inlet slit and a mushroom ventilator are provided in the cover.

Heavy grilled plates are fitted over the radiators and fan assemblies on each side of the engine. These are hinged and secured by recessed Allen screws.

8. ENGINE

The engine is centrally mounted at the rear of the tank with the flywheel end forward. Circular rubber mountings which surround the front and rear crankshaft bearings are used. Engine torque is transmitted through the forward mounting.

Maker	Maybach	Model	H.L. 210 P.45
Engine No.	46064		
Type	$60°V$ 12 cylinder petrol		
Rating	650 Metric H.P. (642 British B.H.P.)		

The aluminium crank case and cylinder block casting houses a circular web crank shaft in seven roller bearings. The cylinder liners are of the wet type having two rubber sealing rings, with the usual drain hole between them. At the top, a flange recessed into the cylinder block gives the necessary location and a slight spigot stands up into the combustion chamber. Pistons are of aluminium and are carried on steel connecting rods machined all over and forked to permit left and right banks to share the same journal. An interesting feature of design noted here is that the web of the "H" section of the forked connecting rod is in line with the crankshaft. The forked rod carries a bearing shell which bears on the full length of the crank pin and receives on its outside diameter the unforked rod from the opposite bank. The big-end nuts are serrated on their circumference instead of being hexagonal.

The camshaft and all auxiliaries are driven by straight spur timing wheels from the opposite end of the crank shaft to the flywheel, which is of steel, machined all over and with starter ring teeth machined on it. There is no detachable starter ring. A normal torsional oscillation damper is fitted at the timing end of the crankshaft outside the crank case.

The cylinder heads, which are of cast iron, and one to each bank have hemispherical combustion chambers.

Valves
Two valves, one inlet and one exhaust are provided for each cylinder. They are operated by a single overhead camshaft to each bank through the medium of rockers. Each rocker is a steel stamping and is mounted upon an eccentric bush, the rotation of which enables tappet clearance to be adjusted. The bush is locked in the desired position by means of a slotted quadrant attached to it working on a set screw and washer in the rocker pillar. The exhaust valves are sodium cooled, but there are no valve seat inserts.

Carburettors
The aluminium inlet manifold of each cylinder head is mounted in the Vee between the banks. Each mounts two down draught Solex Duplex carburettors, type 52 JFF 2 - 2U 2046. These carburettors are of the twin choke type with exposed jets.

Governor
In each inlet manifold a longitudinal shaft controlled by the engine governor carries a butterfly opposite each carburettor butterfly, thus completely over riding the driver. The governor is of the centrifugal type driven from the timing gears and incorporated in the drive to the water pump. The inlet manifolds have drain holes to deal with excess wet fuel.

Air Cleaners
Carburettor air is drawn from the engine compartment, having first passed through two centrifugal pre-cleaners via flexible trunks and thence via a breeches pipe through three oil bath type cleaners which are mounted immediately above the carburettors.

The pre-cleaners are of the vertical tube type with tangential intakes at the sides and the outlet at the top. The oil bath cleaners are of orthodox pattern with annular gauze element.

Petrol Pumps

Four Solex mechanical type petrol pumps each incorporating a bowl type filter are mounted at the nearside rear of the engine. An electric pump is provided for priming. A manual priming pump is mounted on the fighting compartment bulkhead and supplies fuel direct to the inlet manifold.

Exhaust

The exhaust manifolds which are mounted on the outside of each bank are of cast iron and each deals with three cylinders. The rear manifold on each side is spigotted into the leading one. A sheet metal outer cover runs the full length of the engine on each side to provide an air duct for manifold cooling. Two silencers are vertically mounted on the tail plate. Hinged flaps are fitted to their outlets which are normally secured in the open position but are closed for submersion.

Fuel Tanks

There are four petrol tanks, two at each side of the engine compartment. The top tank in each side is of wedge shape and the lower is rectangular. The total capacity of the tanks is approximately 125 gallons.

The tanks on each side are coupled, the upper wedge shaped tanks feeding the lower by gravity. The filler caps are accessible on each side by the removal of a circular B.P. screwed cover. An asbestos screen is fitted to the engine side of each rectangular tank.

Cooling

Water - Radiators, centrifugal pump and four fans.

Ignition

The cylinder head of each bank carries a 6 cylinder Bosch magneto, driven by a spur pinion and idler from the camshaft timing wheel. These magnetos have an automatic advance and retard device which enables the rotating magnets to flick over in a retarded position below normal engine tick over revs. This produces a fat spark no matter how slowly the engine is turning over. The ignition leads pass through a short screened hose direct from magneto to cylinder head cover of each bank, thus reducing to the minimum the amount of screening required.
Totally enclosed 14 mm. Bosch sparking plugs are fitted, one per cylinder.

Starters

Two starters are fitted - one electric and one inertia. The Bosch 24V axial motor is mounted on the starboard side of the engine at the forward end and immediately above it a Bosch hand operated inertia starter, also of the axial type. The hand crank for the inertia starter, is carried in suitable clips on the tail plate, the orifice being covered by a B.P. sealing plate when it is not in use.

Accumulators

The accumulator consists of two 12V 150 amp/hrs batteries stowed on the hull floor astride the propeller shaft immediately ahead of the engine bulkhead.

They are normally connected in parallel but a series/parallel switch permits a change over to 24V for starting.

Radiators

There are two film type radiators mounted transversely at the rear of the engine compartment - one on the near side and one on the offside.

The radiators are coupled and a common filler cap is provided in the nearside unit. A pressure relief valve is mounted on the offside radiator and a balance pipe maintains equal pressure in the two radiators.

Relief valves are fitted in the water inlet and outlets to the engine to avoid air locks when external hot water circuit is in use. The capacity of the water system is approximately 16 gallons.

Water Pump
Water returning from the nearside radiator enters the engine cooling system at an oil/water heat exchanger, mounted at the rear nearside of the engine from which a pipe leads to the water pump. The output from the pump is directed into the cylinder block water jacket from whence it is circulated through the cylinder heads. The outlets from the cylinder heads are coupled and from them the water enters the top of the offside radiator, from the bottom of which it is directed to the top of the nearside radiator.

Fans
A twin fan assembly is mounted transversely at each side of the rear of the engine compartment. The fans are of radial flow type and are mounted in aluminium housings bolted to the radiators. A two speed drive is taken off the timing gears and a short universally jointed shaft carries this drive to the fan drive housing which is mounted on the rear plate of the engine compartment. In this housing the drive is split and taken on each side transversely to each fan assembly through universally jointed shafts. An oil pump is mounted on the housing and supplies oil from the fan drive casing to each fan assembly. The level of the oil in the housing is checked by means of a dipstick accessible when the engine hatch is open and is replenished through a filling orifice in the fixed portion of the engine compartment cover.

Lubrication
The engine sump is dry and a pressure fed lubrication system is used. The pressure pump draws oil from a cannister mounted on the offside of the engine and directs it into a gallery in the crankcase casting, from which it is led off to the cylinder heads and timing gears. The crankshaft receives oil under pressure through a muff which is piped to the pressure gallery. The connection from the oil container to the pressure pump is via oil-ways in the crankcase casting. The scavenge pumps, which are set at opposite ends of the engine, have a common output into the heat exchanger from whence it is returned to the oil cannister. The oil capacity is 28 litres (6.1 gals.)

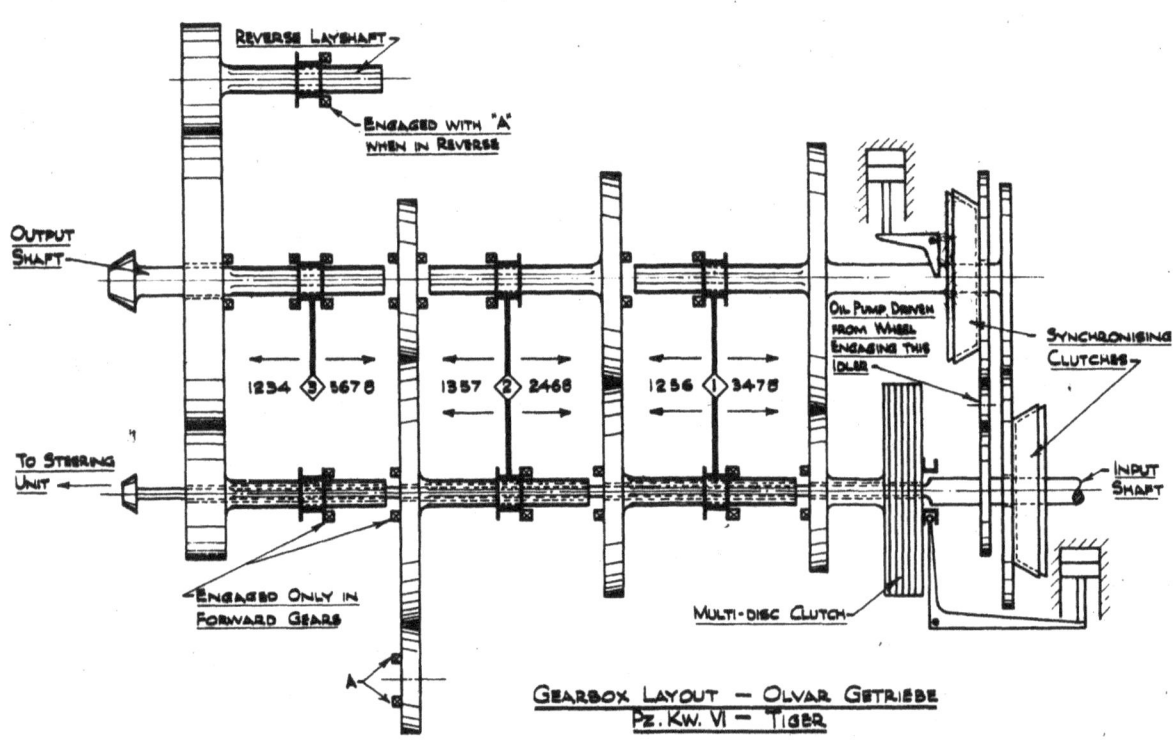

GEARBOX LAYOUT — OLVAR GETRIEBE
Pz. Kw. VI — TIGER

9. GEARBOX AND TRANSMISSION

From the flywheel a universally jointed shaft takes the power to the turret base junction which is used as a centre bearing for the propeller shaft by the mounting of a short shaft in it. This shaft has companion flanges and another universally jointed shaft conveys the power to the gearbox input coupling. The output flanges from the gearbox and steering unit are coupled to the final drive assemblies by short shafts which at their outer ends carry the brake assemblies. These shafts are connected to the companion flanges by muff couplings.

The gearbox is manufactured under "Maybach" license by Olva-Getriebe and provides eight forward speeds and four reverse speeds with pre-selected hydraulic engagement. The gears are arranged on a main shaft, lay shaft and reverse lay shaft, although, in fact, both main shaft and lay shafts consist of four short lengths of shaft each carrying a gear and each able to be engaged or disengaged by a dog clutch. The rearmost dog clutches on both main shaft and lay shafts are controlled by selector forks mounted on a common shaft in such a manner that when one dog is engaged the other is free. The movement of these selector forks is controlled by a double acting hydraulic cylinder mounted on top of the gearbox. Likewise, the central pair is operated by another cylinder. The remaining dog clutch on the lay shaft is operated by a third cylinder, but has engagement with a different gear at each end of its travel thus it has no neutral or free position. The remaining dog clutch on the main shaft and the dog clutch on the reverse are operated together by a hand lever, so that in the forward position of the hand lever the dog on the main shaft is engaged and that on the reverse shaft free, with the exact opposite for the rear position of the hand lever, whilst in the intermediate position of the hand lever both dogs are free. Thus for forward drive, once the hand lever has been placed in the forward position, all changes of gear are effected through the operation of the hydraulic cylinder.

The movement of the gear change lever through its quadrant causes the rotation of a valve which determines the distribution of oil pressure to the appropriate hydraulic cylinder for the ratio required. Side pressure on the gear change lever then admits pressure to that cylinder and affects the gear change.

In reverse the procedure is similar but only the four lowest ratios are available. With the exception of the final output gear and the main shaft and reverse shaft gears meshing with it, all gears are of helical type.

An extension of the input shaft carries a small bevel for controlling the speed of the steering differentials.

At the input end of the main shaft is a multi-disc clutch, which can be disengaged by the admission of hydraulic pressure to a cylinder, the piston of which operates a withdrawal fork. The same withdrawal fork is operated by a clutch pedal. A small cone clutch on the input side of the main shaft and the rear end of the layshaft are geared together and operated by hydraulic pressure giving synchronisation of the lay shaft and engine speeds.

An easily accessible oil filter is provided which serves both gearbox and steering unit which have a common oil level.

A filler cap and a dipstick are provided on the gearbox. The oil capacity is 32 litres (7 galls.).

A metal strip on the gearbox cover bears the following figures:

1 2 3 4 ⟨3⟩ 5 6 7 8   1 3 5 7 ⟨2⟩ 2 4 6 8
    1 2 5 6 ⟨1⟩ 3 4 7 8

which are explained as follows:

The figures within the diamonds correspond to the hydraulic cylinder of each selector. The figures on the left of the diamonds in each case represent the number of the gear engaged with the respective selectors in the forward position. The figures on the right of the diamonds represent the gear engaged with the selectors in the rear position.

The table thus gives the position of each set of selectors for each gear.

The overall ratios from the gearbox input flange to the steering unit output flanges, including bevel reduction on the gearbox output shaft are;

8th	.98 - 1
7th	1.45 - 1
6th	2. 1
5th	3.16 - 1
4th	4.86 - 1
3rd	7.15 - 1
2nd	10.2 - 1
1st	15.4 - 1

The four ratios of reverse correspond to but are lower than the four lowest forward gears.

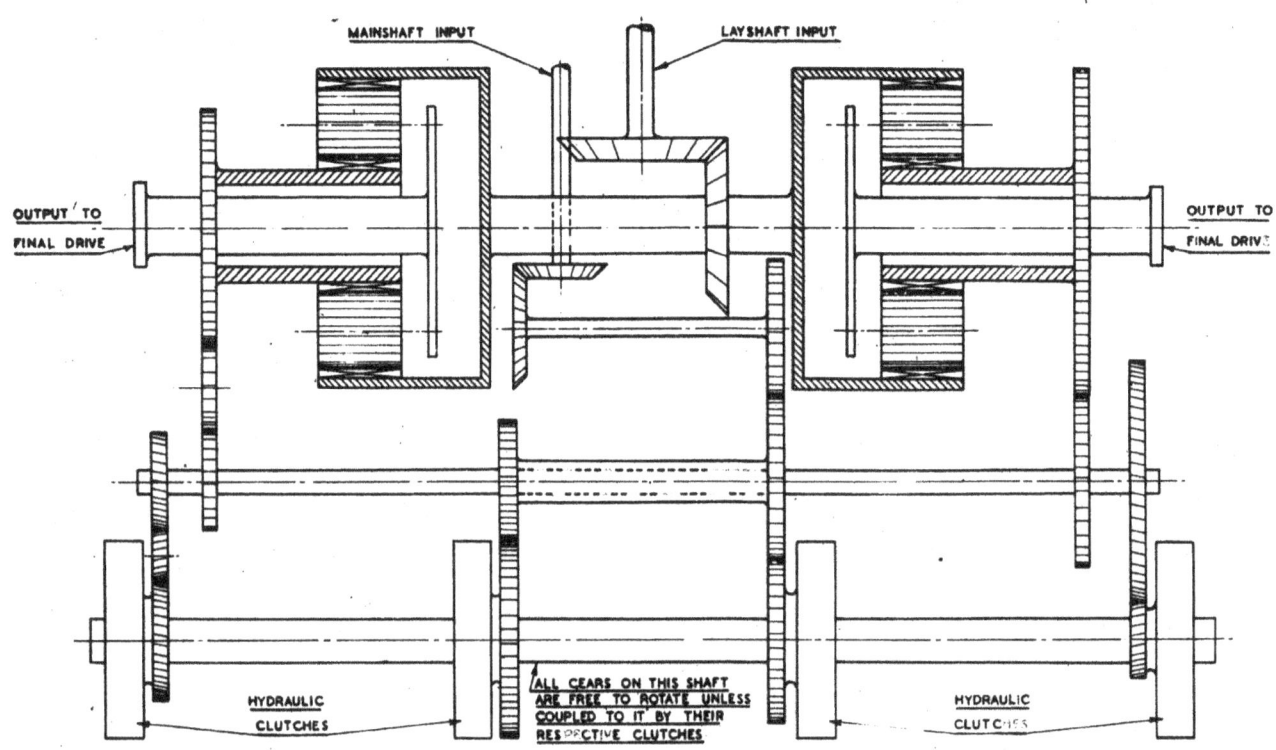

LAYOUT OF STEERING UNIT — PZ. KW. VI.

10. STEERING

From the gearbox the drive is transmitted through a bevel gear on the main gearbox output to a hydraulically operated steering unit controlled by a steering wheel.

The transverse bevel shaft so driven carries an epicyclic train at each end. The annuli of the epicyclics are positively driven with the shaft, whilst the planet carriers of each train are integral with the output flange to the final drive.

Steering is effected by imposing different speeds upon the sun wheels of the epicyclics. The direction and speed of rotation of these sun wheels and the selection of right or left hand side is dependent upon the engagement of four hydraulically operated multi-disc clutches. These clutches connect to the sun wheels through a two speed lay shaft meshing with a small bevel on an extension of the gearbox input shaft. A choice of two ratios may thus be imposed at will upon the sun wheel of the epicyclic, the annulus already rotating at a multiple of engine speed dependent upon the gear engaged.

When no drive is taken from the gearbox layshaft, i.e. when the gears are in the neutral position, a drive is still obtained from the gearbox input shaft via a small bevel and the steering unit layshaft. Thus with the engagement of the appropriate steering clutch opposing rotations of the left and right sun wheels are obtained. As the annuli of the epicyclics are positively secured to a common shaft they are unable to rotate in opposite directions consequently the opposing rotations of the sun wheels necessitate opposing rotation of the planet carriers which are integral with the output flanges to the final drive. A neutral turn is thus obtained. The overall reduction between the gearbox input and the output to the final drive reduction gear is 117:1

Oil pressure from a pump is admitted to the required steering clutches through ports in the steering assembly casing, the opening of which is controlled by piston valve. Movement of the piston valve is governed by the driver's steering wheel. In this way two distinct radii of turn are available for each gear engaged, and identical for right and left turn. A mushroom-shaped knob on the gearbox casing operates hydraulically a brake on one section of the main shaft, thereby eliminating clutch drag and making the neutral turn more positive.

The tank can also be steered when required by steering levers on each side of the driver which operate the right and left brake assemblies.

11. FINAL DRIVE

The final drive assemblies are bolted directly to the hull from the outside and contain two stages of reduction :

        (a) A straight spur reduction, and
        (b) An epicyclic.

The steering unit output shaft drives the small pinion of the spur reduction which meshes with the large pinion. The large pinion is mounted on the same shaft as a smaller pinion, which is the sun wheel of the epicyclic train. The planet carrier mounts the driving sprocket, and the annulus is rigidly secured to the final drive casing. The overall ratio is 10.55 : 1. Each final drive casing, which is a steel casting, has its own drain plug and filler plug, and a third plug which gives the the correct oil level. The oil capacity is 8 litres (14 pints).

12. BRAKES

On each steering unit output shaft there is mounted at the outer end a brake assembly, the stationary member of which consists of two circular discs held back to back by tension springs and expanded as required by a cam and lever operated by either the brake pedal or the hand brake lever or the appropriate steering stick. The rotating member consists of two cast iron saucers, well ribbed, and bolted rim to rim so as to encompass the stationary member.

Operation of the cam lever separates the brake discs until they bear upon
the breaking surface of the saucers. After which a limited rotation
produces a Servo effect. There is no adjustment for these brakes.
The brake is very effective but high temperature results from prolonged
application. Friction surfaces are metal to metal.

13. SUSPENSION

The tank is mounted on solid rubber tyred bogie wheels $31\frac{1}{2}"$ diameter
carried on crank arms, the opposite ends of which fit into plastic
bearings in the hull. Movement of these arms is resisted by torsion
bars coupled to them at one side of the tank, anchored to the hull at
the other. The suspension arms on the starboard side of the tank are
trailing, whilst those on the port side are inclined forward, thus
making room for both sets within the hull.

The bogie wheels are so arranged as to carry three tyres per suspension
arm, and these are placed singly and in pairs in such a way that the
wheels of the adjacent arms overlap. Thus for eight crank arms on each
side of the hull, there is a total of 16 bogie wheels carrying one tyre
each and four bogie wheels carrying two tyres each, giving a total of
24 tyres, in every case arranged with three per axle. The outer wheel
is detached from each axle when the narrow track is used. The bogie
wheels are arranged in the following manner on their crank arms, working
in each case from the outer edge of the track towards the centre:

	1	2	3	4	5	6	7	8
1st Crank Arm	Single bogie	-	-	track horn.	Double bogie twin tyres		Track horn	-
2nd Crank Arm		Single bogie	Single bogie	track horn.	-	-	Track horn.	Single bogie

3rd, 5th and 7th
crank arms as No. 1

4th, 6th and 8th
crank arms as No. 2.

The rear idler 27" diameter runs between the track horns. The vertical
movement of front and rear suspension arms on each side is restricted
by rubber blocks (mounted on the hull side). The nipples for
lubrication for all of the torsion bar bearings are grouped together
and piped to their bearings.

14. TRACKS

The cast steel track is of orthodox design but of unusual width ($2' 4\frac{1}{2}"$).
A further unusual feature is that the track lugs are offset in relation
to the tread, the track pins are spaced at $5\frac{1}{4}"$ centres and are retained
by spring rings fitted into half-round grooves at each end which are
countersunk into recesses cored in the track shoe casting. The track
shoe consists of a main transverse bar on the track pin centre line
with a light well ribbed plate to the next track pin bosses. The inside
of the track shoe forms a smooth surface upon which the bogie wheels run.
The teeth of the driving sprocket engage circular bosses surrounding
the track pin, one set on the inside of the track, the other set on a
line between the first and second bogie wheels from the outside of the
second suspension arm.

When it is desired to reduce the overall width of the tank to a minimum,
a narrow track is fitted. This is identical with the track just
described except that the outer portion is removed. The track is thus
made symmetrical on the sprocket, the overall width of the track and
sprocket being equal.

With the narrow track, only two tyres on each suspension arm were supported and the outer one in each case is therefore removed, together with its hub extension. This results in a material reduction of overall width whilst still retaining a satisfactory suspension and track arrangement. A set of track tools, including spare retaining rings, is carried on a bracket on the rear hull plate.

<u>Track Adjustment</u> - Tensioning of the tracks is provided by the cranked mounting of the rear idler wheels. The draw bolts, by means of which the adjustment is made, are internally mounted and are accessible from outside the vehicle by the removal of a domed B.P. cover at each side of the tail plate. The covers themselves locking the adjustment when in position.

15. INSTRUMENTS AND CONTROLS

The driver's controls comprise :

Steering wheel	- controlling the power steering
Steering levers	- working on the vehicle brakes (for use only when power steering is inoperative)
Handbrake lever	- On the left, operating vehicle brakes
Footbrake pedal	- For right foot " " "
Clutch pedal	- Operating engine clutch mechanically, but with power assistance when engine is running. A handwheel situated at the Driver's right rear provides adjustment.
Accelerator Pedal	- For operation by right foot.
Starter Carburettor	- At right rear of driver's seat.
Gear controls	- These are described in Para.9 "Gearbox"

The driver's seat may be adjusted longitudinally, the angle of its back is adjustable and may be lowered to a horizontal position for ease of access or exit.

The instrument panel is mounted on the right of the driver above the gearbox and carries the following:

(i) A revolution counter recording up to 3500 r.p.m.
    (3,000 to 3,500 marked in RED)
    (1,300 to 2,500 " " GREEN)
(ii) A speedometer - calibrated to 100 K.p.h.
(iii) An oil pressure gauge - calibrated to 12 Kg/cm^2
(iv) A water temperature gauge - from 40 - 120°C
(v) Ignition switch and warning light.
(vi) Lighting switches and fusesboxes.

In the pannier space to the left of the driver is an electrically operated gyroscopic direction indicator. This is identical with that found in certain Pz. Kw. III's and IV's.

16. ELECTRICAL EQUIPMENT

The accumulator consists of two 12V barreries with earthed negative. The batteries are carried on the hull floor astride the propeller shaft immediately forward of the engine bulkhead. The battery master switch and the necessary junction boxes are mounted on the bulkhead.

The two batteries are normally connected in paralled but are connected in series for operation of the 24 V starter motor by a solenoid operated series-parallel switch.

All crew positions are adequately illuminated by individual lighting. Rotary converters and transformers supply the necessary step-up in voltage required to drive the gyroscopic direction indicator and to supply the wireless system.

The wireless and intercommunication arrangements are of the standard type usually found in German Tanks.

No external lamps are present on this vehicle although the wiring and brackets are present.

Illumination is provided for the following instruments:

    (i) The graticule of the binocular sight
   (ii) The bubble of the clinometer
  (iii) The gyroscopic direction indicator
   (iv) The driver's compartment panel.

17. FIRE FIGHTING EQUIPMENT

In the event of fire in the engine compartment, temperature elements (two above and one each side of the engine) close the electric circuit of an automatic C.T.C. fire extinguisher mounted on the fighting compartment bulkhead, and illuminates a red lamp in front of the driver. An instruction plate round the lamp says "When there is a fire in the engine, throttle down immediately to idling speed". A clockwork mechanism in the fire extinguisher allows a 7 seconds period of operation which will be extended for a further 7 seconds period if the temperature elements have not cooled sufficiently. This process will be repeated until the extinguisher is empty. The warning light goes out as soon as the temperature elements are below operating temperature. The C.T.C. is delivered through four jets situated alongside each heat element and fed by piping from the extinguisher. In the event of electrical failure the extinguisher can be operated mechanically by means of a plunger on top. The extinguisher reservoir has a car type air valve and a $0 - 10$ Kg/Cm^2 pressure gauge.

Normal type C.T.C. extinguishers are provided on the radiator top covers and on the turret floor, with suitable retaining straps.

18. VENTILATION

A mushroom type ventilator is provided in the hinged engine cover plate. A Sirocco fan mounted at the flywheel end of the engine draws air from the bottom of the engine compartment for cooling. Air is also drawn by this fan from the casing surrounding the gearbox and is fed into ducts surrounding the exhaust manifolds to the point where the manifolds join the silencers. The ducts then convey the air to the suction side of the radiator fan assemblies.

A further mushroom type ventilator is fitted in the top front plate between the driver's and hull gunner's access hatches. This ventilator provides an air flow to the rear of the gearbox and removes fumes caused by the firing of the hull M.G.

An electrically driven fan is mounted in the turret roof above the loader, and expels the fumes resulting from the firing of the turret armament.

19. DEEP WADING AND SUBMERSION ARRANGEMENTS

The vehicle is equipped for a limited under-water performance to a depth of approximately 15 feet. This feature is achieved by the sealing of the entire tank except for a small compartment on each side of the main engine compartment, containing the radiators.

During submersion air for the engine and crew is admitted through a standpipe mounted above the engine compartment, the top of which is approximately 16 feet above ground level.

The following provision is made to keep the tank watertight for submersion:-

(i) All hatches have rubber sealing rings and screw clamps.

(ii) All vision slits have rubber seatings for their glass blocks and cam operated clamps.

(iii) The ball mounting of the front machine gun has a rubber edged external cover retained by screw clamps.

(iv) The ventilator between driver and hull gunner screws onto a rubber seating.

(v) A pneumatic sealing ring is provided to render the turret ring joint watertight. The tube is recessed in an annular groove formed in the turret ring and its seating. It is inflated through a valve which projects downwards through the superstructure top plate in the forward corner of the fighting compartment on the nearside.

(vi) The vision openings for the binocular sights are filled by rubber plugs mounted on a hinged plate attached to the sight.

(vii) The turret machine gun opening is sealed with a rubber plug mounted on a wooden rod and expanded in position by rotation of a handle.

(viii) The gun mantlet joint is sealed by means of a rubber lined frame clamped in position. A canvas muzzle cover reduces the entry of water in the barrel and one round in the breech prevents water entering the tank.

(ix) A rubber lined cover fits over the outlet of the turret ventilating fan and is tightened down by six screws clamps.

(x) A plate normally carried on the hull top plate, behind the driver, fits over the main air inlet to the engine compartment and shuts it off.

(xi) The subsidiary air inlet to the engine compartment incorporates a sealing plate which screws down on to a rubber seating.

(xii) All engine compartment cover plates have rubber seals.

(xiii) Each length of the extension pipe is rubber sealed so that the only means of entry for air is through the top of the extension pipe.

(xiv) The exhaust outlets have clapper valves, but exhaust back pressure is relied on to exclude water.

(xv) A rubber lined screw clamp seals the machine carbine port.

(xvi) The pannier spaces on each side of the engine compartment, which house the petrol tanks, radiators and fan assemblies, are completely sealed from the main engine compartment by a longitudinal vertical plate running the full length. The appropriate pipe connections and fan drive are thus the only connections to the main engine compartment.

At the point where the air ducts pass through from the engine compartment to the radiator compartments, butterflies are fitted which can be closed by a lever on the fighting compartment bulkhead for underwater travel, the same lever operating a third butterfly which allows the manifold cooling air to return to the top of the engine compartment when the other butterflies are closed.

During submersion, water takes the place of air for cooling the radiators, greatly simplifying the problem of keeping the engine compartment watertight and the engine cool. The petrol tanks are of course exposed to the water but a cock on the fighting compartment bulkhead changes over the vent pipe so that the tanks are vented into the engine compartment.

In the event of water entering the vehicle in spite of the above arrangements, a bilge pump mounted below the turret prevents it from rising to a level at which it can cause harm. The pump is driven from the rear of the gearbox from the same output as the power traverse.

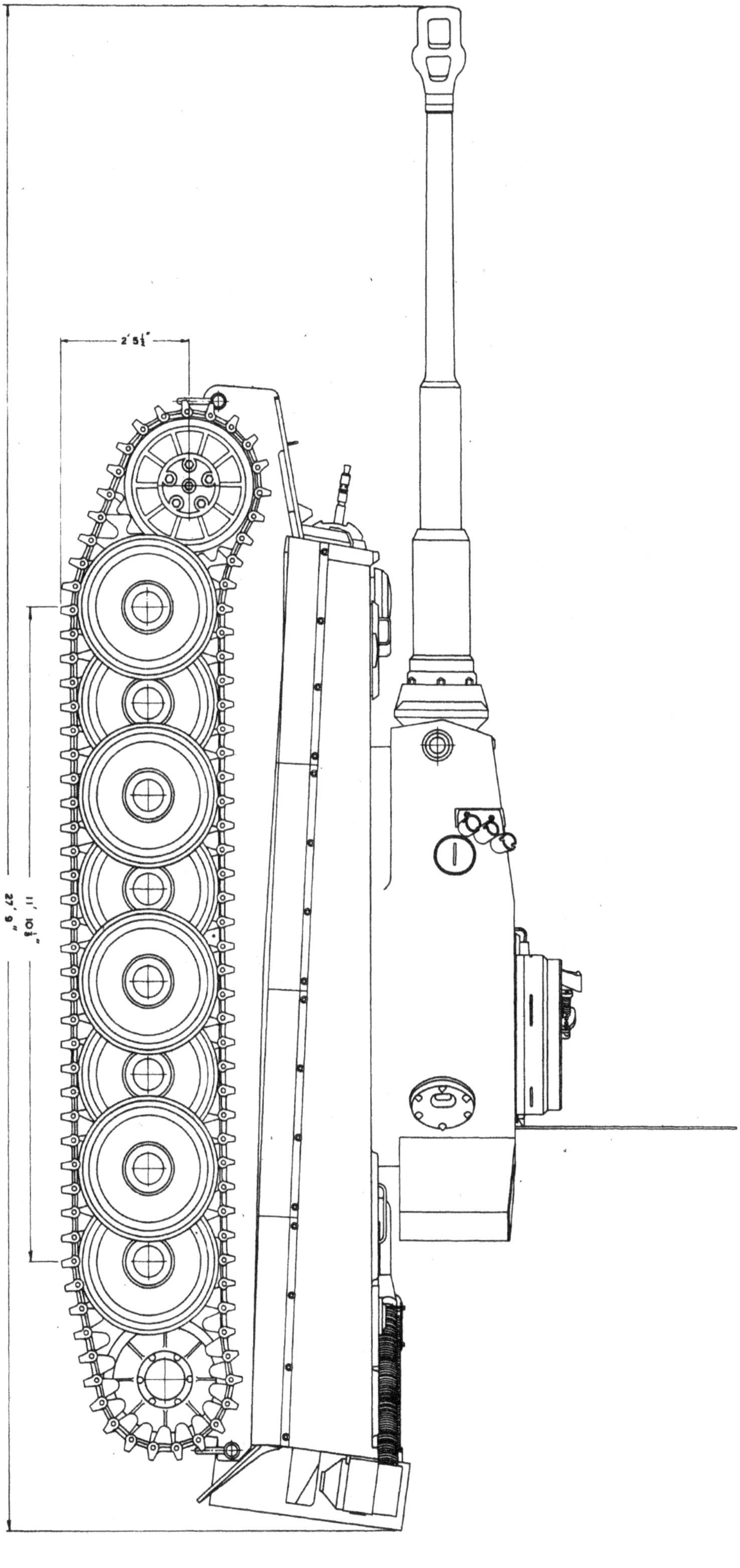

SIDE ELEVATION
WIDE TRACKS

2' 5¼"

11' 10⅜"

27' 9"

29

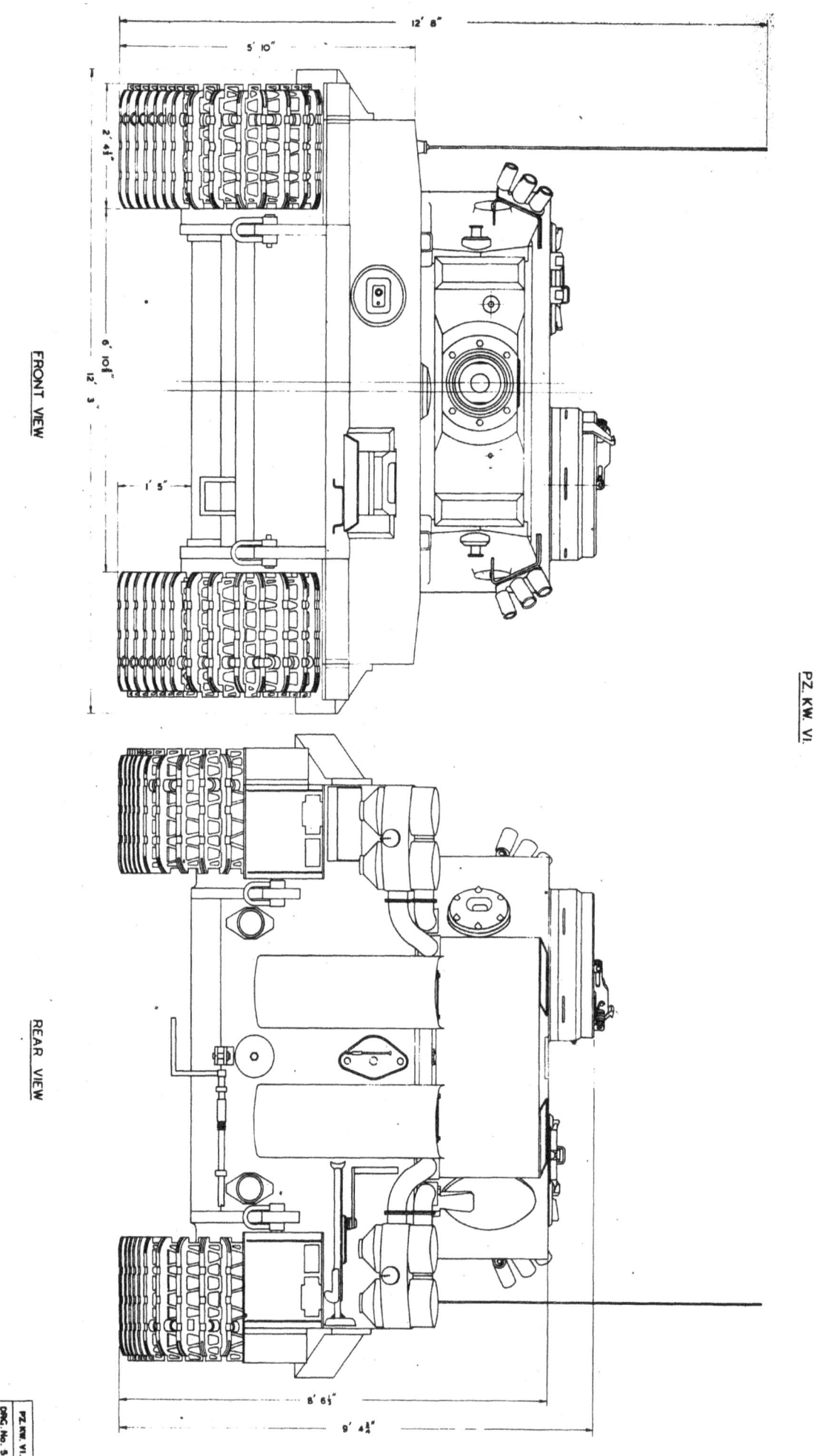

RESTRICTED

The information given in this document is not to be communicated, either directly or indirectly, to the Press or to any person not authorized to receive it.

REPORT ON
Pz Kw VI
(Tiger)
Model H

PART I.
General Description

[Editor's note: The Preliminary Report was the only report on Tiger 131 produced with its own cover (on a green, thicker paper than its interior). All other reports were printed without covers, and thus begin at their respective title pages, as on this page. This particular report's foreword (overleaf) reveals an intent to print all reports on standard paper in which holes could be punched so that they could be threaded into a hard folder.

Each report was printed to start on a right-hand page, and finish on a left-hand page, so that the reports would appear to run together as chapters in one volume (a "book," according to the foreword overleaf). No contents page was produced and no pages were numbered: consequently, the pages were easy to lose or fall out of order. This helps to explain why the contents of the surviving copies vary. Most of the surviving bound copies do not include the Preliminary Report, perhaps because its distribution was narrower, or its cover discouraged hole-punching and -threading.]

Military College of Science
SCHOOL OF TANK TECHNOLOGY
Chobham Lane   Chertsey

January 1944

FOREWORD

An example of the Pz. Kw. VI (Tiger) was brought to this country from North Africa in October 1943 for the purpose of detailed examination. With the tank there is a considerable quantity of spare components and these will greatly facilitate the work of examination and the preparation of the report.

Whilst much of the work is being carried out by the School of Tank Technology, it is clearly desirable that specialist firms and other organizations should in some cases be called in to assist. In ensuing sections of this report, therefore, the source of information is always indicated.

The desirability of consolidating all the available information into one publication is obvious, and the responsibility therefore of progressing reports and final publication has been vested with the Foreign Vehicle Section of S.T.T.

The publication of the completed book will take a considerable time. On the other hand it is obviously essential that all data should be made available to the appropriate Branch Heads of D.T.D. and others, as soon as it becomes available. Consequently it has been decided that the report shall be issued in parts of which this forms the first. Each part will be published and distributed as soon as it becomes available.

All parts will be presented in uniform style, so that they may be collated into a suitable loose leaf binding which is being prepared for the purpose.

Major J.D. Barnes, R.T.R.
Mr. D.M. Pearce, B.A. (Cantab.)

INTRODUCTION

The Pz. Kw. VI was introduced into service by the enemy in the Autumn or Winter of 1942, and appeared in North Africa in January 1943 and later in Sicily and on the Russian front.

The vehicle which has been examined is a Pz. Kw. VI (H) or Sd. Kfz. 182 and is also known as the "TIGER". This model is known to have been developed by Henschel u Söhne G.m.b.H.

The "TIGER" is of course outstanding by reason of its being the heaviest A.F.V. in general service, scaling approximately 56 tons in battle order. Its main armament is an 8.8 cm. gun, whilst its heaviest armour (on the front vertical plate) is 102 mm. Another feature of outstanding tactical interest is its deep wading facilities, and limited under water performance, to a depth of approximately 15 ft.

Its size and weight, however, impose certain tactical disadvantages, the most outstanding being the restriction on transportation due to its width, and its limited radius of action, due to heavy fuel consumption, (stated by the enemy as 2.75 gallons per mile on normal cross-country running).

The workmanship appears to be of a high order, and the design has been executed freely from the drawing board, in general unhampered by the utilisation of existing components. There are exceptions however and certain points of detail design appear unnecessarily elaborate and costly to manufacture.

An interesting development in German A.F.V. construction is the introduction of plate interlocking in addition to the normal stepped jointing. This method has no doubt been made necessary by the use of thicker armour.

The steering unit is in principle similar to the "Merritt-Brown" with the further refinement of a twin radius of turn in each gear. This adoption of a fully regenerative steering system is a distinct departure from the simple clutch/brake system hitherto employed on German tanks. The weight of the "TIGER" no doubt enforced a radical change in the steering design and the adoption of this system is therefore of interest. The gearbox has much in common with other Maybach pre-selective units, and probably the outstanding merit of this design is the provision of a large number of forward ratios (in this case eight) in a relatively compact main casing. This use of a fully automatic change speed operation is in distinct contrast with current Allied practice.

The transmission and steering units are extremely complicated and undoubtedly costly in man/hours to produce. The resultant light control of such a heavy vehicle may be some justification, since those who have driven the tank comment favourably on this feature.

As yet there is no indication that the Germans favour a compression ignition engine and the Pz. Kw. VI is powered by a V-12 Maybach petrol engine. This engine which has undoubtedly been expressly designed for a heavy tank, is a logical development of the Maybach V-12 type 120 TRM used in the Pz. Kw. III and Pz. Kw. IV and is similar in general design. As this engine represents the very latest German practice it merits close study, and it must be conceded that the design has achieved its purpose in a great measure. It is compact, light and very accessible.

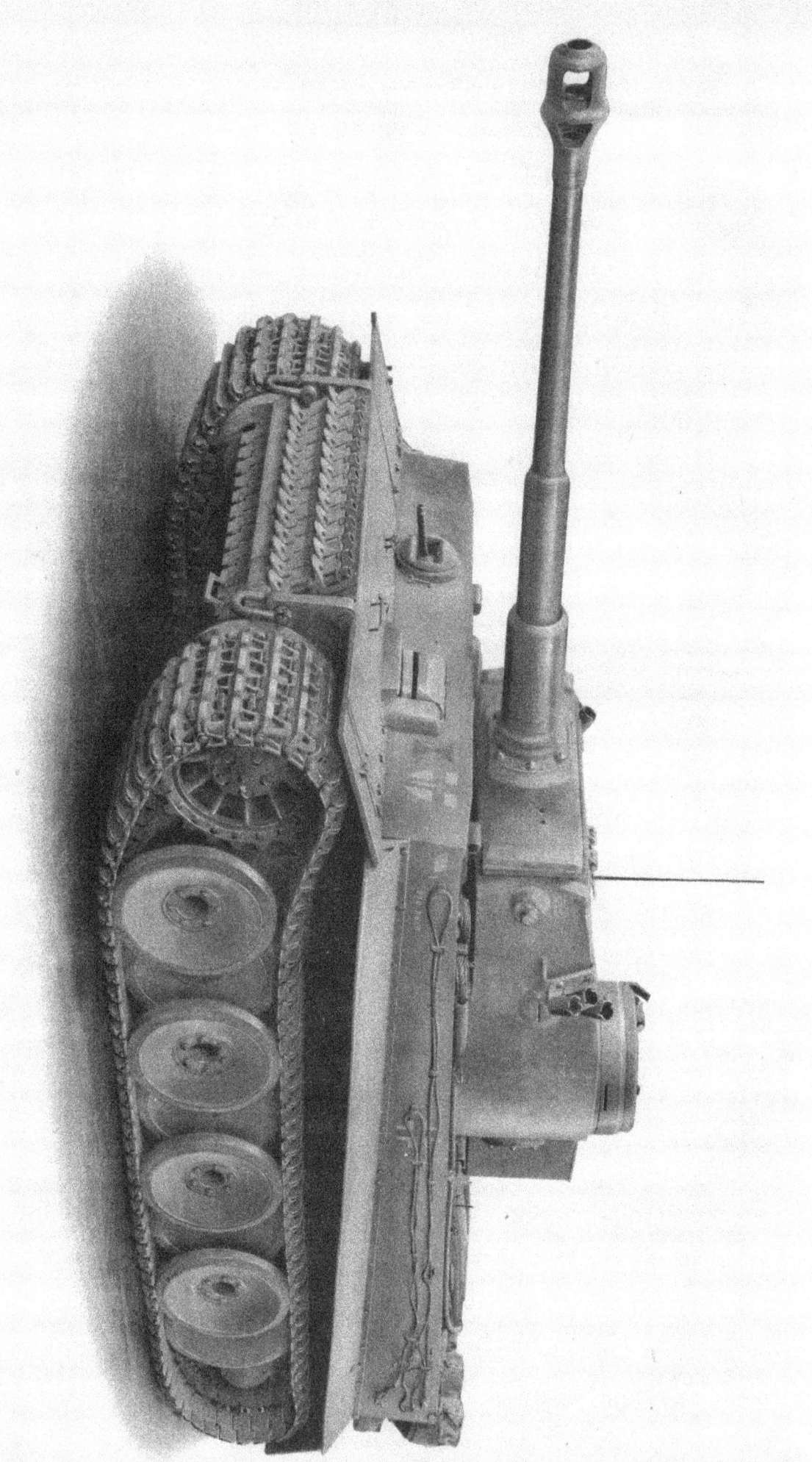

GENERAL DESCRIPTION

As compared with other A.F.V's in service, the "Tiger" is outstandingly well armed and protected. Designed to carry an 8.8 cm. gun and constructed of very heavy armour plate, the vehicle is naturally of exceptional size and weight and it is therefore somewhat surprising to note how it is, to a certain degree, dwarfed by the main armament.

Viewed from the side with the turret at 12 o'clock, the 8.8 cm gun extends beyond the nose of the tank by about a quarter of its length, and the length from the muzzle brake to the mantlet is rather over half the total length of the vehicle.

From the front aspect the great width and extremely wide tracks present a clean formidable appearance, whilst from the rear, the abnormal height of the flat tail plate carrying the large cylindrical silencers and air pre-cleaners, present by contrast an ungainly and untidy appearance.

The use of heavy armour plate has imposed the necessity of employing flat plates wherever possible and the number of plates has been kept to a minimum to facilitate manufacture. This results in a simple box like contour.

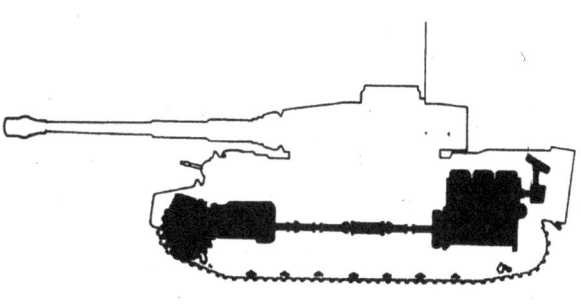

Both the superstructure and engine compartments are high and the former overhangs the tracks at each side. This arrangement permits of adequate turret ring diameter to accommodate the 8.8cm. gun. Apart from the tail plate already referred to, the exterior is of generally clean and simple lines.

A notable departure from past German practice is the welding of the superstructure to the main hull; in previous German designs a bolted joint has been used.

The turret also is of simple outline, the vertical sides and rear being formed of a single rolled plate, whilst the mantlet is a steel casting of rectangular section. A conventional German type of cupola is mounted on the nearside of the turret roof.

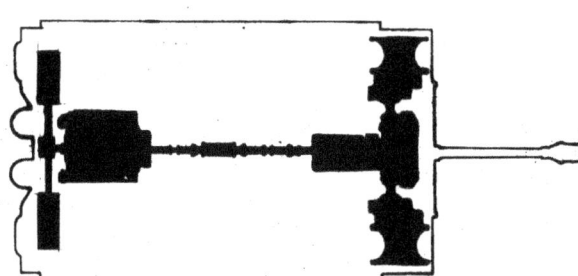

Circular hatches are provided in the superstructure top for the driver and hull gunner. There are three hatches in the turret - a rectangular hatch for the loader in the roof, and two circular hatches, one in the cupola top and one in the turret side.

Massive cast manganese steel tracks of comparatively small pitch are driven by the front sprockets - consistent with normal German practice. Adjustment of the track tension by rear idler is accessible through the tail plate, and the mechanism is all housed within the hull.

The vehicle is sprung on torsion bars. The bogie wheels are arranged to overlap each other thus increasing the number of spring units and resulting in a soft suspension. This arrangement is not altogether unexpected since it has previously been encountered on German tracked vehicles, and its merits are obvious, particularly when dealing with the suspension of an unusually heavy vehicle.

Even distribution of the weight on the tracks is achieved by the use of triple rubber tyred bogie wheels. In order to accommodate the 16 torsion bars on the hull floor, trailing suspension arms are used on one side and leading arms on the other.

The mechanical layout follows orthodox German practice although the elaboration and refinement in design of certain components has been carried to an exceptional degree. The engine is accommodated centrally at the rear and drives forward through a propeller shaft below the turret floor to the gearbox which incorporates the clutch. Bolted to it is the steering unit set transversely in the nose of the tank. A bevel drive is introduced in the steering unit and each track is driven through a final reduction gear in each sprocket. A radiator and twin fan assembly is installed in a separate compartment each side of the engine. Below each compartment two petrol tanks are carried.

Arrangements for wading and total submersion of the tank are necessarily somewhat elaborate, but have evidently not been incorporated as an afterthought. All hatches and doors are rubber sealed, whilst the turret ring is sealed by an inflatable rubber tube. The main air supply for the engine and crew is taken through a demountable telescopic standpipe mounted over the engine compartment. During submersion, the fan drives are disconnected and the radiator compartments flooded.

The excessive width of the vehicle in battle order necessitates special preparation for rail travel. Narrow tracks are substituted and the outer bogie wheels removed as are the track guards and air pre-cleaners.

TANK PREPARED FOR RAIL TRAVEL.

The general layout of the fighting and driving compartments is shown in the perspective drawing. The seating arrangements for the crew follow the normal German practice. In the three man turret the gunner sits on the nearside of the gun with the Commander immediately behind him and the loader sits on the other side of the gun and faces to the rear. The commander is provided with a cupola in which are five vision slits. In the hull the driver sits in the nearside and the hull gunner, who also operates the wireless, sits opposite in the offside.

Although the turret is unusually spacious, the breech mechanism of the 8.8 cm. gun reaches nearly to the rear wall dividing the compartment in two. The mechanism is of the semi-automatic falling wedge type and is, broadly speaking a scaled up version of the smaller tank guns. It is electrically fired by a control on the elevating handwheel. A 7.92 mm. machine gun is mounted coaxially on the offside and is fired mechanically by a foot pedal.

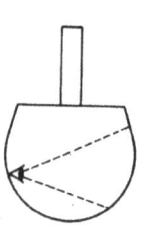
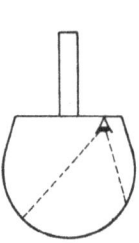

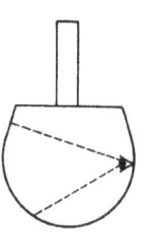

The gunner is provided with a binocular telescope and a turret position dial indicator to his left. The gun is balanced by a large coil spring housed in a cylinder in the offside front of the turret. Elevation and hand traverse are controlled by handwheels to the right and left of the gunner, and an additional handwheel may be used by the commander to give assistance. The hydraulic power traverse is controlled by the gunner by a rocking foot plate.

Around the vertical sides and rear of the turret are various small boxes, brackets and straps for stowing such items as gasmasks, glass blocks, microphones etc., as well as junction and fuse boxes for the turret electrical gear.

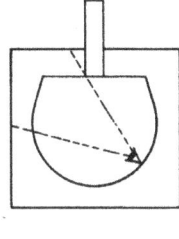

The turret floor rotates with the turret and is suspended on three steel tubes. In the centre is a domed cover for the drive to the hydraulic unit which is bolted to the revolving floor. The drive is taken to the turret rack through shafting and universal joints. Also mounted on the revolving floor is a rack for spare petrol cans and a fire extinguisher. The gunner's seat is carried on a welded tubular extension on the elevating gear, and is situated forward over the hydraulic unit. To the rear on the engine bulkhead are mounted the petrol taps, certain other engine controls and the automatic fire extinguisher unit.

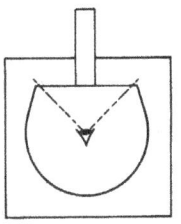

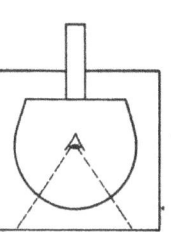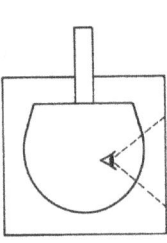

Ammunition for the 8.8 cm. gun is stowed in bins at each side of the fighting compartment. The remainder is stowed under the turret floor and alongside the driver.

The driver is provided with a steering wheel which controls hydraulically the controlled differential steering unit. When the engine is not running this unit is inoperative and orthodox steering levers controlling skid disc brakes may be used. These brakes are also the vehicle brakes and are coupled to a foot pedal and parking brake lever. Other controls are normal. The driver's visor may be closed by a sliding shutter operated by a large handwheel, and a fixed episcope is provided in the escape hatch. A standard German gyro-compass and instrument panel are situated to the right and left respectively.

The 7.92mm. machine gun for the hull gunner is held in a ball mounting in the offside of the front vertical plate. It is fired by a hand trigger and sighted by an orthodox telescope. The wireless sets are carried on a shelf to the right of the hull gunner.

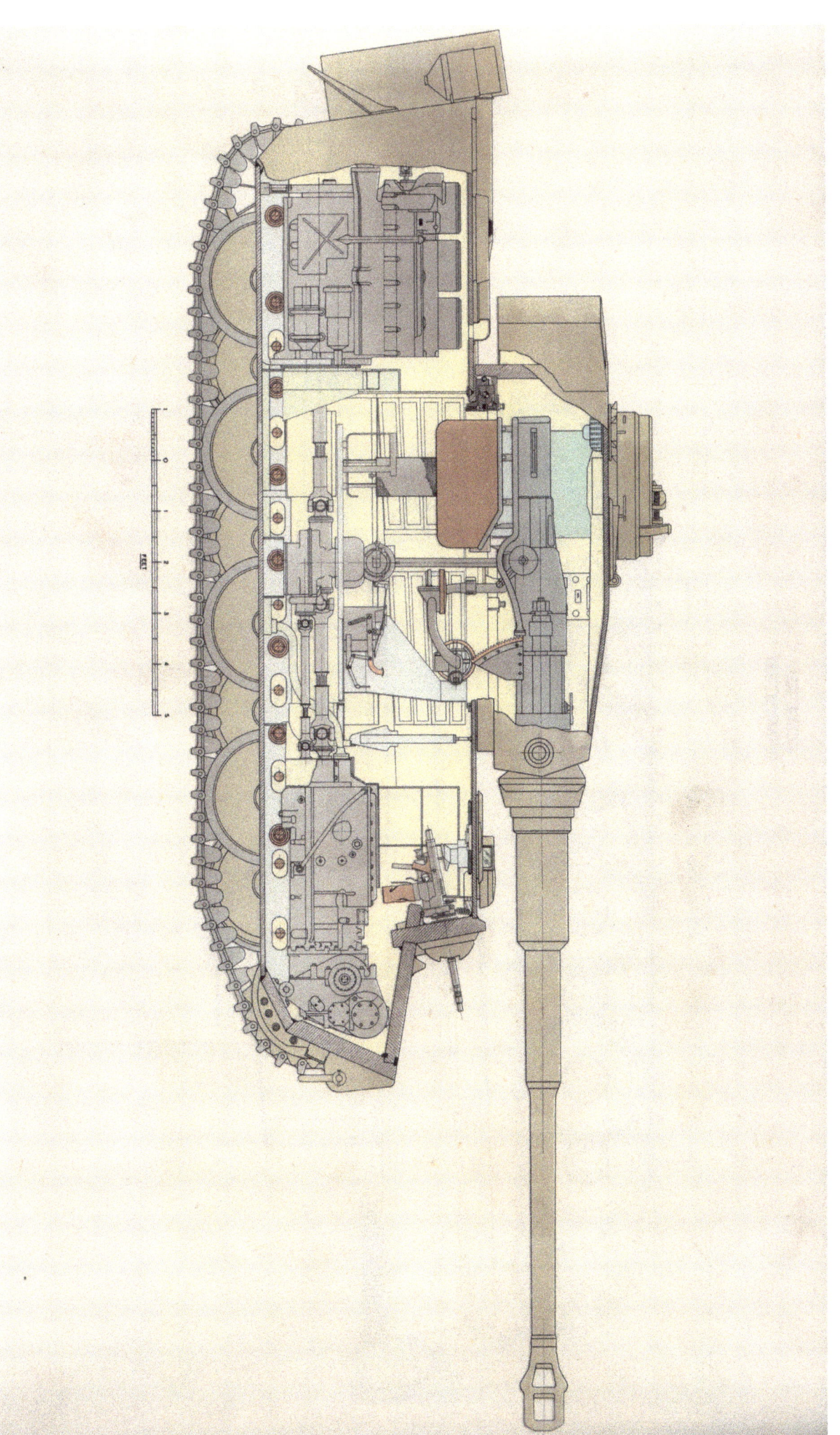

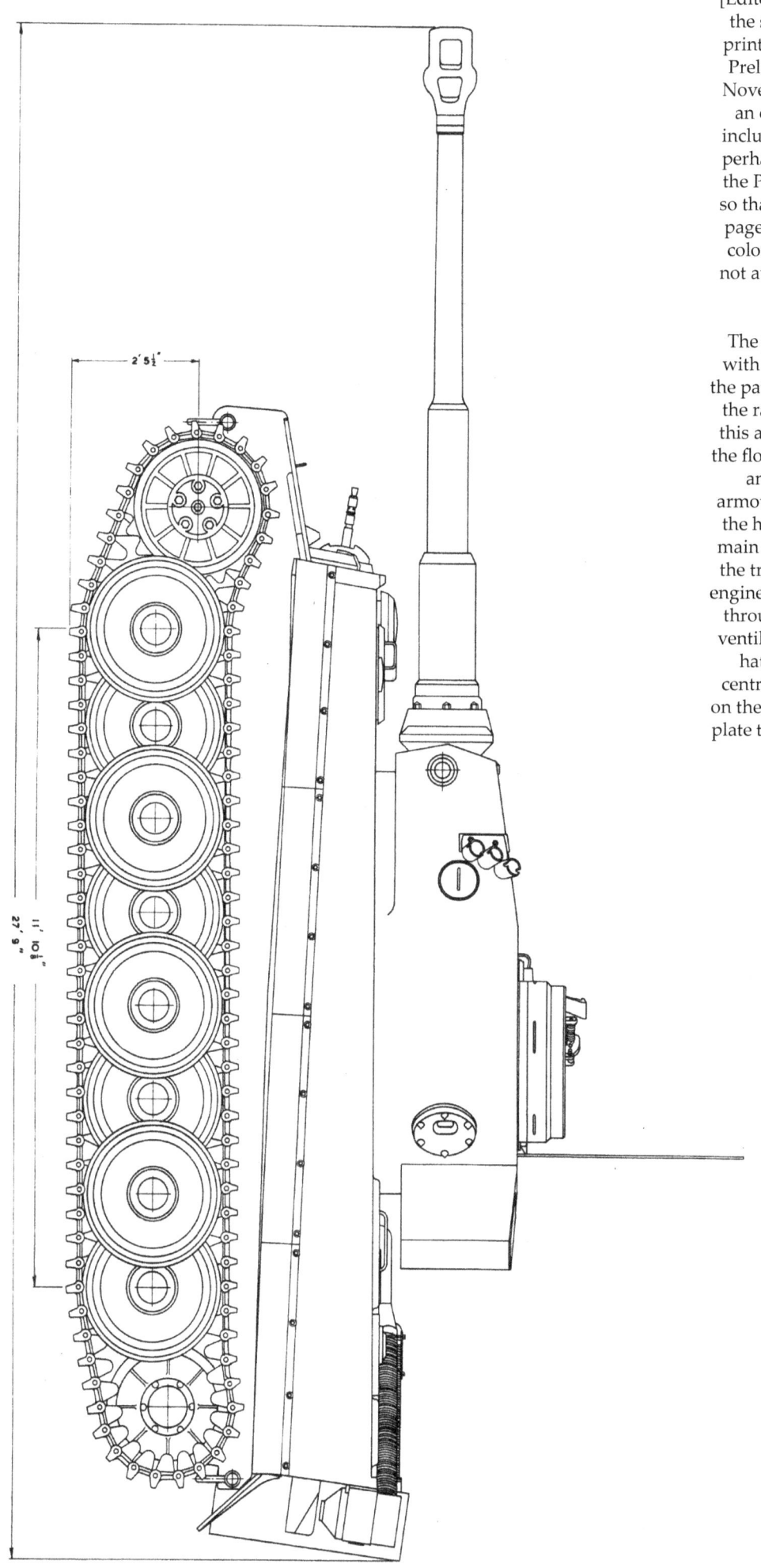

[Editor's note: These are the same drawings as printed in Lidderdale's Preliminary Report of November 1943, except an overhead plan is included. The plan was perhaps excluded from the Preliminary Report so that it would fit in 24 pages. Presumably the colour paintings were not available as early as November.

The plan is annotated with arrows to suggest the path of air flow across the radiators, although this annotation ignores: the flow from the hatches and the foremost armoured ventilator (on the hull roof below the main armament), under the transmission, to the engine compartment; and through the armoured ventilator on the engine hatch and the four centrifugal air cleaners on the exterior of the rear plate to the engine itself.]

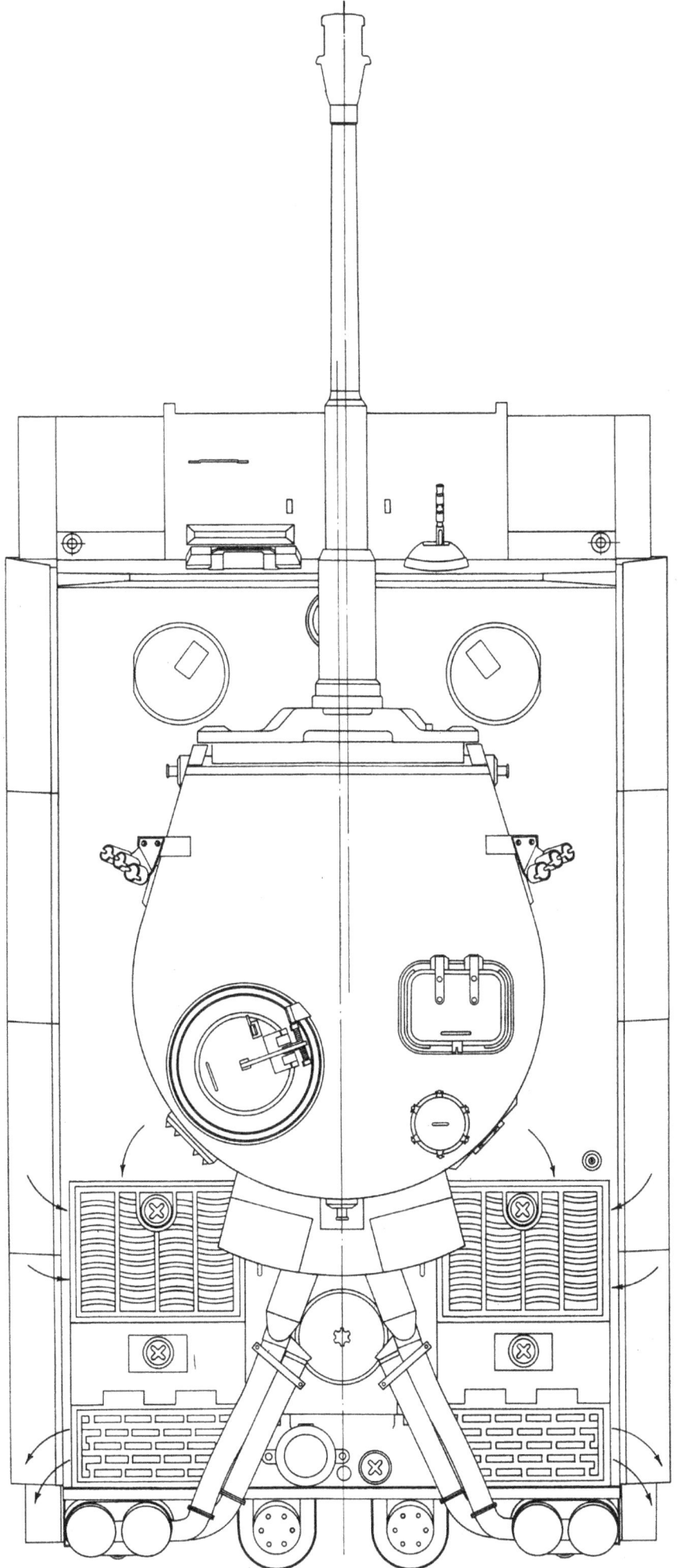

PLAN
WIDE TRACKS

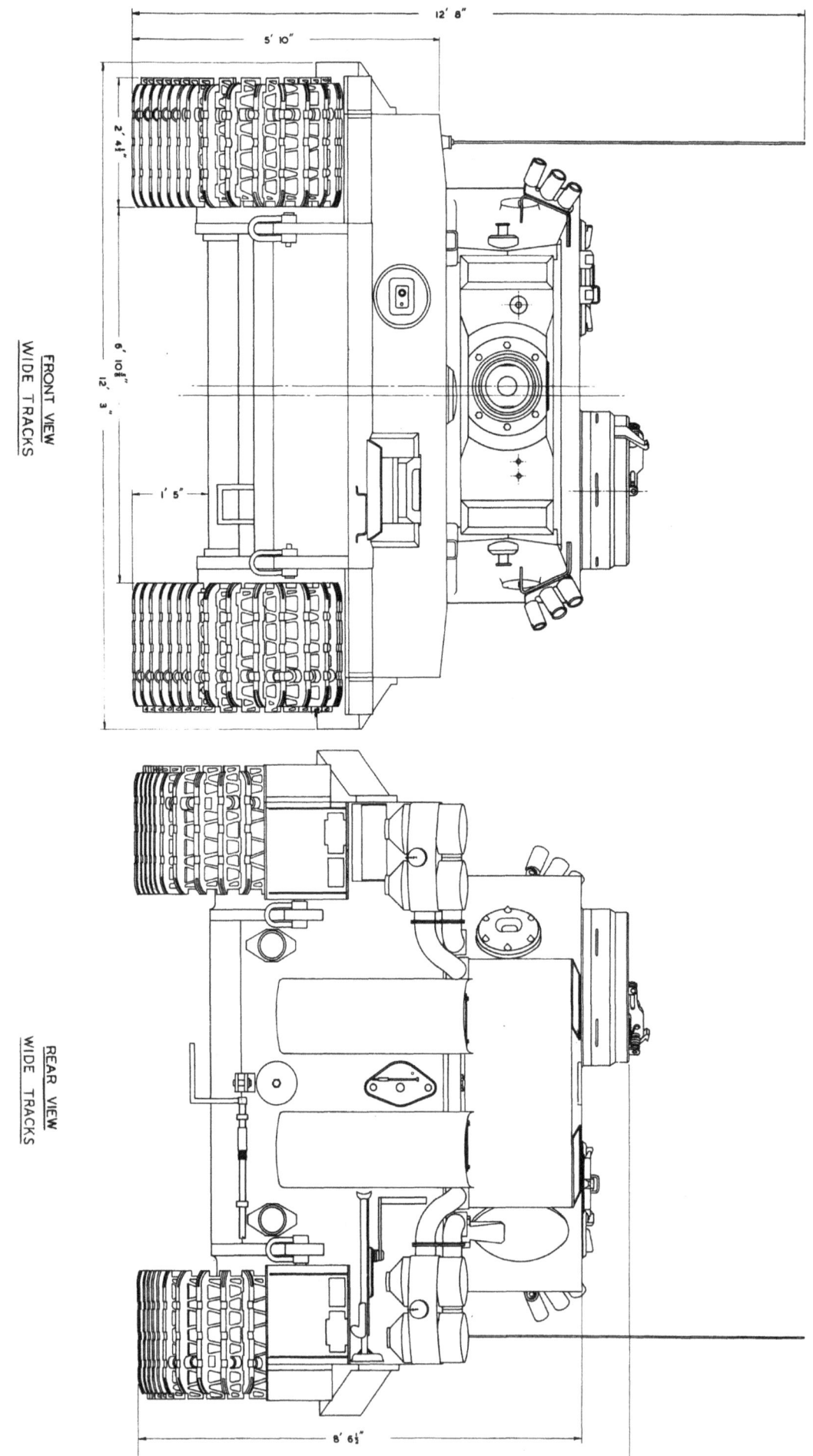

GENERAL SPECIFICATON

TYPE   Panzerkampfwagen (Pz. Kw.) VI.   Model "H" Sd.Kfz. 182

DIMENSIONS

WIDE TRACKS FITTED

Weight (in battle order)	56 tons
Length (excluding gun)	20' 8½"
" (including gun at 12 o'clock)	27' 9"
Width (overall)	12' 3"
Height	9' 4¾"
Ground Contact	12' 6"
Track Centres	9' 3½"
Ground clearance	1' 5"

NARROW TRACKS FITTED

Weight (partially stowed, less crew)	50 tons 5 cwt.
Width (overall)	10' 4"

Other dimensions as for wide tracks.

ARMAMENT

One 8.8 cm. tank gun KwK 36 electrically fired and one 7.92 M.G. 34 co-axial in turret.
One M.G. 34 in front vertical plate.
One 9mm. machine carbine stowed.
Six Nb. K. Wg. 90 mm. smoke generators - three each side of turret.
Three minethrowers - unknown calibre mounted on superstructure roof.

TURRET TRAVERSE

All round hand and power traverse. Power traverse hydraulic unit driven by take-off from main gearbox through auxiliary gearbox. Hydraulic unit consists of variable delivery vane pump supplying a vane motor, both housed in single casting on turret floor. Pump delivery varied by altering eccentricity for speed and direction. Additional control giving two positions of eccentricity on motor - in effect a two-speed gear.

SIGHTING

Turret armament - binocular telescope T.Z.F. 9(b)
Hull M.G. - Telescope K.Z.F. 2.

AMMUNITION

8.8cm. - 92 rounds (mixed APCBC, H.E. and A.P.40)
7.92mm. - 34 belts each 150 rounds.

ARMOUR

Vertical and near vertical plate thickness - 60-100 mm.
Horizontal and near horizontal plate "   - 26- 60 mm.

No facehardened armour used and as distinct from previous German practice, armour is comparable in hardness to British machineable quality plate.

All welded construction, embodying stepped joints, austenitic welding and total plate interlocking.

CREW

In Turret
    Commander
    Gunner
    Loader

In Hull
    Driver
    Hull Gunner/Wireless Operator

Total   Five

POWER PLANT

Engine

Manufacturer	Maybach
Model	H.L. 210
Type	60° V/12 cylinder - petrol
Rating	650 metric H.P. (642 British B.H.P.)
Bore	125 mm
Stroke	145 mm
Normal capacity	21,400 cc.
Cylinder block and crankcase	Single aluminium casting
Cylinder Heads	Cast Iron
Valves	Overhead - two per cylinder - exhaust sodium cooled.
Valve operation	Single gear driven overhead camshaft to each bank.
Carburettors	4 - Solex type 52 JFF 2
Governor	Centrifugal max speed.
Air Cleaners	2 centrifugal pre-cleaners 3 oil bath cleaners
Lubrication	Dry sump Oil pumps: Gear type - 2 scavenge 1 pressure Oil capacity: 28 litres (6.1 gals)
Ignition	2 Bosch impulse starter magnetos - one to each bank. One Bosch 14mm. plug per cylinder. Fully screened.
Starters	One Bosch 24V axial starter. One Bosch inertia starter.

Engine Cooling System

Radiators	2 gilled tube type mounted one each side at rear of engine compartment.
Fans	2 pairs - axial flow type - gear driven. Two speeds.
Water pump	One - centrifugal type mounted between cylinder heads.
Cooling System Capacity	Approx. 16 gals.

Fuel System

No. of tanks	4 - 2 each side of engine compartment
Total capacity	Approx. 125 gallons
Petrol pumps	4 Solex mechanical type One electric pump for priming One manual pump injects fuel direct to manifold for cold starting.

CLUTCH

Multi-plate incorporated in gearbox. Hydraulic control.

GEARBOX

Type:	Maybach Olvar - preselector
Operation:	Four pairs of gears in constant mesh. Dog clutch engagement. Hydraulic control. Synchronising cone clutches on input and output shafts.
No. of speeds:	8 forward - 4 reverse

Gear Ratios:

1st	15.4	:	1
2nd	10.2	:	1
3rd	7.15	:	1
4th	4.86	:	1
5th	3.16	:	1
6th	2.11	:	1
7th	1.14	:	1
8th	0.98	:	1

STEERING

Regenerative controlled differential type. An epicyclic train to each sprocket. Annulus driven by gearbox output. Sun wheels driven from gearbox input. Planet carriers form output to final drives. Speed and direction imposed on sun wheels controlled through gearing by hydraulic clutches giving two radii of turn in either direction in each gear. Clutches hydraulically controlled by steering wheel.

Emergency Steering - Orthodox steering levers control disc brakes on each output shaft, enabling the vehicle to be steered when engine is not running.

BRAKES

Emergency steering brakes serve as vehicle brakes operated by foot pedal and hand lever.

FINAL DRIVE

Spur gear reduction to epicyclics housed in sprockets.

SPROCKETS

Steel castings with twin detachable rings.

TRACKS

Wide.

Type:	4/5 lugs
No. of links per track	96
Material:	Cast Manganese steel
Width:	$28\frac{1}{2}''$
Pitch:	5.125"
Pin diameter:	1.1"
Weight of link with one pin:	66.375 lbs.
Pin retention:	Circlips
Track Pressure:	14.7 lbs/sq.in.

Narrow

Width:	$20\frac{1}{2}''$
Weight of link with one pin:	$46\frac{1}{2}$ lbs.
Track Pressure:	20.4 lbs/sq.in.

TRACK ADJUSTMENT

By rear idler mounted on cranked arm. Drawbolt adjustment accessible through tail plate.

SUSPENSION

Triple overlapping wheels independently sprung on torsion bars. Trailing suspension arms on offside - leading arms on nearside. When narrow tracks are fitted for transportation, outer wheels from each unit are removed.

No top rollers fitted, the track being returned on the wheels.

Wheels

Type:	Steel disc type with solid rubber tyres
No.	Eight each side
Diameter:	$31\frac{1}{2}''$

Torsion Bars

No.	16
Diameter	55mm. and 58mm.
Effective Length	1644.6 mm. ($5'\ 4\frac{3}{4}''$)

Shock Absorbers

Hydraulic piston type on front and rear wheels only, housed in the hull.

ELECTRICAL EQUIPMENT

Accumulators - Two 12 volt, in parallel for normal supply and in series for starting.

Dynamo - One 12 volt - voltage regulator

Wireless Equipment - W/T, L/T and Intercom. Power supplied through rotary converter.

AUTOMATIC FIRE FIGHTING EQUIPMENT

Bimetal thermostats at points in engine compartment energize a solenoid which opens the delivery valve on a bottle containing C.T.C. under pressure.

From the delivery valve the extinguishing fluid is piped to nozzles at the requisite points.

A clockwork time switch trips the solenoid circuit, limiting the period of operation to seven seconds.

The cycle is repeated until the temperature at the thermostats is sufficiently reduced.

WADING AND SUBMERSION

Full provision for wading and submersion to approx. 15ft. All doors, hatches, etc., have rubber seals. The turret ring is sealed by inflatable rubber ring.

Fan drives disconnected and radiator compartments flooded. Air supply to engine and crew via a telescopic standpipe erected on top of engine compartment. Bilge pump driven by engine through power traverse auxiliary gearbox. Engine exhausts directly into water through non-return flap valves on top of silencers.

RESTRICTED

The information given in this document is not to be communicated, either directly or indirectly, to the Press or to any person not authorized to receive it.

REPORT ON
PzKw VI
(Tiger)
Model H

PART II

ARMAMENT, FIGHTING ARRANGEMENTS, STOWAGE
AND POWER TRAVERSE

SECTION I

ARMAMENT

Military College of Science
SCHOOL OF TANK TECHNOLOGY
Chobham Lane   Chertsey

January 1944

PART II

ARMAMENT, FIGHTING ARRANGEMENTS, STOWAGE AND POWER TRAVERSE.

SECTION I.

ARMAMENT

INTRODUCTION

The 8.8 cm.(3.46-in) gun is mounted on a 70½-in. internal diameter ring and has 360° traverse. It is provided with 92 rounds of ammunition. This gun, known as the Kw.K 36, should not be regarded as a development of the Flak 18 and 36 A.A./A.Tk guns, but as a parallel development with the 7.5cm. Kw.K 40 (long) and follows the well known principles of German tank gun design. The only similarity to the Flak 36 lies in the ammunition and ballistics.

The standard Flak 18 and 36 ammunition is fired, except that it is fitted with the C/22 electric primer instead of the C/12 percussion primer.

The combination of a muzzle brake, long recoil (22.8 ins) and a heavy vehicle (approximately 56tons) results in a stable gun platform, thus avoiding one of the difficulties of observation of fire at present being encountered in British tanks.

In addition to the Kw.K 36, the armament of the tank comprises two M.G. 34 7.92 mm. Machine guns, one co-axially mounted with the 8.8 cm. gun, and one in a ball mounting on the offside of the front vertical plate.

A curious feature is the provision of a clinometer in conjunction with a simple type azimuth indicator, graduated in clock hours only, as on the Pz.Kw.IV with 7.5 cm. Kw.K (short). On the Pz.Kw.IV with 7.5 cm. Kw.K 40 (long), however, there is an elaborate azimuth indicator graduated in clock hours and mils, with a split pinion drive but no clinometer. Thus, neither of these vehicles has complete equipment for turret down shooting, although this is known to be practised by the Germans.

It is surprising that no attempt has been made to protect the ammunition from splinters, though there is good protection against dust.

The Germans appear to have discarded tail smoke apparatus in favour of turret mounted generator dischargers, obviously as a result of examination of British A.F.V's. As no extra generators are stowed, beyond those in the dischargers, and as the fitting of the primer is not a quick operation, they obviously cannot be reloaded after firing, until coming out of action.

By comparison with those of present British tanks, the turret is fairly roomy and comfortable. It is observed that the standard of workmanship and design in the armament is of a very high order and shows no deterioration when compared with early German designs.

February, 1944   Lieut. P.L.Gudgin, R.T.R.

8.8 cm. GUN KW. K 36.

AND MOUNTING

DIMENSIONS AND REFERENCES

Length of chamber	23.6 ins.
Length of rifling	161.1 "
Length of Bore	184.7 " (53.3 cals)
Depth of breech opening	9.6 "
Length of Piece	194.3 " (56.1 cals)
Additional length of Muzzle Brake	15.1 "
Overall Length	209.4 "
Angle of breech block guides	1.5°
Diameter at base of cartridge case	4.06 ins.
Diameter at rim of cartridge case	4.56 "
Bore	3.46 "
Rifling - No. of grooves	32, with uniform right hand twist
Depth of grooves	1.5 mm.
Width of grooves	5 "

References :-

Notes on Enemy Weapons No. 33)
) For Flak 18
M. I. 10., Summary No. 63/3A)
) and Flak 36
M. I. 10., Summary No. 81/2)

Construction

The weapon has a detachable breech ring provided with two gun lugs, the right hand one being of open type to facilitate removal of the buffer cylinders without removing the gun. (See photo. in Part I.)

Breech Mechanism

The breech mechanism is a scaled-up version of the standard German tank gun pattern, as fitted on the 7.5 cm. Kw. K. 40, 5 cm. Kw. K 39 etc. (See Part I.)

It incorporates the usual falling wedge breech block, (which has two drillings in the lower portion for lightness), electric primer firing, and S.A. operation by means of separate clock springs for opening and closing. The electric firing pencil is of very robust construction, and has external insulating bushes.

Muzzle Brake

This is of double baffle type, secured by means of a locking ring, and a tab washer. The rear baffle has a renewable insert.

Internal diameter
    of rear baffle - 95 mm.

Internal diameter
    of forward baffle - 105 mm.

Weight, complete
    with locking ring - 124 lbs.

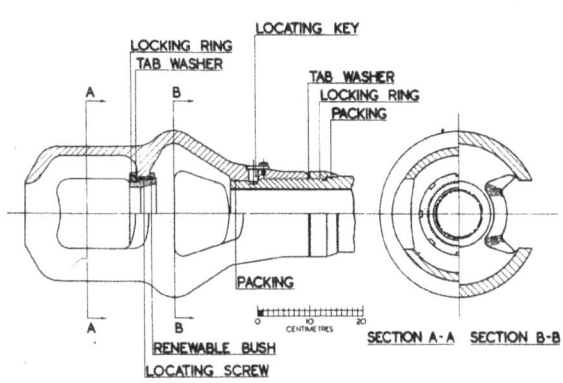

MUZZLE BRAKE
WEIGHT INCLUDING LOCKING RING 124 LBS.

Cradle

The cradle is of standard welded construction and is generally very similar to that on the 7.5 cm. Kw. K 40 (long), but on a larger scale. The left hand gun lug is provided with bronze shoes and runs in an anti-rotation guide inside the left side plate of the cradle. A deflector guard is bolted to the cradle; it is not hinged and effectively divides the fighting chamber into two separate unequal compartments. The deflector guard carries a small capacity (approximately 10 cases) empty cartridge bag on three brackets. The recoil indicator is bolted inside the left side plate.

The gun port water seal is operated by a knob on top of the cradle above the 8.8 cm. gun.

Recoil Gear

The recoil gear is of standard German tank gun pattern; it consists of a hydraulic buffer on the right of the gun, and a hydro-pneumatic recuperator on the left. A spring-loaded hydraulic reservoir with the usual hydraulic safety switch is mounted transversely beneath the gun. The reservoir is much larger than that mounted in previous types of tanks. The stencilled "Braun Ark" on both cylinders indicates that the fluid used therein is an equal mixture of "Bremsflussigkeit braun" (brown buffer fluid) and "Bremsflussigkeit arktisch" (arctic fluid), for use in temperate climates.

The piston rods are nutted to the gun lugs on either side of the breech ring. The right hand gun lug is open and allows the sideways removal of the buffer cylinder. The recoil indicator is graduated from 500 mm. (19.69 inches) to 620 mm. (24.4 inches) with the "Feuerpause" (stop) at 580 mm. (22.8 inches).

The recuperator air pressure was measured and found to be 54 kg/cm^2 or 766.8 lbs/in^2, approximately 54 atmospheres.

The recoil system appears serviceable.

Firing Gear

The Kw. K 36 uses the standard German electric primer type firing system. It is operated by means of a segment shaped trigger bar mounted on the same axis behind the elevating handwheel and parallel with the handwheel rim. (See Part I). It is a 12 volt system supplied from one of the vehicle batteries. The circuit is shown under Electrical Arrangements.

Safety Devices

Standard German electrical safety devices are provided, which prevent firing of the gun if the breech is not closed, the buffer empty, or the gun not fully run out. A mechanical safety switch, of the type fitted in the Pz. Kw. III and IV is mounted near the top right hand side of the breech ring. This switch breaks the firing circuit each time the gun is fired; the gun cannot then be fired until the loader has reset the switch. There is no deflector guard safety switch since the guard does not fold.

Mounting

    Maximum elevation   16° 41') Limited by stops on
    Maximum depression   7° 15') the rear face of mantlet.

The mounting is of the external mantlet type. The mantlet is cast in one piece and consists of a large rectangular external shield of approximately the same size as the front of the turret, behind which is a cylindrical portion, roughly hollowed out at the back, working inside the turret. There are two designs of mantlet, apparently in parallel production - one is flush finished on the front face (as on the tank under examination), the other has a raised portion round the telescope openings.

Each turret side wall forms a cheek, carrying a fixed spherical trunnion; these trunnions fit into split spherical bushes in the sides of the cylindrical inner mantlet. The trunnions are continued outwards through the cheeks of the turret walls to form two lifting points for the turret. The front of each cheek is chamfered away above and below the trunnion axis to allow for the elevation and depression of the mantlet. The 8.8 cm. Gun is offset 4 inches to the right. Splash proofing appears to be adequate.

Balance

The piece is mounted very far forward, and the mounting is considerably muzzle heavy. This is counter-acted by means of a large cylinder, containing a strong compression spring (with adjustable compression), horizontally mounted above the right hand side of the turret ring to the right of the loader. The spring is compressed by a piston, the piston rod is connected through a system of levers to a small subsidiary compression cylinder and to the right hand side of the cylindrical inner mantlet. The diagram shows the linkage positions with the mantlet horizontal.

Elevating Gear

The elevating gear is of sector and pinion type, the sector having external teeth. It is driven by a handwheel on a transverse axis underneath the gun, and turned by the gunner's right hand. This handwheel is mounted on a tubular swan-necked steel arm which passes under the gun and is welded to the forward offside turret platform support. Drive is transmitted from the handwheel to the elevating pinion by means of a universally jointed shaft inside the hollow arm, a bevel gear, and a worm and worm wheel.

    Radius of handwheel $4\frac{3}{8}"$
    Maximum obtainable elevation   16° 41' (18 turns)
    Maximum obtainable depression   7° 15' ($6\frac{3}{4}$ turns)

    Total Arc   23° 56' ($24\frac{3}{4}$ turns)

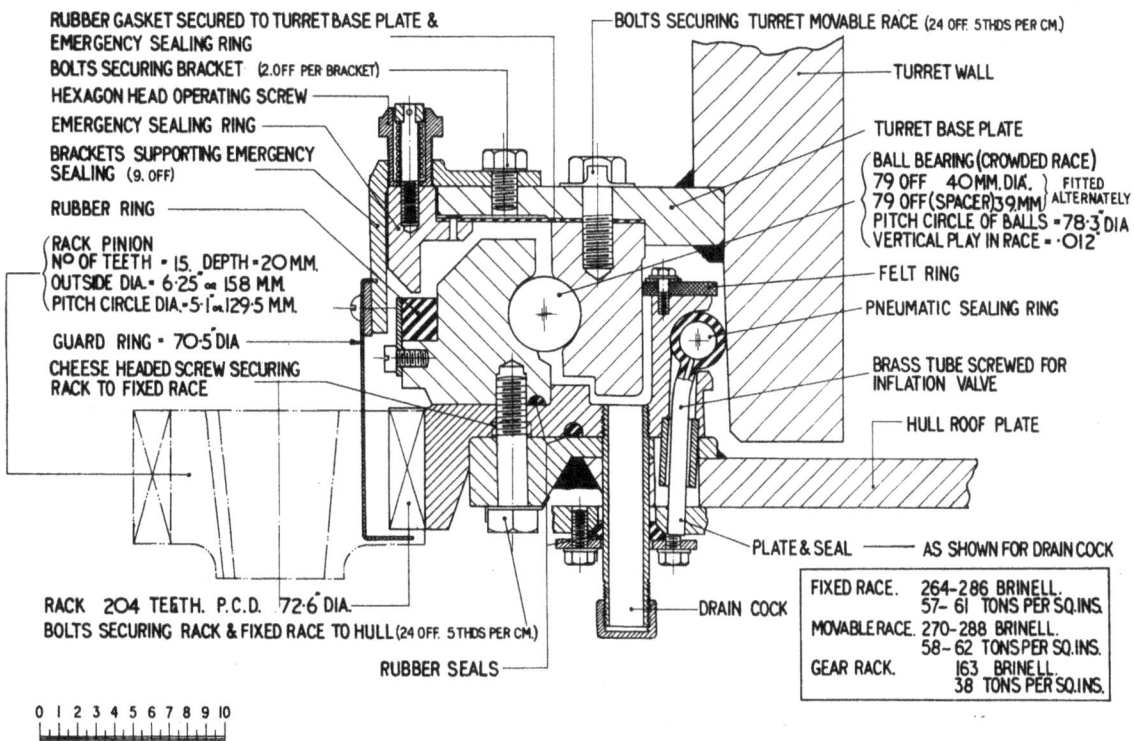

Composite section of turret suspension

    Ratio - approximately 1°/turn

    Maximum workable elevation - 11° (approx)

    Maximum workable depression - 4°   "

    Total Arc   15°

Clearance between sector and sector pinion .004 ins. At maximum depression, the breech ring fouls the elevation lock, and at maximum elevation the deflector guard fouls the water cans on the floor. When firing, therefore, the maximum workable elevation and depression is considerably smaller than the maximum possible.

The elevation lock consists of two hooks, pivoted from the turret roof which engage studs on either side of the breech ring, and a screw clamp which presses on the top of the breech ring and forces the studs into the hooks. In the locked position, the gun is horizontal. This rather complicated arrangement prevents chatter when travelling.

<u>Turret Suspension</u>

The turret is carried on a vertical bearing, of the crowded ball race type. There are 79 load carrying balls of 40 mm. diameter and 262 grammes weight, and 79 spacer balls of 39 mm. diameter and 241 grammes weight. The stationary race is on the inside and the moving race on the outside.

The turret rack is in one piece and has the following dimensions:-

Root circle diameter	186.4 cm.	(73.4 ins)
Pitch circle diameter	184.4 cm.	(72.6 ins)
Addendum circle diameter	182.4 cm.	(71.8 ins)
No. of teeth	204	
Diameter to centre of balls	198.8 cm.	(78.3 ins)
Vertical play in turret race	.012 of an inch.	

The turret ring is sealed by means of an inflatable rubber tube (of 1.14-ins external diameter deflated) carried in an annular groove on the outside of the stationary race. Above this, is a felt ring clamped to the stationary race. The joints between the various components of the stationary race are sealed by rubber sealing rings.

There is no external protection of the turret ring joint, apart from that afforded by the projection of the front vertical plate above the superstructure roof. Adequate splash protection is provided by the sectional shape of the turret ring.

Traverse Gear

Full traverse of the turret through 360° is provided, both by power and hand.

Hand Traverse - the hand traverse is provided with two wheels, one for use by the gunner and an auxiliary wheel for the commander. They are inter-connected by means of universally jointed shafts, but the commander's handwheel may not be turned without first disengaging the plunger type lock on the gunner's handwheel.

Both wheels are geared with considerable reduction into the turret rack through a gearbox above the gunner's handwheel.

Radius of gunner's handwheel	- $5^{1}/5"$
No. of turns of gunner's handwheel for 360°	- 720 ($\frac{1}{2}$°/turn)
Radius of commander's handwheel	- 4"
No. of turns of Commander's handwheel for 360°	- 595 (.6°/" approx.)

Power Traverse - the turret may be power traversed by the engine through a hydraulic unit consisting of a variable delivery pump and motor. The drive to the unit is taken from a power take-off at the rear of the gear box, through an auxiliary gearbox situated centrally below the revolving turret floor and vertical shaft passing through the floor. The unit itself is bolted to the turret floor. The drive from the unit is taken to the turret rack through bevel gears and shafting. The auxiliary gearbox is provided with a gear lever situated on the hull gunner's side of the gearbox.

The hydraulic unit in the centre of the turntable floor carries two control levers, one of which operates a multiplate clutch on the input shaft and the other a two speed motor control.

The gunner's main traverse control consists of a rocking footplate under his right foot. To traverse right it is rocked forward, to traverse left, backward. Variable speeds forward and reverse are obtained, within the limits of the 2-speed control, according to the angle to which the footplate is rocked. The footplate is in a comfortable position, but the arc of movement (24°) is too large for comfortable operation, especially by the heel.

A full technical report on the power traverse components and performance details will be found in Section V.

It will be noted that, as all the hydraulic mechanism is contained in the turret, the complication of a rotating hydraulic joint is avoided and no disconnection is required when removing the turret. The dog clutch on the vertical drive shaft comes away, leaving the base junction in position on the hull floor.

There is no Broadside Indicating System fitted in spite of the large overhang of the gun barrel (9 ft. 6 ins.) Neither was it present on the Pz.Kw.IV, Model G, with the long 7.5 cm. Kw.K 40, although it appeared on all earlier tanks.

A plunger type traverse lock is provided under the superstructure roof in the forward near side of the fighting compartment, by means of which the turret may be locked in the 12 o'clock, 6 o'clock and 11 o'clock positions. It consists of a spring loaded plunger, which engages in recesses drilled in the turret skirt and is engaged or disengaged by means of a lever.

CO-AXIAL MACHINE GUN

This is the M.G. 34 and has the new type feed block (used on the infantry M.G. 34 for taking 50-round belt drums). This gives feed from left hand side only. For details of this gun, see M.I.10 Summaries Nos. 110/2/C and 66/4. Also "Notes on Enemy Weapons No. 5.," and "Enemy Weapons, Part I."

Cradle

The cradle is exactly similar to that on the Pz.Kw.IV, incorporating a spring buffer and carrying two belt bags (one full and one for empty cases). It supports the firing linkage and also the belt guide, with check pawl, to prevent the belt " running back ". Vertical and lateral zeroing adjustments are incorporated and provision is made for swinging the M.G. body clear for changing barrels.

Firing Gear

This is of the rod and lever type and is operated by a foot pedal situated above the power traverse control footplate. It is placed for use by the gunner's right foot, thus the M.G. cannot be fired when the turret is being traversed by power.

AUXILIARY MACHINE GUN

The auxiliary M.G. 34 is of the same type as the co-axial, with the new type breech block and is mounted in the offside of the front vertical plate. The mounting is of the standard German ball type, the Kugelblende 100 (the 100 is believed to be the thickness of armour used in the mounting), with a fixed hemispherical external mantlet. It is similar to that on the Pz. Kw. IV, the ball being inserted from the outside. It incorporates a head pan and a compensating tension spring anchored to the superstructure roof to counteract the breech heaviness of the mounting. This gives the same fault as that on the Pz. Kw. IV, Model G, of pulling the gun off, upwards and to the left.

The travelling lock is identical with that on the Pz. Kw. IV and locks the gun pointing slightly downwards and to the left.

Elevation	$-20°$	Traverse left	$-15°$
Depression	$-7°$	Traverse right	$-15°$
Total Arc	$-27°$	Total Arc	$-30°$

SIGHTS

Main Armament

Telescope - Sighting of the turret armament is done by means of an articulated, binocular telescope, type T.Z.F.9 (b), mounted on the left of the 8.8 cm. gun. It is a binocular development of the T.Z.F.5 series with similar optical characteristics, and has adjustable interocular distance ($2\frac{3}{8}$" - $3\frac{3}{8}$") by rotation of the cranked eyepieces. These are geared together by two toothed sectors giving a 1 : 1 ratio. The interocular distance may be locked by means of a knurled knob above the right hand eyepiece. The telescope is of stationary eyepiece type, the eyepieces being slung from the roof on a strengthened support, and locked in it by a pin. The lenses are bloomed, and this fact, taken in conjunction with the " (T) " marking, tends to confirm our previous surmise that the "(T)" indicates bloomed lenses. Contrary to previous reports, the telescope is not a coincidence rangefinder, a separate instrument being carried for this purpose.

War Office T.I. Summary No. 115 gives the following data :-

Magnification	-	x 2.5 (approx)
Field of view	-	$23°$ (approx)
Overall length	-	33 inches (approx)
Overall width	-	$11\frac{3}{8}$ "
Weight	-	49 lbs. 14 ozs.
Exit Pupil dia:	-	6 mm.

The telescope in the vehicle under examination was numbered '171'.

Parts of other telescopes, Nos. 97, 74 and 53 were also received. All had the "T" marking, and bloomed lenses, but none was complete or serviceable. The eyepieces were removed from No. 53 to make No. 171 complete.

No. 171 is the only instrument so far examined with a number greater than 100. There appear to have been minor changes in design after the first 100 models - for example, the aiming marks in the first 100 were of normal type, consisting of complete triangles, whereas on this model the bases of the smaller triangles are not put in.

The caps on the graticule adjusters on this telescope are of a different design from the previous ones.

The graticules in both telescopes are illuminated from the same light source by means of a divided prism inserted in the centre of the graticule box.

The inside of the telescope bodies are smoked to prevent reflection.

There is a graticule with horizontal and vertical adjustment in each telescope. They are of standard pattern except for the omission of the bases of the triangular aiming marks in later models. The later models also have a vertical line below the central aiming mark in the left hand telescope. The purpose of the left hand telescope graticule is not clear, unless it serves as a battle sight, to be set at given ranges before going into action. It may be moved sideways in and out of view by means of a lever on the left rear of the graticule box. A standard type range scale for 8.8 cm. and M.G. is provided in the right hand telescope. It is adjustable to give ranges from 0 - 4000 metres (in hundreds) for the 8.8 cm. gun and from 0 - 1200 metres (also in hundreds) for the M.G. Range is put on by means of a standard type lever vertically mounted under the telescopes. The range scale and aiming mark glasses do not appear to be bloomed. It should be noted that the graticule adjustment controls are most inaccessible, and adjustment is difficult when the telescope is mounted.

An adjustable browpad of standard German type is provided. There is no open sight, contrary to earlier German practice.

Another report on this instrument has been prepared by the Aberdeen Proving Ground, Project No. FMFC-108, which contains photographs, data and a drawing of the original pattern of graticule.

Clinometer - A clinometer on the left side of the cradle is held in position at the top by means of a stud and at the bottom by a spring-loaded plunger. The stud is on an adjustable eccentric, to which is welded a knurled disc with seven drillings. The disc is locked in position by a bolt which may be threaded into one of three drillings in the cradle and through any of the seven drillings in the disc. As received, the bolt was in position in the centre drillings in both disc and cradle. When the disc is turned, alteration of 1 mil is caused in the relative elevation of clinometer and gun. Thus, a total adjustment of 9 mils is possible in the clinometer mounting by using a combination of both sets of drillings.

The clinometer arc is graduated on the left hand side from 0 to 400 mils (25°) of elevation, in black figures, and from 0 to 100 mils (5.6°) depression, in red figures. On the right of the arc there is a range scale (presumably for use with H.E. shell) graduated from 0 - 80 (in hundreds of metres). The range of 8000 metres corresponds approximately to 151 mils (8.5°) on the left hand scale.

Provision is made for the illumination of the bubble, but the bulb and wiring are deficient on this instrument. The bulb seems to be smaller than that normally used in German instruments and is probably a pea bulb.

An alternative position for the clinometer is provided outside the left cradle side plate, to the rear of the first position. In order to mount it here, the securing pins have to be reversed.

Auxiliary M.G.

The hull machine gun is sighted by the standard episcopic sighting telescope K.Z.F.2 (See C.I.A. Sketch No. 129 Sheet 6).

Magnification	-	x 1.75
Field of view	-	18°
Length	-	380 mm.
Weight	-	7 lbs.

FIRE CONTROL

A single dial target position indicator, similar to that on the Pz. Kw.IV with 7.5 cm. Kw. K (short), is fitted on the turret ring to the left of the gunner. It is graduated from 1 to 12 in clock hours and carries a pointer driven off the turret rack by means of a pinion and universally jointed shafts. In addition, there is a toothed indicating ring, also graduated from 1 to 12 and with 360 teeth, inside the cupola driven off the turret rack.

A sighting vane is incorporated in the front episcope in the cupola.

It is known from examination of burnt-out "Tigers" that a rangefinder is also sometimes carried, but whether this is universal or merely applies to a proportion of tanks is not known. No mention of it is made in captured stowage lists for this tank and none was found in the tank under examination, but two fixed tubular supports on the turret roof, one in front of and one behind the cupola, seem to be standard fittings, and their internal diameter corresponds to the ground mounting for this rangefinder.

From examination of a badly burnt specimen (marked Cxn. Kf 50995. E.M. 34*), taken from a "Tiger", the rangefinder would appear to be the E.M. 34, of coincidence type, with a base length of 70 cm. (27.56 ins), a magnification of x11 and giving ranges from 200 to 10,000 metres (219 to 10936 yards). Full particulars, drawing and photographs are contained in M.I.10 Summary No. 75 and Middle East A.F.V. Technical Report No. 13.

It is believed that a scissors telescope (type S.F.14.Z) is carried, and it is probable that the pivoted tubular bracket under the right hand side of the cupola is used for mounting this. Part of the mounting appears to be deficient, so the telescope could not be fitted.

AUXILIARY ARMAMENT

Smoke Generator Dischargers

These are mounted in two sets of three, one on each forward side wall of the turret. The top discharger of each set has an elevation of 30° and is on a parallel axis with the keel line of the tank. The centre dischargers have an elevation of 35° and are inclined outwards with their axes at 15° to the keel line. The bottom dischargers also have an elevation of 35°, but are inclined further outboard with their axes at 30° to the keel line.

The discharger cups are of 95 mm. internal diameter and of 150 mm. internal length. They are of Nb.K.Wg type and are electrically fired from six push buttons, in two sets of three, on the turret roof on each side and forward of the cupola.

They fire the Nb.K. 39 90 mm. smoke generator, six of which are carried, one in each discharger. No spare generators, primers or discharger spares are carried.

Machine Carbine and Ports

The machine carbine is assumed to be the 9 mm. M.P. 38 or 40, and is vertically stowed on the offside rear of the turret wall. Earlier models of the Pz. Kw. VI had two machine carbine ports, similar to those in the Italian tanks M.11/39 and M.13/40, at 4 o'clock and 8 o'clock in the turret wall.

These ports are closed by means of a rotating armoured shutter operated by a lever. The shutters contain an eccentrically positioned aperture, which may be moved into or out of register with a similar sized aperture in the turret wall.

In later models, including that under examination, the 4 o'clock port has been removed and replaced by a large circular loading or escape hatch which swings downwards and outwards and may be opened (but not closed) from the inside. It is locked by a vertically sliding bar held by two screw clamps. As it cannot be closed from the inside, it obviously cannot be used for the jettisoning of empty cases in action.

Signal Pistol

This is the 27 mm. (1.032 in.) Walther signal and grenade pistol (Kampfpistole) and is stowed on the left hand turret wall behind the commander's traverse wheel. It is rifled and carries a small dial sight for use with H.E. Grenades.

Descriptions of this pistol and its ammunition will be found as follows :-

    Pistol - Enemy Weapons, Part V

    Pistol and Ammunition - M.I.10 Summary No. 101

    Ammunition - M.I.10 Summaries Nos. 65 and 112.

"Minenabwurfer"

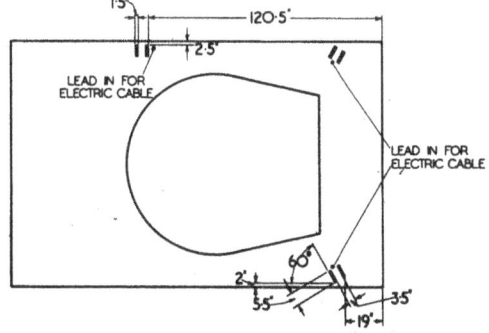

Provision appears to be made on the nearside rear, and the near and offside front of the superstructure roof for the fitting of three "Minenabwurfer" or mine-droppers. They appear to be electrically fired from the fighting compartment, the leads being connected to a switch in the centre of the rear bulkhead. The mine droppers and the switch are deficient on this vehicle. Their exact function is unknown and no details are available, but from examination of a photograph (STT No. 4069) they would appear to consist of a small cylinder, similar to the smoke generator dischargers on the turret. The mountings are fixed, that of the rear thrower pointing outboard at 90° and those of the forward throwers at 45°, to the keel line, and elevated at approximately 30°. The mine thrower can only be a single shot weapon, with no means of reloading in action once fired.

AMMUNITION

SUMMARY

The following ammunition is carried on this tank :-

Calibre & Type	No. of Rounds
8.8 cm. Kw. K 36	92
7.92 mm. M.G. 34	5,100 (34 - 150 rd. Belts)
27 mm. Signal Pistol	24 (12 white, 6 red, 6 green)
90 mm. Nb.K.39 Smoke Generators	6
9 mm. Machine Carbine	An unknown number, in 32-round magazines.

8.8 cm. AMMUNITION

Where Stowed	No. of Rounds
Left of driver	6
Offside of forward compartment	16
Nearside of forward compartment	16
Forward offside of fighting compartment	4
Forward nearside of fighting compartment	4
Aft offside of fighting compartment	16
Offside floor of fighting compartment	4
Nearside floor of fighting compartment	4
Under turntable, offside (may only be removed when turret is at 12 o'clock	6
Aft nearside of fighting compartment	16
TOTAL	92

[Editor's note: This image was placed upside down, relative to the photographer's attitude. It is reproduced here exactly as oriented and placed in the original report, except with a higher-resolution copy of the original photograph.]

All rounds are horizontally stowed, lying fore and aft, alternately nose and base forward, in unarmoured sheet metal bins with folding doors.

The rounds stowed on the fighting compartment floor are retained at their bases by rests, sliding vertically in grooves in the bin sides. The rests may be lifted, pushed back and dropped into grooves out of register with the rounds as the latter are removed.

The neck of each round sits on a pivoted spring loaded rest which may be swung sideways into the side of the bin when the round is removed to facilitate access to the lower rounds. As the majority of rounds are stowed high up in the vehicle, they are more vulnerable than those in British A.F.V.'s which are stowed low down in armoured bins.

Normal Flak 18 and 36 ammunition is used in this gun, fitted with C/22 electric primers instead of C/12 percussion primers. According to a captured document (M.I.10 letter A/M564) the types and proportions of ammunition in use in the N. African campaign were H.E. (25%) A.P. 38 (A.P.C.B.C.) (66%) and A.P. 40 (9%). For a total of 92 rounds these proportions give 23 rounds of H.E., 61 rounds of A.P.C.B.C. and 8 rounds of A.P. 40 per tank. In the tank under examination only A.P.C.B.C and H.E. (with percussion fuze) rounds were found. Both the A.P.C.B.C. and H.E. have smoke tracers.

Any of the undermentioned types of ammunition may be used, however, although H.E. with time fuze is not likely to be encountered.

Type	A.P.38 A.P.C.B.C	A.P.40	H.E/A.Tk (Hl.Gr Patr 39)	H.E (Percussion Fuze)	H.E. (Time Fuze)
M.V.(ft/sec)	2657	3000	1968	2690	2690
Weight of Round (lbs)	33.75			32	31.75
Length of Round (ins)	34.21			36.69	36.69
Weight of Projectile (lbs)	20.75	16	16.75	20.3	20.06
Length of Projectile (ins)	14.49			15.55	15.55
Filling (lbs)	3 T.N.T		1.5	1.9 Cast Amatol	1.9 Cast Amatol
Fuze	Base 222		A.Z.38 St.	Nose (percussion) A.Z.23/28	Nose (clockwork) Zt.Z.s/30
Propellant Charge (lbs)	5.34 diglycol Nitro Cellulose	6.14 diglycol	2.6 diglycol	5.34 diglycol	5.34 diglycol
Weight of Core (lbs)		4.25			
Length of Core (ins)		5.5			
Diameter of Core (ins)		1.375			

Cartridge Case

Weight	-	3.06 kg.	(6.75 lbs.)
Length	-	569 mm.	(22.4 ins.)
Diameter at neck	-	90 mm.	(3.54 ins.)
Diameter at base	-	103 mm.	(4.06 ins.)
Diameter at rim	-	115 mm.	(4.56 ins.)

Capacity :- 3650 cc's

Design No. 6347

These base markings are typical of those found on the ammunition in the tank at the time of examination.

An elevation scale for the Kw. K 36 firing H.E. with percussion fuze will be found at Appendix "A" to Part I of this report.

For further information on the ammunition for the Kw. K 36, see the following :-

A.P.C.B.C. (A.P. 38)	-	Enemy Weapons, Part V (Appendix "F"). M.I.10 Summaries Nos. 80/3, 98/3 and 72/3 and Appendix "E".
A.P.40	-	M.I.10 Summaries Nos. 72/3 and Appendix "E", and 107 M.I.10 Summary (14/9/43) 1/2 No. 17.
H.E./A.Tk	-	M.I.10 Summary No. 111/6.
H.E. (Percussion Fuze)	-	Handbook of Enemy Ammunition, Pamphlet No. 1 (sec.ii.) M.I.10 Summary No. 80/3 C.
H.E. Shell (Time Fuze)	-	Handbook of Enemy Ammunition Pamphlet No. 1 (sec.ii.) Enemy Weapons Part IV (Appendix "E"). M.I.10 Summary No. 72 (Appendix "D").

7.92 mm. AMMUNITION

Fighting Compartment

Where Stowed		No. of Belt Bags (150 rds)
Forward bulkhead	- Offside side plate	1
Rear Bulkhead	- Nearside, bottom	1
Rear Bulkhead	- Nearside, higher up	5
Rear Bulkhead	- Centre bottom	3
Rear Bulkhead	- Offside bottom	1
Rear Bulkhead	- Offside top	1
Offside turret wall (behind loader)		4
On Gun		1
Total in Fighting Compartment		17

Hull Gunner's Compartment

Where Stowed	No. of Belt Bags (150 rds).
Rear bulkhead, above pannier	4
Offside wall, above pannier	8
Front vertical plate, above pannier	4
On Gun	1
Total in hull gunner's compartment	17

Total in tank - 34 belt bags (5,100 rounds).

This total agrees with that in the captured stowage list, which gives 32 belt bags, not including one at each gun. Each belt contained a mixture of A.P. trace and A.P. incendiary rounds of 1937 and 1938 manufacture in the approximate ratio of 50 rounds of A.P.I. in each belt. Two belts, however, consisted of ball (with green annulus and varnished steel cases) and A.P. trace (with coppered steel cases) of 1942 manufacture, in the ratio of 75 : 25.

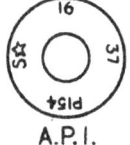
A.P.I.

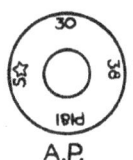
A.P.

These markings on the bases of the rounds are typical.

For further data on 7.92 ammunition, See C.I.A. Foreign Ammunition Chart, Lines "C" and "D".

SMOKE GENERATORS

These are the Nb.K.39, 90 mm. generator, and use the C/23 electric primer, a miniature version of the electric C/22 fitted on the 8.8 cm. ammunition. No spare smoke generators are carried.

SIGNAL CARTRIDGES

These are stowed in two metal containers on the rear of the turret ring on the right hand side of the commander.

MACHINE CARBINE 9mm.

An unknown number of 32-round magazines are stowed in a removable container beside the machine carbine on the offside of the rear turret wall.

APPENDIX "A" TO SECTION I, PART II
OF REPORT ON PZ. KW. VI (H)

ELEVATION SCALE

-for the-

GERMAN TANK GUN 8.8 cm. Kw.K 36.
Firing H.E. with Percussion Fuze

(Taken from Clinometer)

RANGE (metres)	T.E (mils)	RANGE (metres)	T.E (mils)	RANGE (metres)	T.E. (mils)
200	1.6	3600	38.0	6550	101.6
400	3.0	3700	39.7	6600	103.1
600	4.5	3800	41.3	6650	104.8
800	6.4	3900	42.6	6700	106.3
1000	8.0	4000	44.2	6750	107.6
1100	9.3	4100	45.5	6800	109.2
1200	10.0	4200	47.4	6850	110.8
1300	11.0	4300	49.5	6900	112.2
1400	12.0	4400	51.5	6950	113.7
1500	13.1	4500	53.5	7000	115.1
1600	14.2	4600	55.5	7050	116.9
1700	15.3	4700	57.6	7100	118.2
1800	16.5	4800	59.7	7150	119.8
1900	17.5	4900	61.8	7200	121.3
2000	18.5	5000	63.9	7250	122.8
2100	19.8	5100	65.9	7300	124.3
2200	20.8	5200	68.0	7350	125.9
2300	22.0	5300	70.0	7400	127.3
2400	23.0	5400	72.0	7450	128.7
2500	24.2	5500	74.0	7500	130.3
2600	25.8	5600	76.0	7550	132.2
2700	26.8	5700	78.2	7600	134.0
2800	28.0	5800	80.5	7650	136.2
2900	29.2	5900	83.2	7700	138.0
3000	30.4	6000	86.0	7750	140.1
3100	31.5	6100	88.3	7800	142.2
3200	32.7	6200	91.3	7850	144.2
3300	34.0	6300	94.1	7900	146.3
3400	35.2	6400	97.2	7950	148.3
3500	36.6	6500	100.2	8000	150.6

RESTRICTED

The information given in this document is not to be communicated, either directly or indirectly, to the Press or to any person not authorized to receive it.

REPORT ON
Pz Kw VI
(Tiger)
Model H

PART II

ARMAMENT, FIGHTING ARRANGEMENTS, STOWAGE

AND POWER TRAVERSE

SECTION II

FIGHTING ARRANGEMENTS

Military College of Science
SCHOOL OF TANK TECHNOLOGY
Chobham Lane   Chertsey

January 1944

[Blank page, as per original report]

PART II

ARMAMENT, FIGHTING ARRANGEMENTS, STOWAGE AND POWER TRAVERSE

SECTION II

FIGHTING ARRANGEMENTS

INTRODUCTION

The fighting arrangements in this vehicle are, to a large extent, of standard German design. Notable innovations are the offsetting of the commander's position and cupola to the nearside (following British practice), the rotating turret floor and the provision of a seat for the loader.

Although crew comfort has been given great consideration during design, in actual fact the commander's and gunner's positions are somewhat cramped. On the other hand the loader's position is roomy by comparison with that in recent British tanks, partly on account of the absence of ammunition stowage on the turntable.

February, 1944.   Lieut. P.L. Gudgin (R.T.R)

FIGHTING CHAMBER, LAYOUT AND CREW ACCOMMODATION

Leading Dimensions of Fighting Chamber

Height of roof above turret ring	- 25½ ins.
Depth of turret ring	- 7¾ "
Turret platform to turret ring	- 28¼ "
Headroom in turret	- 61 "
Additional headroom in cupola	- 10½ "
Total headroom	- 71½ "
Distance between trunnions	- 54⅞ "
Distance of trunnion axis from centre of turret	- 49½ "
Height of trunnion axis above top of turret ring	- 9½ "
Height of front of roof above trunnion axis	- 16 " (approx)
Floor to trunnion axis	- 45 " (approx)
Ground to trunnion axis	- 82 "
Offset of axis of 8.8 cm. gun to right of turret centre	- 4 "
Internal diameter of turret ring	- 70½ "
Diameter of turret platform	- 57½ "
Internal diameter of cupola	- 18 "

LAYOUT AND CREW ACCOMMODATION

For the first time, the commander's position is offset to the near-side behind the gunner. A pressed sheet metal guard plate is bolted to the roof of the turret on the commander's right hand side, which protects him from the left deflector guard side plate, and possible injury to his right elbow by the recoil of the gun.

Commander

The commander's seat is mounted on a pillar bolted to the turret ring at 7 o'clock. There are two seats on the same pillar, one above the other. The upper one (52" above the turret platform) is used for observing out of the top of the cupola, and when not in use may be folded down, to form the backrest of the lower seat, by operating a lever on the right hand side of the pillar against the compression of a spring. The lower seat (36" above the turret platform) may be folded up when not in use. Two footrests are provided, as described below.

Gunner

This seat is non-adjustable and is mounted 21¾" above the turret platform on an extension arm welded to the hollow casing of the elevating handwheel shaft.

Below the seat is welded a footrest 18¼" above the turret platform for use with the commander's lower seat. The back-rest is secured to the power traverse drive casing which also carries the footrest for the commander's upper seat, 26½" above the turret platform.

Loader

For the first time, the Germans have in this tank, seriously considered the seating and comfort of the loader. His seat is mounted on the off-side of the fighting chamber, 22½" above the turret platform. It is pivotally mounted on the elevation gearbox and normally faces to the rear. When not in use, however, it may be lifted and swung forwards under the gun. It is not adjustable for height.

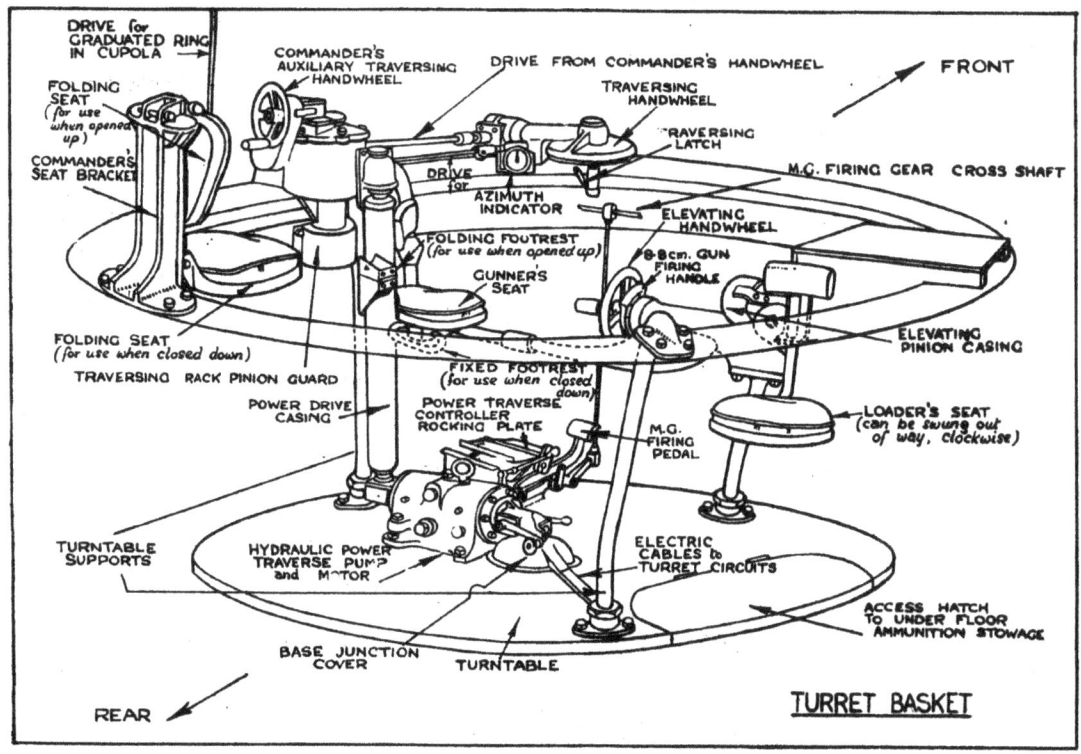

Driver

    The driver has an orthodox seat of tubular metal construction. It is mounted on the forward near side of the hull floor, is adjustable longitudinally and has a ratchet adjustment for the backrest (see diagram).

Hull Gunner

    This is a fixed non-adjustable seat of orthodox type on the off side floor of the forward compartment. The backrest is hinged to the hull sideplate and may be lifted out of the way to facilitate rapid exit from the turret through the forward compartment, or vice versa.

    All seats are fitted with comfortable sponge rubber seats and backrests.

VISION

Commander

    Five vision slits (size $7\frac{1}{4}" \times \frac{5}{8}"$) around the cupola. These are provided with standard fixed laminated glass blocks, 94 mm. thick; no protective shutters are fitted. A sighting vane is incorporated in the front episcope.
    One machine carbine port at 8 o'clock in nearside turret wall.

Turret Gunner

    Binocular sight T.Z.F.9 (b)

    One vision port, with slit $5" \times \frac{3}{8}"$ at 10 o'clock in nearside turret wall. Both this and the loader's slit have a replaceable laminated glass block (70 mm. x 150 mm. x 94 mm.) and no B.P. shutters.

Loader

    One vision port at 12 o'clock in offside turret wall (similar to gunner's).

    One loading and escape hatch at 4 o'clock in offside turret wall (or one machine carbine port in earlier models). It is believed that an episcope is located in front of the loader's hatch in the latest models.

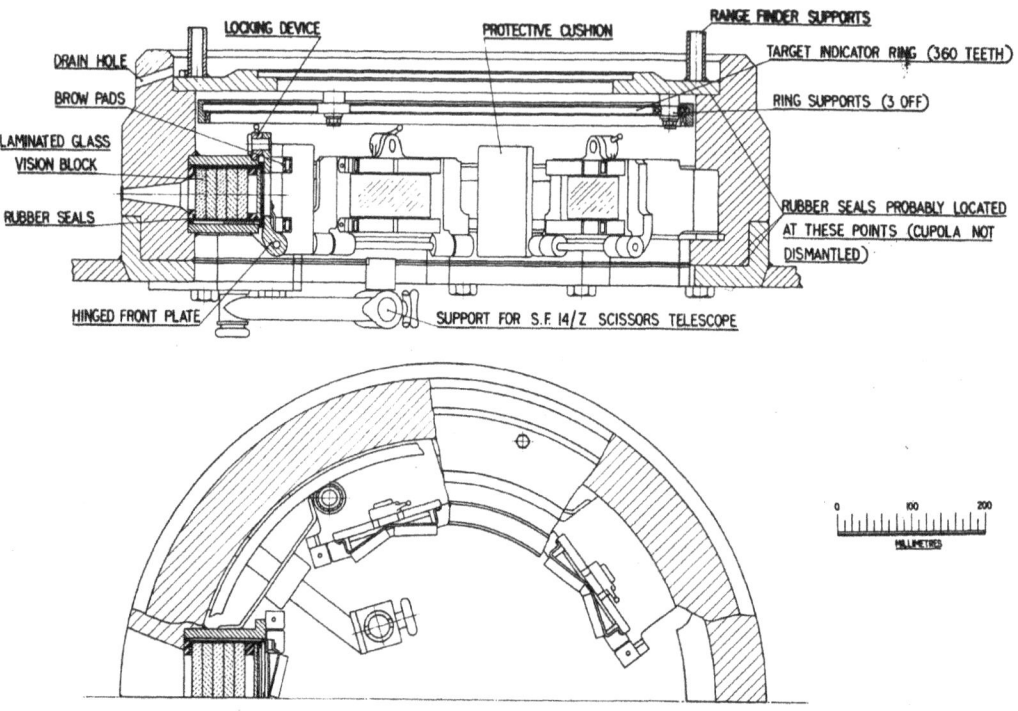

Section through Cupola

Hull Gunner

One sighting telescope K.Z.F.2.

One episcope in a circular hatch in superstructure roof. Both this and the driver's episcope have plastic casings and renewable prisms. The windows measure 5"x1½" and the length has been increased by a rubber faced distance piece to 11". Both episcopes are fixed facing forward and outboard, at an angle of about 30° to the keel line of the tank and have armoured hoods.

Driver

One visor in the front vertical plate, with a double sliding shutter (operated by a handwheel on the right of the steering wheel) and a replaceable laminated glass block (70 mm. x 240 mm. x 94 mm.).

Two holes for the driver's episcope K.F.F.2 in the front vertical plate have been plugged and welded. The episcope has also been deleted in a captured stowage list, though it was present on a Pz. Kw. VI. examined on the battlefield in N. Africa by the writer.

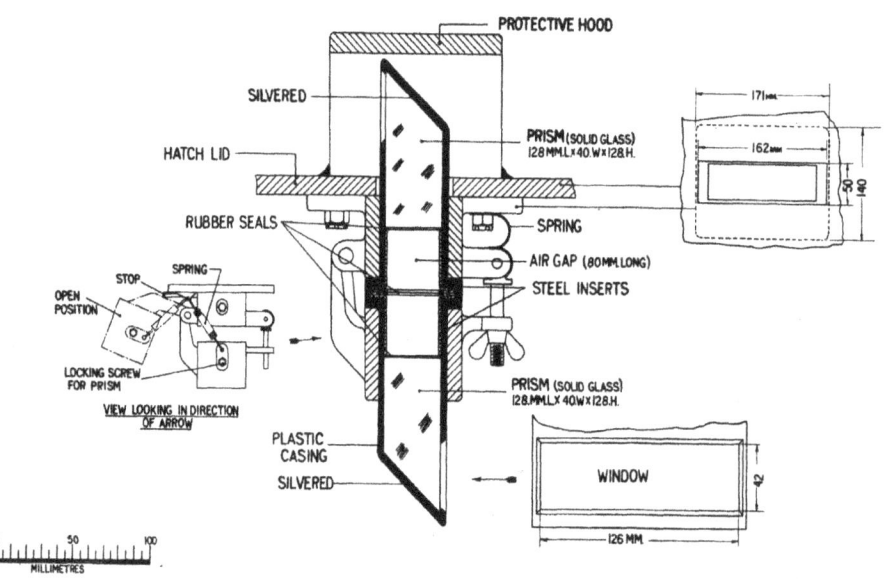

Driver's & Auxiliary Gunner's Episcope

> **RESTRICTED**
>
> The information given in this document is not to be communicated, either directly or indirectly, to the Press or to any person not authorized to receive it.

REPORT ON
PzKw VI
(Tiger)
Model H

PART II

ARMAMENT, FIGHTING ARRANGEMENTS, STOWAGE

AND POWER TRAVERSE

SECTION III

STOWAGE

Military College of Science
SCHOOL OF TANK TECHNOLOGY
Chobham Lane   Chertsey

January 1944

[Blank page, as per original report]

PART II

ARMAMENT, FIGHTING ARRANGEMENTS, STOWAGE AND POWER TRAVERSE

SECTION III

STOWAGE

INTRODUCTION

The stores and fittings stowed in this vehicle show little variation from those previously found in British or German tanks. The chief difference is the provision of accessories for deep wading and the method of attaching fittings to the turret walls. The latter is worthy of especial note.

The items have been carefully positioned to achieve ease of access and maximum freedom of movement for the crew.

Two lists of items are given - first, a list of those fittings, stores etc. found in the tank under examination, and second, a captured enemy official kit list, with ordnance reference numbers.

This Section has been compiled in collaboration with Major Shaw, D.C.M., R.T.R., V/GD Branch, D.T.D.

February, 1944.   Lieut. P.L. Gudgin, (R.T.R.)

[Editor's note: Major Shaw is listed above with a DCM (Distinguished Conduct Medal), which he must have earned on active service earlier in the war, while serving with the Royal Tank Regiment (RTR). His affiliation is given as DTD (the Ministry of Supply's Department of Tank Design), which employed many active Army personnel. The "V/GD Branch" is difficult to interpret, because the Ministry of Supply was restructured every few months and left no other records with this particular term or person. Perhaps the "V" is an abbreviation for "Vehicles," and "GD" means "Gun Design." In practice, DTD led no design work: it advised, inspected, and remediated commercial designs.]

STOWAGE

1. INTERNAL

(a) Fighting Chamber

All stowage fittings in the turret are welded, not directly to the turret wall but to vertical strips approximately $\frac{1}{4}$" clear of the wall. These are welded at the top to the turret roof and at the bottom to the turret ring. Thus, a hit on the wall will not cause the fittings to be projected into the turret, unless directly hit by the projectile.

Item	No.	Where Stowed	Item in captured Equipment Table
Breathing tubes	2	In containers, front nearside turret roof	C. 47
Breathing tube	1	In container, front offside turret roof	C. 47
Plug for machine gun port	1	Front offside turret roof	C. 11
Pivoted bracket (scissors telescope ?)	1	On right of cupola " "	
Container for gun history sheets	1	Nearside turret side wall	
Gunner's respirator	1	" " " "	
Signal pistol	1	" " " "	C. 43
Container for binoculars	1	Nearside rear on turret ring	
Stopper for machine carbine port	1	Nearside rear turret side wall	C. 12
Commander's respirator	1	Rear turret wall	
Water bottle	1	" " "	
W/T headset and microphone	2	In boxes on turret wall	C.52, 53 & 54
Glass blocks for vision ports	4	Rear turret wall	C. 27
Hatch keys	2	" " "	C. 36
Containers for signal cartridges	2	" " "	C. 46
Carrier for M.G. ammunition container	1	Offside " "	C. 29
Machine carbine	1	" " "	C. 40
Water bottle	1	Offside turret side wall	
Loader's respirator	1	" " " "	
Projectile ejector (Entlader)	1	" " " "	C. 57
Holder for M.G. bipod box	1	" " " "	C. 19
Water bottle	1	" " " "	
"Baggage" container	1	" " " "	
Fire extinguisher	1	Front of turret platform	63
Box	1	Front of turret platform under gunner's seat	
Box for 8.8cm Breech spares	2	Front of turret platform	C. 1
5 gallon water cans	3	Rear " " "	64 & 65
Stowed position turret M.G	1	Nearside of turret platform	
Wire basket	1	Nearside of turret platform (under commander's seat)	
M.G. spare barrels, in case	2	Offside of front bulkhead	C. 39
Spare prism	1	Nearside of front bulkhead	C. 25
Box for M.G tools	1	Rear of offside wall	C. 13

(b) **Auxiliary gunner's compartment.**

Respirator	1 Offisde pannier side wall	
Spare prism	1 " " " "	C. 25
M.G. spare barrels in case	2 " " " "	C. 39
Box for M.G. Tools	1 Offside of front bulkhead	C. 13
Breathing tube	1 Centre of front bulkhead	C. 47
Water bottle	1 Front wall, on right of M.G.	
Spare prism	1 " " " "	C. 25
First aid kit	1 On pannier roof, offside	C. 42
M.G. spares box	2 " " "	C. 38
Clips for offside headlamp when stowed.	Offside superstructure roof.	

(c) **Driver's Compartment.**

Clips for nearside headlamp	Nearside superstructure roof	
Vision blocks (spare)	2 Offside above instrument panel	C. 26
Breathing tube	1 Offside of front bulkhead	C. 47
W/T headset & microphone	2 Offside floor, behind seat	C. 52, 53 & 54
Water bottle	1 Nearside of front bulkhead	
Spare prism	1 Nearside of front bulkhead	C. 25
Respirator	1 Nearside pannier wall behind seat	
Oil can	1 Nearside floor, behind seat	46
Box for telescope accessories (?)	1 Nearside pannier wall	
Gyroscopic direction indicator	1 Nearside front of pannier roof	C. 44
1 Bin in floor behind seat table.)	(See section II (c) of 3, Enemy Equipment	

2 **EXTERNAL.**

Towrope	2 Offside and nearside, superstructure roof	81
Crow bar	1 Nearside " "	75
Wireless Aerial	1 Offside " "	
Fire Extinguisher (hand)	1 In holder, offside rear of superstructure roof.	80
Jacking block	1 Front offside, superstructure roof	74
Axe	1 Front centre of superstructure roof	76
Wire cutters	1pr Front nearside of superstructure roof	77
Blanking off plate	1 " " "	83
Shovel	1 " " "	79
Spade	1 Centre of front glacis plate	78
Sledge hammer	1 Front centre of superstructure roof	82
Track pulling cable	1 Nearside side plate	73
Track tool box	1 " " rear of track guard	28
Inertia starter handle	1 Offside, rear vertical plate	71
15-ton jack	1 Offside, rear track guard	72
Towing shackles	2 Offside and nearside, rear vertical plate	86
Track links	12 Front vertical plate	
Stowage bin	1 On rear of turret.	

The five or six section cleaning rod for the 8.8 cm gun, when carried is secured externally in the tow rope clips on the superstructure roof. No rods were present on this vehicle. Variations in stowage positions for most of the above mentioned items may be encountered, as, from examination of various photographs, no standard layout would appear to have been fixed as yet.

Certain fittings have been seen on the turret sides arranged vertically in pairs, 5 pairs a side. The purpose of these is unknown and none were found on the tank under examination.

EQUIPMENT TABLE FOR Pz.Kw.VI, MODEL H, MARK H1. (Translation of a captured document).

Serial No.	Description	No. per veh.	Indent Ref & Drawing No.
	I. TOOLS AND SPARE PARTS		
	A. Carried inside vehicle.		
	1. In tank tool box		
1.	Tool box, tank pattern	1	21 B 7641
2.	List of contents for tool box	1	021 St 37083
3.	Spanners DE (8 x 9)	1	)
4.	" (10 x 11)	1	)
5.	" (14 x 17)	1	) DIN 839
6.	" (19 x 22)	1	)
7.	" (24 x 27)	1	)
8.	Spanners, box, hexagonal DE (8 x 9)	1	R 9 5322
9.	" (10 x 11)	1	R 2 5323
10.	" (14 x 17)	1	R 5326
11.	" (19 x 22)	1	R 5331
12.	" (24 x 27)	1	R 5334
13.	Tommy Bar	1	R 5335
14.	Spanner, adjustable, 70 mm.	1	R 5292
15.	Half-round file, bastard, 200 mm. long	1	R 2103
16.	File handle with guard, diam. of handle 23mm.	1	R 2324
17.	Hammer, fitters, wt. 500 g. with handle	1	R 4586
18.	Screwdriver, with handle, blade .05 mm.	1	R2 5152
19.	" blade 1.2 mm.	1	R6 5152
20.	Roll of insulating tape in sealed packing width 15 mm. length 5 m.	1	Commercial Pattern
21.	Fire-point elements.	10	DIN 72581
	2. In engine tool box (Maybach) (attached to engine) Spare parts (incl in tool box)		
22.	Gauge, valve adjustment, contact breaker and point clearance	1	225084/1
23.	Spanner, sparking plug and jet	1	
24.	Sparking plugs	3	W 225 T 1
25.	Washers for sparking plugs (14 x 20)	3	DIN 7603
26.	Spare bowl for petrol pump	1	351 192/1
27.	Washer for above	1	351 193/1
	B. Secured outside vehicle		
	3. In track tool box on tailplate		
28.	Tool box complete	1	021 B 2799 U6
29.	List of contents	1	021 D 2799-49
30.	Track puller	1	021 C 39399 U9
31.	Hammer, fitters, wt. 1500 g. with handle	1	R 45 89
32.	Spanner for track tensioning and for removing covers over track adjusting spindles	1	021 D 2799-6

33.	Drifts for track-pins	1	021 E 2799-8
34.	Steel wire, diam. 1 mm., wt. 100 g. (on wooden fork 021 F 8999-12)	1	021-41099
35.	Pliers, combination 160 mm. long	1	R 4406
36.	Chisel, flat 25 x 16, 200 mm. long	1	R 4145
37.	Securing rings for track-pins	100	HE 2996-4
38.	Spanner for air pipe	1	021 C 2743 U14
39.	Spanner (box) for bogie wheels and sprockets	1	021 E 2799-5
40.	Hollow drift for track	1	021 E 2799-7

4. In bin on back of turret

41.	Track links	10	HB 3008-1
42.	Track pins	10	HE 2996-3

II. AUXILIARY EQUIPMENT

1. Carried inside vehicle

(a) In container on left under driver

43.	"Magnet" inspection lamp 12 V 15 W with protective wire grid and 20' flex	1	021 E 8999-38
44.	Box for above	1	021 E 8999-39

(b) On floor to left of driver

46.	Oil can, capacity 15 litres	1	U 481
47.	Grease gun with flex piping capacity 500 cu.cms.	1	U 548
48.	Coupling (for grease gun nozzle)	1	021 F 9399-64

(c) Behind driver's seat under floor

49.	Cotton waste, 1 lb.	1	
50.	Weather shield (hung on instrument panel)	1	
51.	Spanner, hexagonal for screw filler on power traverse 22 mm. diam., and for screw filler on radiator 32 mm. diam.	1	021 D 2799 U17
52.	Spanner for engine cover plates	1	021 D 2799 U16
52a.	Spanner, hexagonal, for internal engine bolts	1	14 DIN 911
53.	Spanner, for watertight seat on engine cover plates	1	021 E 2799 U14
54.	Filler, oil	1	U 574
55.	Filler, power traverse oil	1	021 E 2799-51

(d) In bin on back of turret

56.	Tarpaulins 1200 x 1800 mm. (6' x 4')	2	HSK No. J 3003

(e) In box (apparatus carried on tank for use in cold weather)

57.	Hose for transfer of warm water with holder	1	R10-104/4-14
58.	Heating equipment with handpump	1	HSK No.J 2838 U1
59.	Blow lamp	1	R 1 5882
60.	Connecting hose for heating equipment, 1200 mm (4' long)	1	HSK No.J 2838 U2
61.	Connecting hose for heating equipment, 1800 mm (6' long)	1	HSK No.J 2838 U2

(f) In satchel

62.	Instructional satchel containing:
	  Maintenance handbook incl. description and
	    working instructions, circuit and layout
	    diagrams
	  Diagram of auto-fire extinguisher circuit
	  Drawing of warm water transfer equipment
	  Drawing of pre-heater equipment
	  Drawing of heating arrangement for fighting
	    compartment
	  Lubricating and maintenance points
	  Lubrication chart
	  Equipment table for chassis
	  Equipment table for superstructure and turret
			HSK No. J 2713
			021 C 2727-17
			HSK No. J 2933
			HSK No. J 2932
			
			HSK No. J 2934
			HSK No. J 3056
			HSK No. J 3076

(g) On turret turn-table

63.	Fire extinguisher (O.T.C), 2 litres, (4 pints) with holder	1	U 1705
64.	Water container, standard Army pattern, capacity 20 litres (5 gals)*	2	574/Army
65.	Container for distilled water, standard Army pattern, contents 20 litres*	1	574/Army

(h) Beside headlamp holder

67.	Screwdriver for headlamp, unstowed	1	021 E 2799-2
68.	Locking ring	1	F 8999-86
69.	Ignition key, Bosch	1	S.A.A3/7*
70.	Cover for ignition key	1	021 F 9299-202

2. Stowed outside vehicle

(a) On tail plate

71.	Handle for inertia starter	1	021 B 2799 U13
72.	Steel jack 15 tons, with ratchet drive	1	U1684/5 at present 3767/6341

(b) On left side-plate

73.	Steel cable, 14 mm. diam x 15 m. long with eye	1	021E 2799 U12

(c) On roof

74.	Jacking pad	1	021E 29399 U4
75.	Crowbar 1800 mm. (5' 10") long	1	R 1843
76.	Axe *	1	R 24
77.	Wire cutters * ≠	1	28 B 41
78.	Spade *	1	29 C 46
79.	Shovel ≠	1	R 4284 DIN betn 120
80.	Fire extinguisher (O.T.C) (2 litres, with holder)	1	U1705
81.	Steel cable, 8.2 m. long 32 mm diam.	2	021 D 2799-45
82.	Sledge-hammer 6 kg (13¼ lbs.) with handle	1	R 4605
83.	Blanking off plate for air split over engine compartment	1	HSK No. J 3032
84.	Duct for warm air	1	HSK No. J 2743 U 1 in box
85.	Transfer hose for warm air	1	HSK No. J 2743 U5 in box
86.	Shackles (on tank)	4	

C. Equipment lists for superstructure and turret of Pz.Kw.VI, Model H1.

1.	Spares box (No.1) for breech of 8.8 cm.Kw.K 36	1	
2.	Cleaning rod head	1	5D 6899-115 U4
3.	Cleaning rod (in 5 or 6 parts) 4 rods 1238mm long	4	HSK J2669 U1
	1 rod 1240mm long	1	HSK J2669 U2
4.	Cover for cleaning rod	1	5C 6899-205
5.	Breech cover for 8.8 cm. Kw.K 36 (canvas)	1	5B 3899-2
6.	Lanyard for fuze key	1	8353
7.	Fuze key for percussion fuze (type A.Z.23)	1	13 E 6615
8.	(deleted) Muzzle Cover (canvas or artificial leather) for Kw. K 36	1	5C 3899-6
8a.	Muzzle covers (expendable)	10	5B 3899-5
9.	Canvas bag for muzzle covers	1	605 C 490
10.	Deflector bag	1	5B 3854 U2
11.	Plug for M.G opening	1	021 D 869
12.	Stopper for pistol port	1	per 021 SE875
13.	M.G spares boxes	2	21 St 7614
14.	Cover for M.G 34	1	021 C 57499-230
15.	Cover for gun mantlet	1	021 C 39099-80
16.	Cover for M.G. mantlet	1	in accordance with Model 4 St.ARF 31441
17.	Cartridge belt bags	32	021 St.39150
18.	Holders for above	2	021 St.37462
19.	Containers for M.G. spares (bipod, butt, foresight bracket) 1 in turret		021 B 7622
	1 in hull		
20.	Sighting telescope (type TZF 9b)	1	027 Gn 185
20a.	Cover for above	1	027-265-267
21.	(deleted) Driver's episcope KFF2 (1 set binoculars)	1 set	027 Gr. 3539
21a.	Dust covers for above	2	021 St.33999-21
22.	M.G sighting telescope, type KZF2	1	027 Gr 5075
23.	Cover for ball mounting, '100'	1	According to Model Wa. proof 6.
24.	Cap for ball mounting	1	HSK J 3098
25.	Prism holders	8	021 D 2746-1
26.	Bullet-proof glass 70 x 240 x 94	3	021 St. 9296
27.	Bullet-proof glass 70 x 150 x 94	11	021 St. 9280
28.	Cover for machine carbine	1	021 C 37499-255
29.	Case for machine carbine magazines	1	01 B 3321
30.	Extraction fan (in fighting compartment) capacity 12-13 cu. in. (approx. 450 cu.ft) per min.	1	
31.	Extraction fan cover (watertight)	1	021 C860 U51
32.	"Out of action" flag (yellow and black)	1	021 D 33477
33.	Smoke discharger, left	1	021 St 41406
34.	" " , right	1	021 St 41407
35.	Switch boxes for Smoke dischargers	2	21 St 7642
36.	Hatch keys	2	6 AKF 31406-1
37.	M.G.34 with tank type barrel sleeve	2	
38.	Ammunition Boxes - M.G	3	
39.	Holders for M.G barrels (each containing 2 barrels)	3	
40.	Machine carbine	1	
41.	M.G spares (butt and bipod)	1 set	
42.	First Aid kit	1	
43.	Signal Pistol	1	
44.	Gyro-direction indicator with lead	1	
45.	Transformer for above	1	
46.	Signal pistol ammunition, 24 rounds	12 white, 6 red, 6 green	
47.	Flexible hose for gas masks	4	
48.	Belt tags for M.G.34	32	
49.	Belt links for M.G. 34	96	
50.	Carrying slings (complete) for M.G.34	2	
51.	Belts filler 34 with box	1	

52.	Headsets, W/T, type B, soundproof	2	
53.	Throat microphone, type A, with 2-point plug and switch	2	
54.	Throat microphone, type B, with 3-point plug and switch	2	
55.	Twin lead, 25 cm. long with cross-piece and three double 20 mm. non-interchangeable plugs	1	
56.	Grease gun with tube, contents 140 cu.cm ($8\frac{1}{2}$ c.in.)	1	U547
57.	Ejector, projectile for 8.8 cm. gun	1	5E 6899-40
58.	Clinometer for 8.8 cm. gun	1	
59.	Spanner for M.G. 34	2	
60.	Muzzle covers for M.G. 34, expendable	4	
61.	Brushes for cleaning M.Gs.	2	
62.	" " "	4	
63.	Grease box for 2 oz. lubricating grease	1	J/9441/35 1099-210
64.	Sealing covers	2	4/VI/E 03479
65.	Air pump with tube)	–	4AKF 31406-50
66.	Air pressure gauge in leather case)	–	5AKF 31406-51
67.	Hexagonal box-spanner) ∅	–	5AKF 31406-52
68.	Tension device for compensating spring)	–	
69.	Padlocks	2	

∗	Supplied by unit.
✗	Fitted by Unit.
∅	One of each for five turrets.
✠	On indent from C.O.O., Kassel.

RESTRICTED

The information given in this document is not to be communicated, either directly or indirectly, to the Press or to any person not authorized to receive it.

REPORT ON
Pz Kw VI
(Tiger)
Model H

PART II

ADDENDA TO SECTIONS I, II AND III.

AND REPORT ON GUNNERY TRIALS

Military College of Science
SCHOOL OF TANK TECHNOLOGY
Chobham Lane   Chertsey

November   1944

[Blank page, as per original report]

PART II

ADDENDA TO SECTIONS I, II AND III.
AND REPORT ON GUNNERY TRIALS.

INTRODUCTION

The Tiger tank was sent for brief Gunnery Trials by Experimental Wing, A.F.V. School. This section contains the substance of their reports: E.O. No. 37/1/157 dated 17th March 1944 and 37/1/171 dated 14th April 1944, together with a few additional points which have come to light since Sections I, II and III of Part II were published.

November 1944.   Major W. de L. Messenger, R.T.R.

ADDENDUM TO SECTION I

8.8 cm. GUN Kw.K.36

AND MOUNTING

BREECH MECHANISM.

The accessibility and ease of stripping are noteworthy. All moving parts can be removed without the use of tools. During firing the action of the semi-automatic gear was extremely smooth and silent.

RECOIL GEAR.

During firing, recoils averaged as follows:-

Projectile	Recoil mm.	ins.
H.E.	520	20.5
A.P.C.B.C.	530	20.9
(Maximum working	580	22.8)

From this it is concluded that the system was functioning correctly. Recoil and run-out were very smooth, the gun coming gently to rest.

FIRING GEAR.

The trigger for the electric firing gear is remarkably light.

MOUNTING.

Studs are provided on the rear face of the mantlet to act as elevation stops.

BALANCE GEAR.

There is a certain amount of "spring" in the linkage, while the various pivots introduce considerable friction when elevating or depressing the gun. Working against the "spring" only, the trunnion friction was $\frac{1}{2}$ to 1 lbs measured at the rim of the elevating wheel, but when the "spring" was taken up the load rose to 23 - 24 lbs due to pivot friction.

ELEVATING GEAR.

Backlash was 16 - 19 minutes at the gun or $\frac{3}{8}$ in. at the rim of the elevating wheel.

TRAVERSE GEAR.

Hand Traverse. The force required to rotate the turret with the tank 0° 56' down at 12 o'clock and 1° 2' down at 3 o'clock was:-

Position of turret.	Traversing. Right.	Left.	Note:
12	½ lbs.	16 lbs.	There is a foul caused
1	12 "	14 "	by damage between 9 and
2	16 "	12 "	10 o'clock when the
3	22 "	6 "	loads rose to 60 lbs.
4	22 "	1 "	right and 45 lbs. left,
5	28 "	½ "	and the turret jammed.
6	20 "	1½ "	At this point it could
7	28 "	1½ "	not be rotated owing to
8	15 "	1½ "	the clutch slipping.
9	28 "	9 "	
10	3 "	9 "	
11	10 "	17 "	

CO-AXIAL MACHINE GUN

CRADLE.

The gun is mounted so close to the 8.8 cm. buffer cylinder that re-arming with a new belt is very difficult.

SIGHTS

MAIN ARMAMENT.

Telescope T.Z.F.9b. The illuminating lamp plugs into a socket in the turret roof, and is controlled by a switch on the board to the gunner's left. The intensity shutter control is too far forward for the gunner to reach. (This difficulty is also experienced on the Pz Kpfw III.)

Experimental Wing, A.F.V.S. suggest that the aiming mark in the left telescope is for use with A.P. composite rigid shot (Pzgr 40).

No jump is allowed for the 8.8 cm. gun, but there is an allowance for +6 mins. with the M.G.

Clinometer. This has the same dimensions as that for the 7.5 cm. Kw. K (short) in Pz Kpfw IV (see report by D.T.D. on Pz Kpfw IV Model E) being 16.4 ins. long and curved at a radius of about 24 ins. The only difference is the scale.

The range of the bubble between the marks on the glass is ½ mil.

FIRE CONTROL.

The approximate characteristics of the S.F.14Z stereo binocular are:-

Magnification	x10	Field of view 5°
Exit pupil	5mm.	Eye relief ½ inch.
Interocular distance		57 mm. or more - as stereo
		58 mm. or more - as periscopic.

Graticule, right eyepiece, in 10 mil squares with 2 mil gaps at 5 mil intervals. Interrupted cross at centre for datum point.

The graticule is illuminated.

A small clinometer graduated in mils is also incorporated.

The S.F.14Z was provided with an adapter by Experimental Wing A.F.V.S. and used during the firing trials.

With the binoculars properly mounted and using the auxiliary hand traverse, the commander has an excellent means of accurately aligning the gun onto a target which the gunner cannot see.

When mounted on an ordinary tripod the performance was very similar to that of the British Stereoscopic Binoculars but the light transmission appeared to be slightly inferior.

It is believed that the instrument should be mounted on a rotating azimuth dial, if so this might explain the absence of a proper azimuth indicator on the turret ring of the tank.

AUXILIARY ARMAMENT

"S" MINE DISCHARGERS.

Examination of further photographs and subsequent inspection of the tank reveal that two further dischargers were at one time mounted on the rear corners of the hull, directed outwards at 45° to the keel line.

AMMUNITION

SUMMARY.

The ammunition capacity is re-stated as follows:-

8.8 cm.

Where stowed.	No. of rounds	Type
Left Pannier.		
Beside driver	6	A.P. or H.E.
Centre	16	A.P. or H.E.
Rear	16	A.P. or H.E.
Right Pannier.		
Centre	16	A.P. or H.E.
Rear	16	A.P. or H.E.
Fighting Compartment.		
Left front	4	A.P.
Left rear	4	A.P.
Right front	4	A.P.
Right rear	4	A.P.
Under Turntable.		
Right	6	A.P. or H.E.
Total	92	

Possible proportions lie between:-

    (a) 92 (100%) A.P. and

    (b) 16 (17½%) A.P. and 76 (82½%) H.E.

Intelligence reports indicate that about 50% of each is carried.

The armour piercing projectiles are low capacity A.P.C.B.C. shell (white tip), not "A.P.38" as stated in Section I of Part II.

7.92 mm.

Where stowed.	No. of 150 rd belt bags.	No. of Rds.
Fighting Compartment.		
On gun	1	
Turret - right wall	4	
Forward bulkhead - right	1	
Rear bulkhead	16	
Total	22	3300
Forward Compartment.		
On gun	1	
In right pannier - vision plate	3	
- side plate	8	
- front bulkhead	4	
Total	16	2400
Grand total	38 belts	5700

This is more than given in the German kit list, but represents the maximum capacity of the stowage fittings.

ADDENDUM TO SECTION II

FIGHTING ARRANGEMENTS

LAYOUT AND CREW ACCOMMODATION.

The shield on the right of the commander protects him from back-flash if flashing ammunition is used.

The flush turntable without coaming and the absence of shielding around it improve access to and ease of handling the ammunition. On the other hand the loader is somewhat handicapped by having no ready use ammunition stowed on the turntable.

COMMANDER.

The commander has three alternative positions:-

(a) Sitting on upper seat - head out.

(b) Sitting on lower seat - closed down.

(c) Standing on turntable - closed down.

Nevertheless, his position is cramped and uncomfortable.

GUNNER.

The gunner is cramped by the legshield and has the most uncomfortable position in the tank. However, the position of the laying controls is good.

DRIVER.

The driver's seat folds back to allow exit into the fighting chamber.

VISION

The fields of view from the vision devices have been mapped by the M.R.C. Physiological Laboratory, and in consequence the section on "VISION" has been re-written to include the gist of their report, and to expand the information previously given in Part II Section II. The original text should therefore be ignored, but reference should be made to the section drawings of the commander's cupola and of the driver's episcope.

It should be noted that all the vision devices are made watertight with rubber seals. All glass blocks and prisms are readily changed, and spares are carried.

COMMANDER.

Provided with a fixed cupola with <u>five vision slots</u> ($7\frac{1}{4}$" x $\frac{5}{8}$") backed by 94mm laminated glass blocks; there are no shutters. A sighting vane is incorporated with the front slot.

A machine carbine port is provided at 8 o'clock in the turret wall.

The cupola field of view on the ground is shown in Fig. I. The firm line represents the nearest point on the ground that is visible from the cupola, moving the head if necessary. The part of the turret structure that limits near vision in a particular direction is indicated on the line. The radiating dotted lines give the boundaries of the field from each slot with the head held centrally opposite the glass blocks without moving. The blocks are numbered clockwise (C1), (C2), etc.

In the Pz Kpfw III and IV commander's vision was outstandingly good (especially when compared with contemporary Allied vehicles), particularly in that he could see near ground all round the vehicle. The distance between the vision device and the edge of the turret, the slope of the turret roof and the height of the device above the general level of the turret roof, are the main factors determining whether or not ground will be seen near the vehicle in any given direction. These various factors were all well balanced in the Pz Kpfw III and IV. The cupola was centrally placed at the rear and narrowest part of the turret and allowed good vision to the rear and sides of the vehicle. Vision forwards was less good because the whole length of the turret was in front of the cupola, but this was mitigated to some extent by sloping the roof downwards from the cupola and further by raising the cupola above the roof. Compared with vision in other directions, commander's near vision forwards is not so important, as vision in this direction is also covered by the driver and hull gunner. In contemporary Allied vehicles the commander's vision device was placed to one side of a square flat-topped turret. This meant that on the whole vision was good in one direction (over the nearest turret edge) and liable to be bad in other directions, because of the distance between vision device and turret edge. The blind zone in the commander's field on the Churchill extended to within 120 feet of the right hand side of the turret. Also, because of the lowness of the periscopes on the turret roof, visual fields were badly obstructed by fixtures such as fans which projected above the general roof level.

In the early models of the TIGER, it appears that the designers did not consider near vision to be so important. The commander's cupola is placed not centrally behind, but to one side of the gun. Vision to the left and rear of the turret is good, but bad to the right and right rear. It should, however, be noted that part of the blind area to the right in the commander's field can be seen through the loader's slot (see Fig. I).

Using the head movement necessary to get the maximum field from each of the constituent vision blocks, a continuous view of the ground round the vehicle is obtained with a slight overlap between the peripheral fields of each block. If one only looks through the centre of each block without head movement, there is a blind zone of 15-20° between it and the next block. The fact that the commander sees through a narrow fixed aperture in front of each block does not mean that the vertical field is reduced, but that the whole available field cannot be seen at once, vertical head movement being needed to cover it all.

The generally cramped position of the commander makes it difficult to turn round and look to the rear. Vision to the right rear is limited by the stowage bin, this limitation could have been reduced by sloping its top surface more steeply as was done on the Pz Kpfw III and IV.

Fig. I. shows clearly that the best approach for tank hunters is from the right and right rear of the turret. If close to the ground they should be invisible when within 100-120 feet of the vehicle.

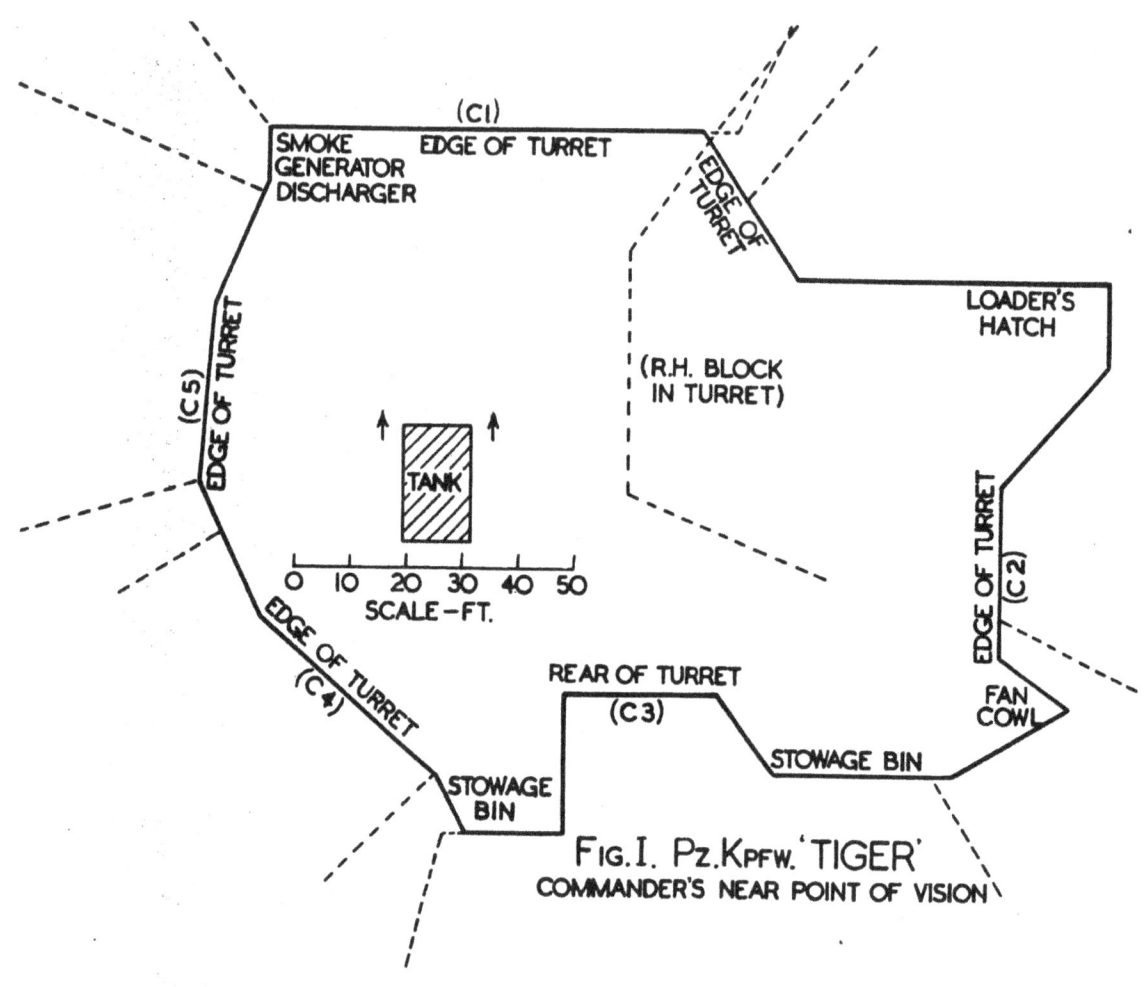

Fig. I. Pz.Kpfw. 'TIGER' COMMANDER'S NEAR POINT OF VISION

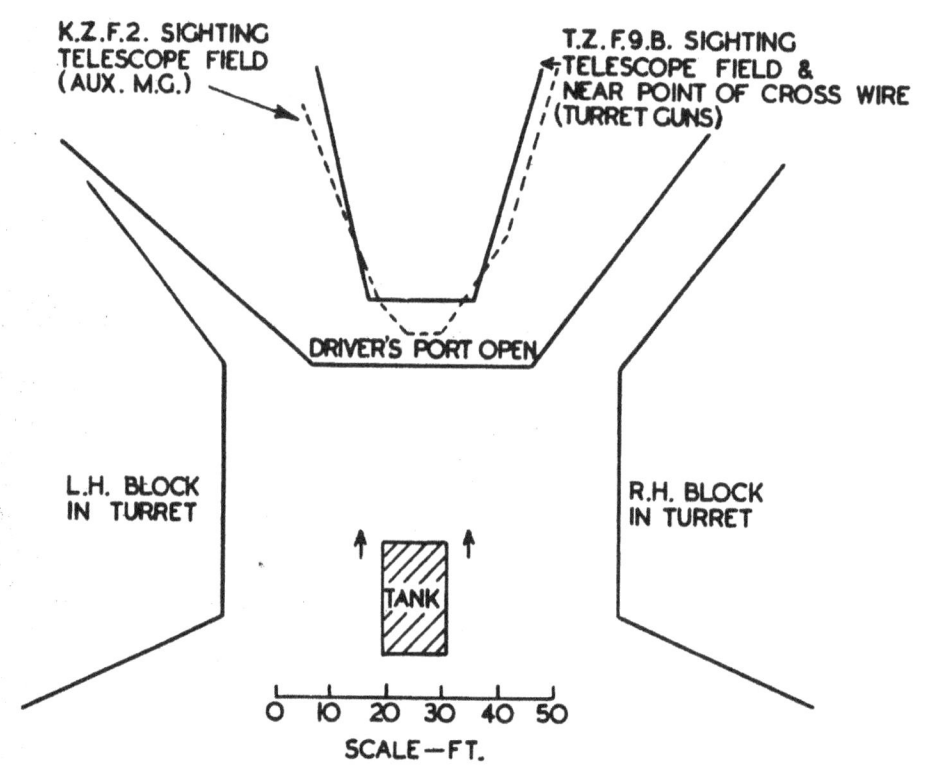

Fig. II. Pz.Kpfw. 'TIGER' NEAR POINT OF LOADER'S, GUNNER'S, DRIVER'S & HULL GUNNER'S VISION.

It would, however, appear from recent photographs that re-design of the cupola to improve observation of the ground near the vehicle has been necessary. It is interesting to note that the new design, as far as can be seen from the photographs, involves the use of eight high episcopes in place of the direct vision blocks. Episcopes have not been used in cupola design by the Germans since the Pz Kpfw II.

TURRET GUNNER (See Fig. II).

Besides the binocular sighting telescope T.Z.F.9b (field of view 23°) in the co-axial mounting (elevation 17°, depression 7°), there is a slot, 5" x 3/8", at 10 o'clock in the turret wall backed by a replaceable laminated glass block (70mm x 150mm x 94mm thick). There is no shutter. This aperture allows a good view to the left, but considerable head movement is required to cover the whole field of view.

The nearest point fire of the gun is 35 feet to the front and sides and 70 feet over the tail.

LOADER (See Figs. I and II).

The loader has a slot similar to the gunner's at 2 o'clock in the turret wall. This covers part of the commander's blind area, but the loader is restricted in obtaining a full field of view rearwards by the kit bin which prevents him moving his head.

Photographs show that later models incorporate what appears to be a fixed episcope, similar to those used in the forward compartment, in front of the loader's hatch. In the present model the loader is uncomfortably blind.

Early models of the tank had a second machine carbine port in place of the loading and escape hatch.

DRIVER (Fig. II).

The normal driving vision aperture is a port in the front plate which may be closed down as much as required by a balanced pair of rising and falling shutters, operated by a handwheel on the right. This is backed by a laminated glass block (70mm x 240mm x 94mm thick). It gives good and adequate vision.

The front plate is bored with two holes for the normal driver's episcope, consisting of a pair of K.F.F.2 cranked telescopes, but the holes have been plugged and welded, and the episcope carrier fittings removed. The K.F.F.2 telescopes have also been crossed out on the stowage list.

There are no side ports, but the hatch carries a fixed episcope facing 45° to the left of the keel line of the tank. The "windows" measure 5" x 1½" and the height is 11" with a 3.2" air gap. Top and bottom prisms are identical and interchangeable. As this was out of order, its field of view could not be mapped, but it is probable that it is partly masked to the front by the upward projection of the edge of the superstructure front plate.

AUXILIARY GUNNER (Fig. II).

Besides the K.Z.F.2 Telescope (field of view 18°) in the ball mounting (elevation 20°, depression 10°, traverse 15° left and 15° right) the auxiliary gunner has a fixed episcope identical to the driver's, but facing outwards to the right. The same remarks apply to this as to the driver's episcope and, unfortunately, its field of view could not be plotted either.

GUNNERY TRIALS.

8.8 cm. AMMUNITION.

    A.P.C.B.C./H.E.   Length   34.21 ins.
                        Weight   33.75 lbs.
                        Point of balance 19.75 ins. from base.

    H.E. fuzed AZ 23/28   Length   36.69 ins.
                        Weight   32.0 lbs.
                        Point of balance 19.75 ins. from base.

The balance of the rounds was bad when picked up in the most convenient way from the bins, being projectile heavy.

Both types were fitted with a smoke trace and use flashless propellent. This gave a large quantity of smoke but no flashes were observed firing in daylight.

FUMES FROM 8.8 cm. GUN.

It was only possible for the M.R.C. Physiological Laboratory to take two snap samples of the fumes in the commander's cupola which were collected in 565 cc. vacuum bottles after firing the 2nd and 3rd rounds in a 5 round burst of H.E. ammunition. These were analysed for carbon monoxide and ammonia. During the trial all hatches were closed, the engine was off but the ventilation fan was running.

RESULTS.

Trial.	Rounds fired.	Conc. NH_3 in parts per million in atmosphere.	%CO in atmosphere.	%CO per 100 parts per million NH_3.
Blank	-	-	.029	-
8.8 cm.	2	150	.850	.565
8.8 cm.	3	191	1.015	.530

This does not provide sufficient data on which to issue a report and M.R.C. merely comment as follows:-

> "Under the exceptional conditions of this trial the fumes drifted slowly through the fighting compartment and contained a dangerous amount of CO. The ammonia was irritating. These results give no information about the gun fumes in a properly ventilated Tiger tank".

BACKFLASH.

Owing to shortage of ammunition available for firing during subsequent demonstrations, electric primers were fitted to the H.E. ammunition which had been supplied with the tank to make up the stowage. This was stated to be Flak ammunition though it was fuzed percussion.

The markings on it were indistinct but it bore the date 1941, and the projectiles were fitted with copper driving bands as opposed to iron.

This ammunition was, as expected, not flashless but gave considerable muzzle flash and large backflashes occurred with 3 out of 4 rounds fired.

The conditions were not conducive to backflash as there was a following wind and the hatches were opened up without the fan or engine running.

This confirms the supposition that the deflector guard fitted on the Commander's side was placed there to protect him against backflash and also may be one of the reasons why the Germans have adopted flashless propellant for their tank guns.

ASSEMBLY OF AMMUNITION.

During trials one round was noticed to hang fire and one misfire occurred. This latter round was broken down and revealed that

(a) the primer had fired.
(b) the silk sleeve and igniting charge had been incorrectly assembled or shaken off.

The silk sleeve showed a good deal of charring where it was folded over the primer opening and had prevented the flash reaching the igniter or propellant.

A further point of interest was noticed in the base fuze and tracer assembly. The fuze is assembled into the shell with a right hand thread and the tracer screws into it with a left hand thread, while the rifling has a right hand twist.

STABILITY.

The tank provides a very stable gun platform for either head-on or broadside stationary firing.

The gun tends to rise due presumably to the suspension settling down for the first two or three rounds fired, but after this remains constant.

During the firing trials a hornet target was engaged at 1100 yards. Correction was given to the gunner for the first round, after which he fired a further 5 rounds without having any observation or moving either the traverse or elevating controls, and secured 5 consecutive hits.

OBSERVATION.

The flashless propellant produces a very large smoke cloud which is dispersed to some extent on each side of the gun by the muzzle brake. There was a following wind throughout the firing trials so that the smoke prevented observation of strike by the gunner at range up to 1600 yards. In most cases, however, the commander was able to observe by seeing over the smoke cloud.

ACCURACY.

The gun appeared to be remarkably consistent.

A shoot of 5 rounds taking a constant aim at a screen target at 1200 yards gave all the shots in an area 16" by 18".

Owing to a fracture of the offside front suspension arm, the tank could not be taken to the new range and firing could only be carried out at ranges up to 1600 yards.

RATE OF FIRE.

The highest timed rate of fire during these limited trials was 4 rounds in 39 seconds. (1st round loaded and timed from firing).

The normal rate of fire is estimated to be from 5 - 8 rounds per minute.

Over a great number of rounds, the availability of a large quantity of ammunition should give this tank a higher rate of fire than in our own heavy gun tanks where the bulk of the ammunition is not so readily accessible.

MOVING TARGETS.

Tracking of moving targets at 1000 yards up to speeds of 15 m.p.h. was done with the tank on level ground.

Hand traverse was easy for all speeds.

Powered traverse on "low" was the best for ease of tracking at all speeds but had a very wide neutral zone.

On "high", speeds appeared a little irregular and it was unsuitable for speeds of 5 m.p.h. or lower. At 10 m.p.h., correction by the hand traverse was necessary.

Five rounds were fired at a target moving at 15 m.p.h., range 1500 yards. Although smoke obscured direct observation by the gunner, 3 hits were scored after corrections had been given by the commander. Laying was done on Low Speed with hand traverse assistance.

CLINOMETER.

A target at 1800 yards was engaged by normal bracketting methods. A hit was obtained with the 4th round.

SUMMARY.

The design has been well thought out and it embodies a number of distinctly original features such as the heavy armament and armour, turret and hull construction, powered traverse layout and facilities for total submersion.

It appears that the user has not had the same influence on it as on British tanks since so many of the items, whilst basically good, are unsatisfactory and could well be improved from the user aspect by slight modification.

The outstanding features would appear to be:-

GOOD POINTS.

1. 8.8 cm gun with its smooth action and easily stripped breech mechanism.
2. Heavy armour and method of construction (welding and front plates projecting above the roof plates).
3. Stability as a gun platform.
4. Ammunition stowage - quantity and accessibility.
5. Electrical firing gear with safety interlocks and novel trigger switch.
6. Flush turret floor without coaming or shields.
7. Binocular telescope with fixed eyepiece.
8. Mounting for periscopic binoculars in cupola and commander's hand traverse.
9. Ability to superimpose hand on power traverse and absence of oil pipes and unions.
10. Ample space for loader.
11. Method of attaching stowage to turret walls (flexible strips).
12. Spring assisted hatches.
13. S-mine dischargers.
14. 2-position commander's seat and backrest.
15. Electrically fired smoke generator dischargers.
16. Handholds on roof to assist gunner.

BAD POINTS.

1. Out-of-balance of gun and turret.
2. Obscuration by smoke from flashless propellent.
3. Ventilation of gun fumes.
4. Lack of intercommunication for loader.
5. Cramped positions of gunner and commander.
6. Powered traverse control - lack of definite neutral position and awkward range of movement.
7. No armouring on bins.
8. Small gun deflector bag.
9. Awkward re-arming of co-axial M.G.
10. Gunner's exit via commander's cupola.
11. Head pad on auxiliary M.G.

The Pz Kpfw VI with its heavy armour, dual purpose armament and fighting ability is basically an excellent tank, and, in spite of the defects noted, constitutes a considerable advance on any tank that we have tried.

Its greatest weakness is probably the limit imposed on mobility owing to its weight, width and limited range of action.

Taking it all round, it presents a very formidable fighting machine which should not be under-rated.

ADDENDUM TO SECTION I.II

STOWAGE

REMARKS BY EXPERIMENTAL WING, A.F.V.S.

A large amount of kit is carried on the tank and yet the interior does not appear unduly cluttered up. The points of particular interest are:-

Internal

1. All fittings are labelled - similar to British practice.

2. Crew equipment is stowed near to their position in the tank and consists of (a) waterbottle, (b) gasmask container and (c) breathing tube.

3. Each M.G. has:-
(i) Its own spare parts box with shaped wooden compartments for the accessories carried therein.
(ii) A box containing bipod and butt for dismounted use.
(iii) Two spare barrels in container.

4. Only one machine carbine is carried. This is understandable since both turret and hull M.G. can be used dismounted.

5. One bin is provided in the turret R.H. top corner for kit and L.H. turret sill plate has a raised coaming forming a "loose" container for use by both the commander and gunner.

6. Ammunition (see also Part II, Section I).
No immediate supply is carried on the turntable but the floor and pannier bins are very accessible for most turret positions.
The method of securing the rounds in the floor bins is simple, quick and accessible. The projectile is held by a separator which swings out of the way; the round is prevented from moving forward by its rim engaging a lip and the rear separators lift up quickly and park in special grooves at the end of the bin. They cannot be removed and so are not lost.
The turntable necessitates the rounds in the rear bins being stowed with the projectiles facing 12 o'clock which is the wrong way round for loading. A changeover of hands is therefore necessary.
The pannier bins, too, work quite well but the outermost rounds require a knack for quick removal. In fact, rapid withdrawal of ammunition necessitates learning the optimum procedure for each batch of rounds. This comes quickly with experience.
Six rounds are held in reserve under the floor and are accessible with the turret at 12 o'clock.
A total of 36 150rd. belt bags (5400 rounds) of M.G. ammunition appear to be carried. This excludes any on the M.G's and is four in excess of that given in the German list. Of the 36 bags, 21 are in the main turret and 15 in the front compartment. The normal British stowage requirement is 15 225-rd liners for the co-axial M.G. and 10 liners for Hull M.G. - total 3625 rounds.
No cross country work was done so we were unable to check the security of the German method of stowing the "Gurtsacke" (belt bag) on rails. The bags were quite easy to handle and would seem to provide an effective dust protector-cum-collector bag.
The belt filling machine was complicated in construction but worked most efficiently when its operation was understood.

External

Gun cleaning rods, spades, axes, shovels are stowed in clips or straps and some of the track tools in a partitioned box.

The general impression was of tidiness in front but a conglomeration of kit and fittings all over the engine compartment.

No track plates were attached to the visor plate.

Some models may be fitted with track plates round the turret between 3 and 5 o'clock, and 9 and 7 o'clock.

The stowage diagrams which follow are based on those by Experimental Wing, A.F.V.S.

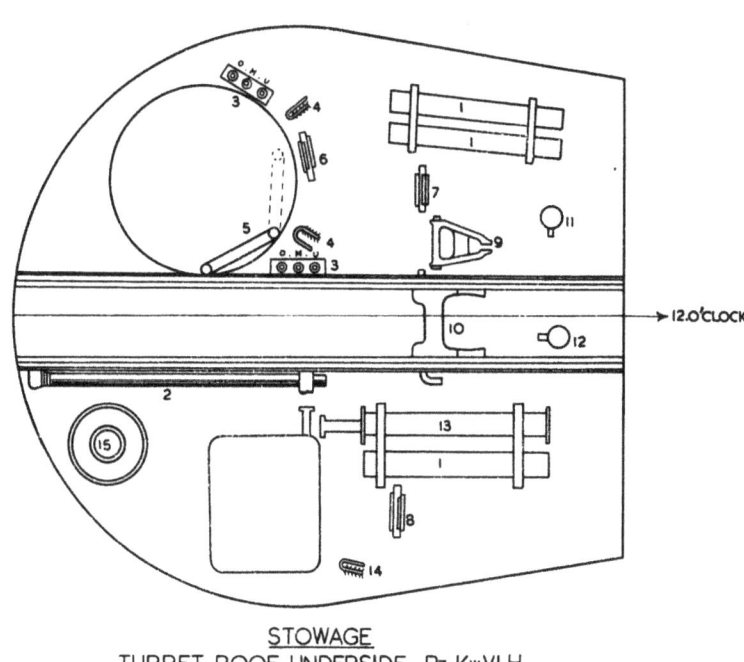

STOWAGE
TURRET ROOF UNDERSIDE Pz Kw VI H

KEY TO DIAGRAM

1. BREATHING TUBES. (ATEMSCHLAUCH)
2. PLUG FOR COAXIAL M.G. APERTURE. DURING SUBMERSION.(DICHTSTOPFEN BEZW M.G.)

FITTINGS
3. SMOKE GENERATOR DISCHARGER SWITCHES. (NEBELKERZEN)
4. COMMANDERS HANDHOLDS.
5. CMDRS SCISSORS PERISCOPE HOLDER.
6. CMDRS FESTOON LAMP.
7. GUNNERS FESTOON LAMP.
8. LOADERS FESTOON LAMP.
9. TELESCOPE SUPPORT BRACKET.
10. GUN ELEVATION CRAMP.
11. SOCKET FOR TELESCOPE & CLINOMETER ILLUMINATION.
12. SOCKET FOR ELECTRIC FIRING CIRCUIT.
13. BALANCE GEAR LOADERS HATCH.
14. LOADERS HANDHOLD
15. EXTRACTOR FAN. 12V. 10A. 6000

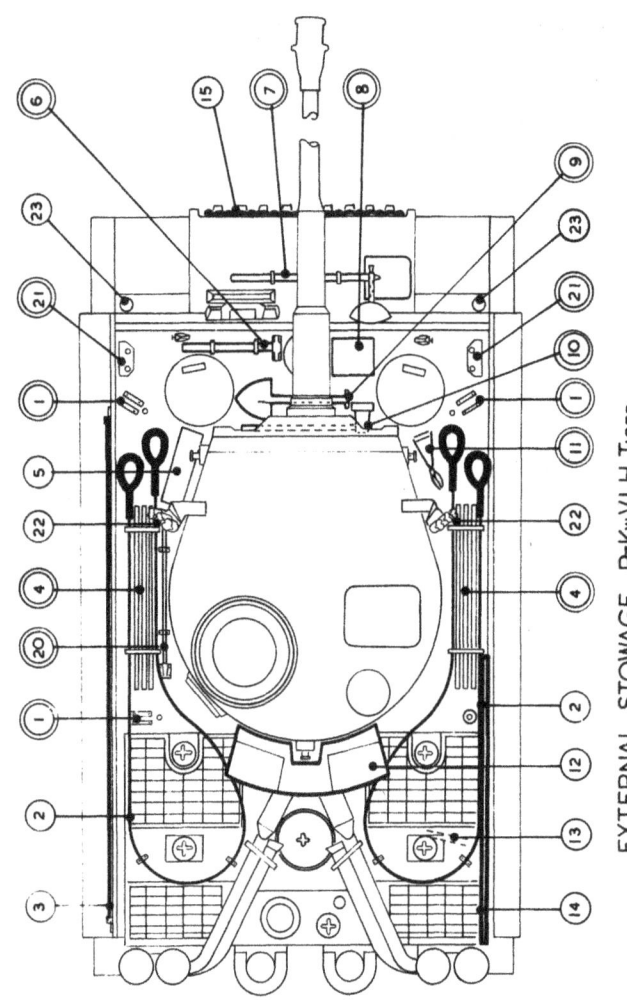

EXTERNAL STOWAGE. PzKw VI.H. TIGER.

KEY TO DIAGRAM

1: ANTI-PERSONNEL MINE ATTACHMENTS.
2: TOW ROPE.
3: 15 WIRE ROPE.
4: GUN CLEANING RODS.
5: BLANKING OFF PLATE FOR AIRSLIT ENGINE COMP'T.
6: SLEDGE HAMMER.
7: SHOVEL.
8: JACKING BLOCK.
9: SPADE.
10: AXE.
11: WIRE CUTTERS.
12: TURRET BIN (10 TRACK LINKS, 10 TRACK PINS)
13: TETRA FIRE EXTINGUISHER.
14: WIRELESS AERIAL STOWAGE.
15: SPARE TRACK LINKS.
20: CROW BAR 5'10"
21: HEAD LAMP POSITIONS.
22: SMOKE GENERATOR DISCHARGERS.
23: HOLE FOR POLE SUPPORTING CAMOUFLAGE (CAMOUFLAGED AS LORRY OR BUS)

ITEMS THUS ◯ TAKEN FROM EXISTING ON VEHICLE.
ITEMS THUS ⬭ TAKEN FROM W O PHOTOGRAPH M 20181.

EXTERNAL STOWAGE - REAR.
PzKw VI.H. TIGER.

KEY TO DIAGRAMS
EXTERNAL STOWAGE

1. ANTI PERSONNEL MINE ATTACHMENTS.
3. 15m WIRE ROPE FOR PULLING TRACKS.
12. TURRET STOWAGE BIN. (10 TRACK LINKS AND 10 TRACK PINS)
16. 15 TON JACK.
17. TRACK TOOL BOX.
18. TOWING SHACKLES.
19. HANDLE FOR INERTIA STARTER.
22. SMOKE GENERATOR DISCHARGERS.

Pz.Kw.VI H STOWAGE
TURRET & FIGHTING COMPARTMENT AT LEFT HAND SIDE

KEY

1. Coaming to form receptacle for Maps etc.
2. Commander's Field Glasses
   Fernglas
3. Plug for Revolver Port
   M.P.Dichtstopfen
4. Signal Pistol
   Leuchtpistole
5. Gunner's Respirator
   Gasmaske
6. Container for Gun & Mounting Book
   Rohr u. Wiegenbuch
7. Coaming to form receptacle for Gunner's Kit
8. Spare Prisms
   Prismeneinsatz
9. Ammn. Panniers each holding 16rds. A.P. or H.E.
10. Ammn. Bins, Vertical, each holding 4rds. A.P. only
11. Stowage Bin, Near-side only
12. Wire Basket for Flags etc.
13. Drive to Cupola Indicator
14. Commander's Hand Traverse
15. Instructions for Sealing Turret
16. Emergency Battery for Firing Circuit
    Not batterie
17. Change-over Switch
    Not/Netz
18. Commander's W/T Sockets
19. Gunner's W/T Sockets
20. Turret Direction Indicator
21. Leads to Near-side Smoke Generator Discharger

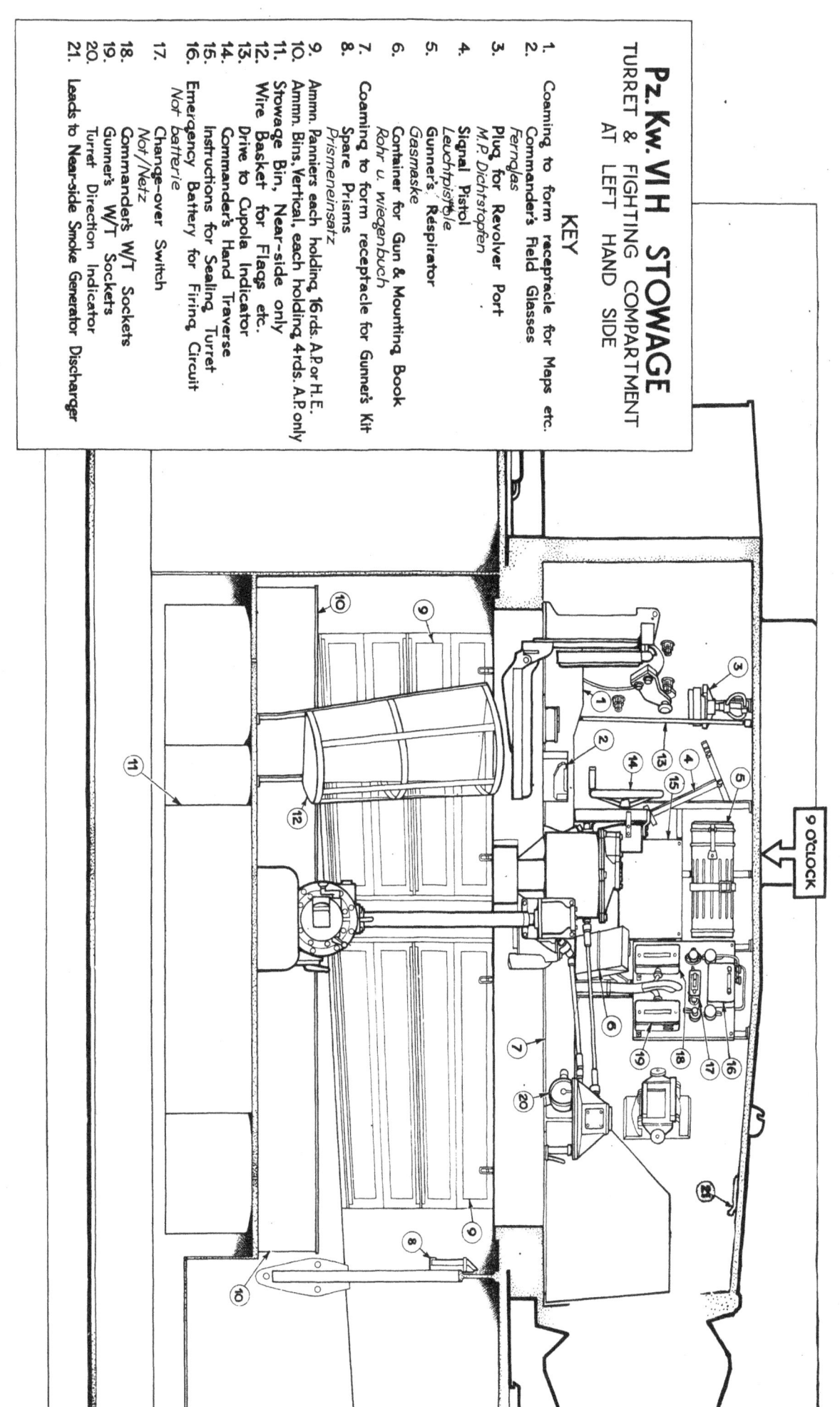

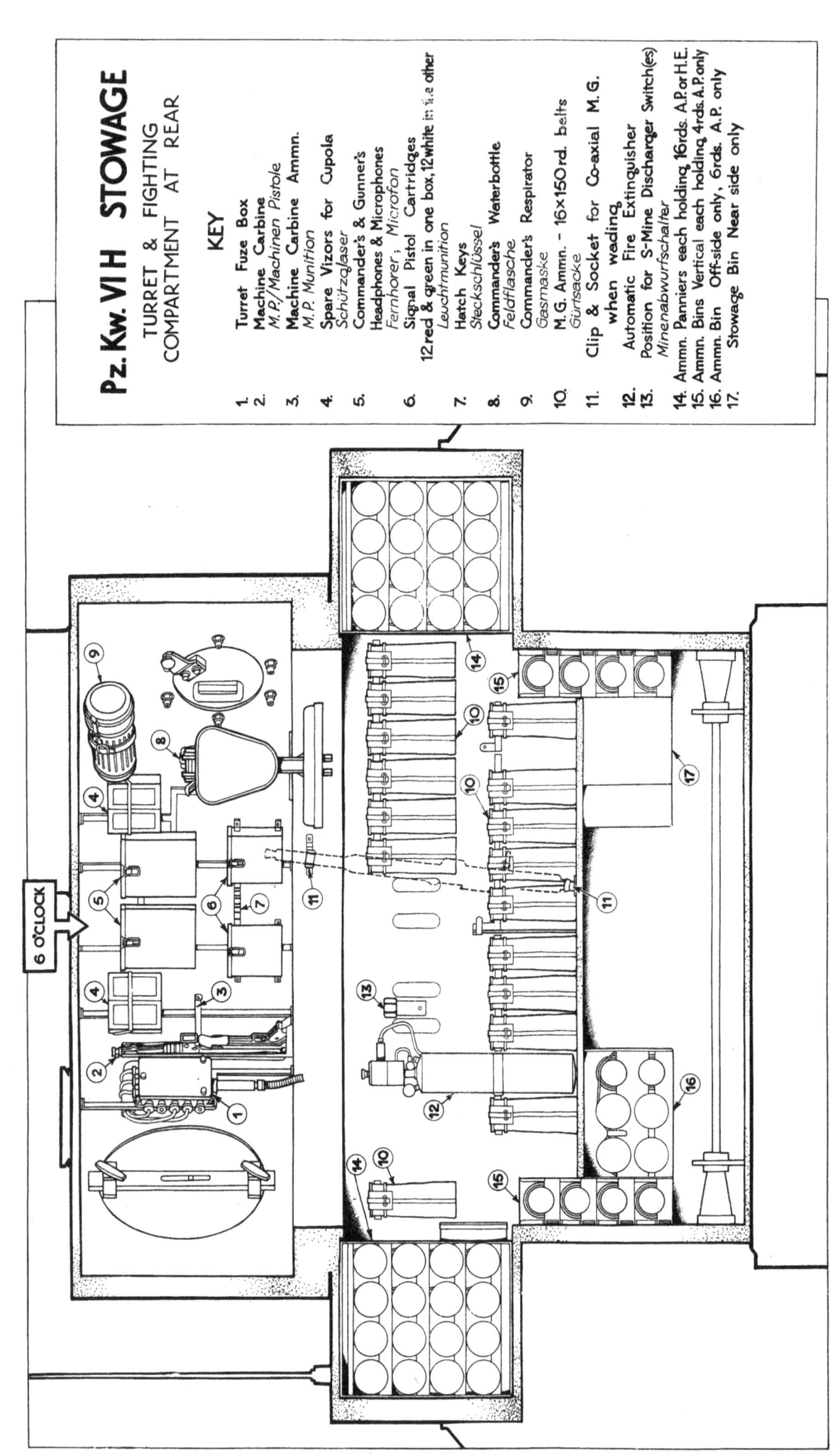

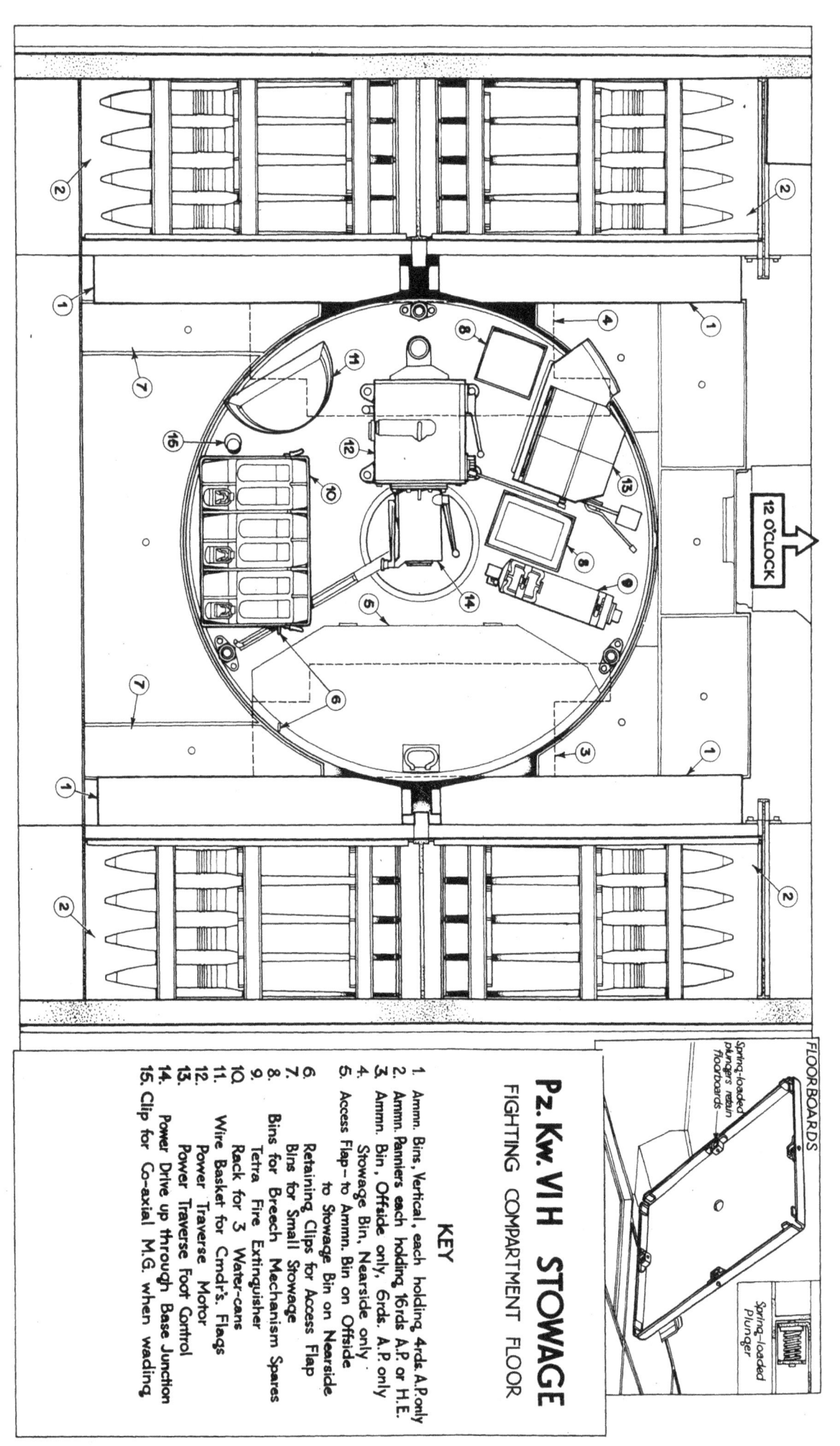

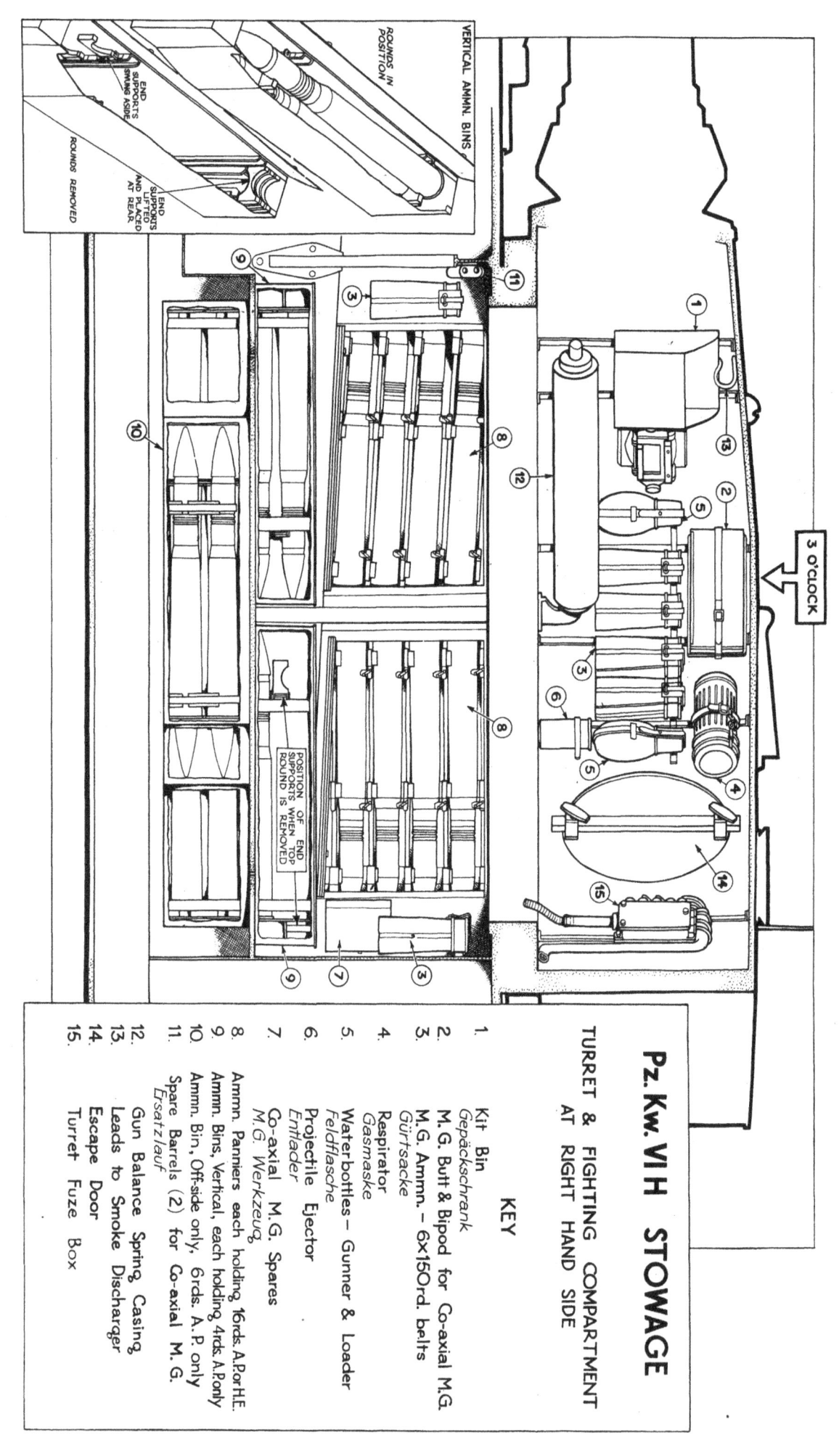

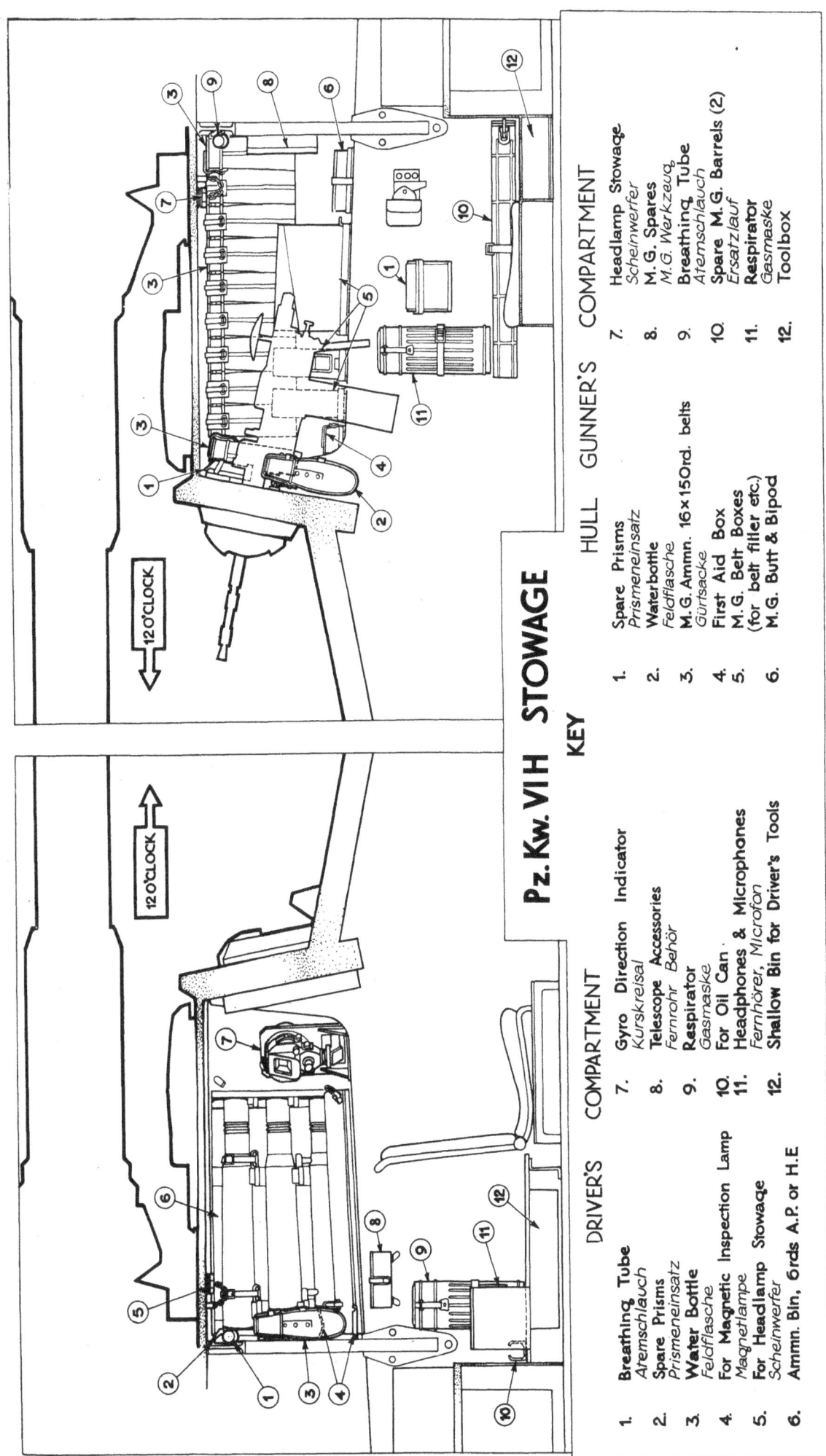

[Blank page, as per original report]

> **RESTRICTED**
>
> The information given in this document is not to be communicated, either directly or indirectly, to the Press or to any person not authorized to receive it.

REPORT ON
PzKw VI
(Tiger)
Model H

PART IV

POWER PLANT

SECTION I

GENERAL DESCRIPTION OF ENGINE.

Military College of Science
SCHOOL OF TANK TECHNOLOGY
Chobham Lane   Chertsey

September 1944

[Blank page, as per original report]

PART IV

POWER PLANT

SECTION I

GENERAL DESCRIPTION OF ENGINE.

INTRODUCTION

In addition to the engine installed in the tank, two spare power units and a quantity of spare parts were shipped from North Africa. The report which follows is based mainly on examination of one of the spare engines, both of which were in a damaged condition.

In one case, failure of big end bearings had caused considerable damage to the crank pins, whilst the other engine had suffered a similar failure with additional damage to one piston and cylinder liner caused by the fracture of a connecting rod. Whilst the tank was undergoing firing trials at Lulworth, its engine also failed in a similar manner, and the recurrence of this trouble would seem to indicate an inherent weakness in design. A composite engine is being built by F.V.P.E., from the spares available with a view to field trials and this may give a better indication of the reliability factor.

The particular engine which was examined in detail, had one or two features which rather suggested that it was an early prototype built before quantity production had commenced.

Various components have been submitted to specialist manufacturers for examination and will therefore be reported upon separately.

A number of parts have also been subjected to material analysis and the results of these investigations are not included in this section.

September 1944.

J.D. BARNES Major, R.T.R.
D.M. PEARCE B.A.(Cantab).
G. BOYD Lieut., R.A.C.

LEADING DATA

Type	HL 210 P 45
Date of manufacture	1942
Engine No.	46064
Bore	125 mm. (4.92 ins.)
Stroke	145 mm. (5.71 ins.)
Stroke/bore Ratio	1.16 :1
Capacity	21.353 litres (1301.2 cu.ins.)
Capacity per cylinder	1.779 litres (108.43 cu.ins.)
Compression Ratio	7 : 1
Rated maximum B.H.P.	650 metric B.H.P. (641 British B.H.P.) at 3000 R.P.M.
Maximum R.P.M.	3000
Mean piston speed at 3000 R.P.M.	2854 ft/min.
Firing order	1 - 12 - 5 - 8 - 3 - 10 - 6 - 7 - 2 - 11 - 4 - 9
Overall length	1220 mm. (4ft. 0 ins.)
Overall width	975 mm. (3ft. 2¼ ins.)
Overall height (excluding air cleaners)	940 mm. (3ft. 1 in.)

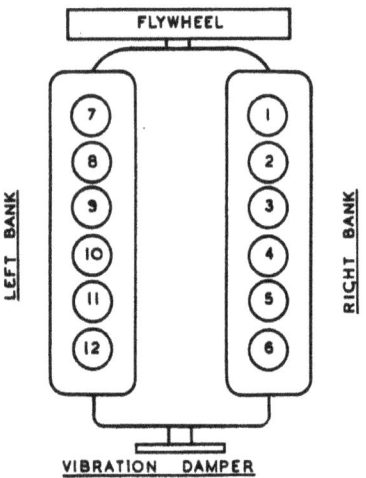

Cylinder numbering diagram.

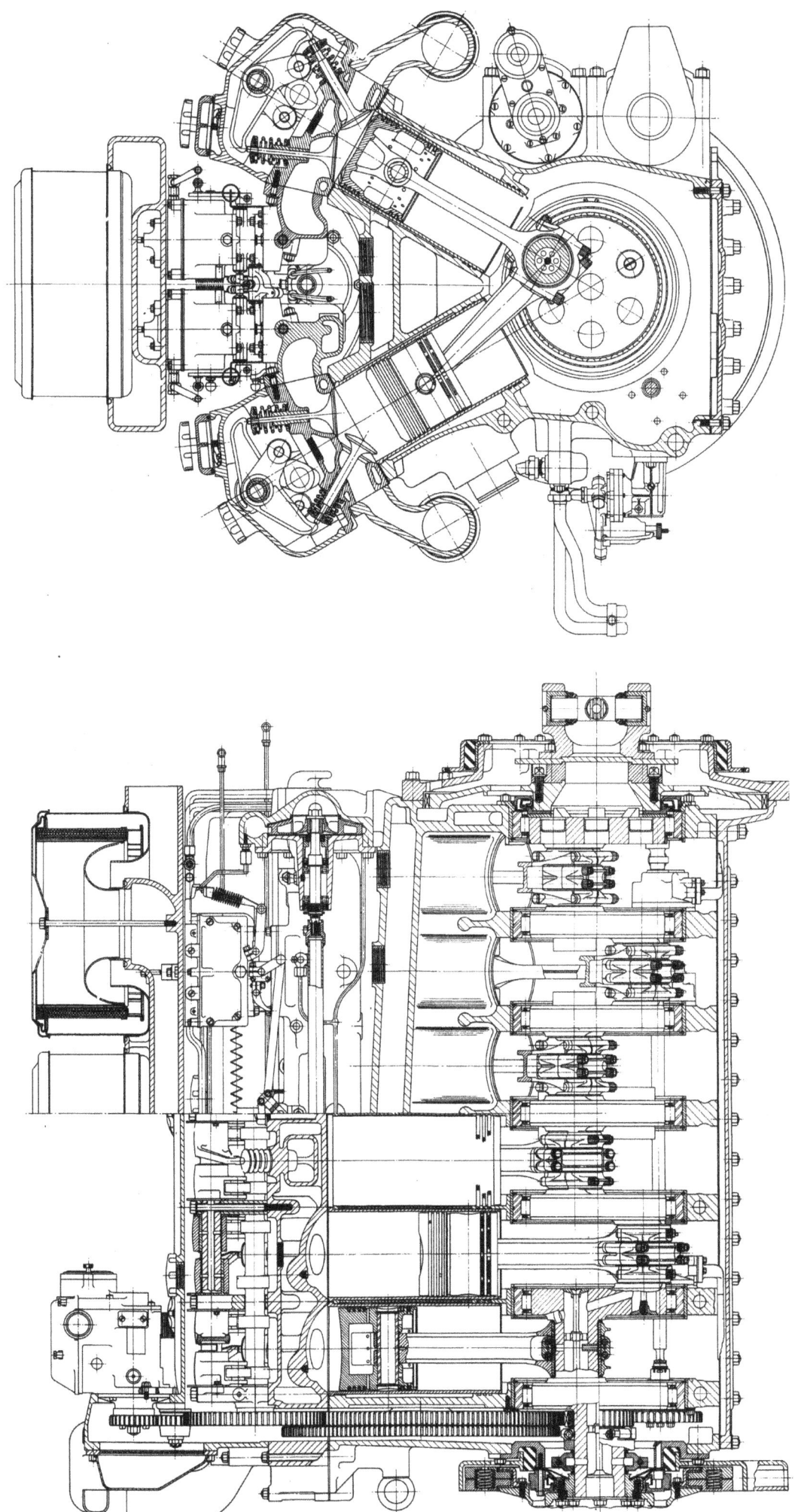

GENERAL DESCRIPTION

The Maybach, type HL.210-P.45, petrol engine of 21 litres, is a 60 degree, Vee - 12 cylinder. The cylinder blocks and crankcase are a single light alloy casting and the cylinders are fitted with wet liners. Cast iron cylinder heads carry one inlet and one exhaust valve per cylinder. The valves are inclined and both inlet and exhaust are driven by a single overhead camshaft to each bank. The inlet valves are of large diameter tulip form, whilst the exhaust are sodium filled.

The camshafts are gear driven from the rear end of the crankshaft. A six cylinder Bosch magneto is provided for each bank, and gear driven from the camshafts. Also driven from the timing gears is a two-speed take-off for the cooling fans, immediately behind which is situated the governor. The governor shaft extends between the banks to drive the water pump which is mounted at the front end of the engine. Four Solex type 52 JFF 2 carburettors are installed between the cylinder banks. Aluminium pressed pistons are carried on forged "H" section rods and copper lead big end bearings are employed. The forged crankshaft has circular webs which form the inner races of the seven large diameter roller main bearings. A friction type vibration damper is carried on the "free" end of the crankshaft. Dry sump lubrication is employed, two gear type scavenge and one delivery pump of similar pattern being driven by a shaft in the crankcase from the timing gears. This same shaft drives the four diaphragm type fuel pumps. The dynamo, also driven from the timing gears, and the electric and inertia starters are carried on the side of the crankcase.

DESIGN

It is at once apparent that the engine was specifically designed by Maybach for use in a heavy tank. It closely follows this maker's previous tank engine practice, and may generally be regarded as a scaled up version of the type HL. 120 as used in the Pz.Kpfw. III and IV.

The chief feature of the design is its compactness, and this aim has no doubt influenced the designer to use roller main bearings, resulting in close pitching of the cylinders and consequent small overall length.

It is considered that the design is generally excellent, achieving small bulk, with high output, and that the apparent unreliability is due to the engine being over-rated. It is significant in this connection that the later Tiger tanks are powered with an engine similar to that of the Panther with an increased swept volume of 23 litres. The larger engine, though very similar in design to the HL 210-P.45, incorporates one or two major changes, notably the substitution of cast iron for aluminium for the cylinder block and crankcase, possibly in an attempt to improve crankcase rigidity.

The installation is very neat, internal drillings and the mounting of the oil tank on the engine have enabled the number of external oil pipes to be reduced to the minimum.

The engine runs in a sealed compartment - to allow the tank to be submersible - and consequently particular attention has been paid to the forced draught over the exhaust manifolds and the direction of air around the front and rear of the engine.

The rubber engine mounting is of a somewhat unusual design, but appears sound. The combustion chamber is of near hemispherical form and an accessible central position of the sparking plug has been achieved by off-setting the single overhead camshaft. The use of sodium cooled exhaust valves is interesting, though the rather unusually heavy section rocker arms are somewhat inconsistent with the generally high standard of finish of the valve gear.
Attention is directed to the very unusual arrangement of the forked connecting rod - the web being parallel to the crankshaft axis. The use of four big end bolts on the blade rod is also noteworthy.

The very unusual mounting of the master timing pinion to arrange for setting of the valve timing was only present on the one engine examined in detail and this together with other small modifications seem to indicate that this particular engine was an early prototype manufactured before large scale production had begun.

The finish and workmanship is everywhere of a high order.

> **RESTRICTED**
>
> The information given in this document is not to be communicated, either directly or indirectly, to the Press or to any person not authorized to receive it.

REPORT ON
Pz Kw VI
(Tiger)
Model H

PART IV

POWER PLANT

SECTION II

DETAILED DESCRIPTION OF ENGINE.

[Editor's note: None of the copies of this title page is dated. The report lacks any introduction, which would have been dated, given the norm in other reports. The report must have been written after the "General Description of the Engine" (i.e., after September 1944). No other documentation survives to explain the schedule of investigation into this engine (the same spare as described in the preceding report) or Tiger 131's engine and engine compartment (which is depicted in this report).]

Military College of Science
SCHOOL OF TANK TECHNOLOGY
Chobham Lane   Chertsey

PART IV

POWER PLANT

SECTION II

DETAILED DESCRIPTION OF ENGINE.

CRANKCASE AND CYLINDER BLOCKS.

Left hand side ¾ view showing liner partially withdrawn

The crankcase and cylinder blocks are a single aluminium alloy casting closed at the base by a simple flat cover. The crankcase extends well below the centre line of the crankshaft. The crankshaft is assembled through the front end wall, and the structure is extremely rigid.

The timing case is cast integrally with the crankcase which is internally divided into seven compartments formed by the walls of the timing case and webs which support the main bearings.

The webs incorporate oilways and are machined to receive steel bands which form the housings for the main bearings. The bands have grooves and circlips to locate the roller main bearings. Nos. 1, 2 and 5 webs are internally drilled and have machined faces to receive the three oil pumps. Nos. 3 and 6 webs and the front end wall are drilled and bushed to support the oil pump driving shaft. A drilling on the rear end of the block face delivers lubricant to the overhead valve gear.

Right hand side ¾ view showing timing case

There are external machined surfaces on the left hand side for four petrol pumps, oil filter (with connections to internal drillings), and unions for external oil pipes. The oil tank is bolted to the right hand side of the crankcase and a machined surface with three drillings in line provides the necessary connections. The central drilling passes to the sump, while the other two continue through Nos. 4 and 5 bearing webs.

Wet cast iron cylinder liners are employed; they are spigotted into the crankcase at their bases and located at the top by a flange seating in an annular groove in the top face of the cylinder block. Water sealing is by three rubber rings.

There are 18 water passages which communicate with appropriate holes in the cylinder head. It is noted that four additional holes in each bank have been blanked off. The timing case has two water passages cored in it for two outlet pipes, whilst at the other extremity of the block there are two passages for the centrifugal pump.

Two water hose connections are provided on the left side of the cylinder block, one to the rear at the base and the other central at the top. Two sets of brackets are cast on this side of the crankcase for the oil cooler and dynamo. Similarly on the right hand side the bracket for the electric starter is cast, whilst that for the inertia starter is bolted. This rather confirms the report that an inertia starter was not fitted to the first 50 Pz.Kpfw.VI tanks.

14 main bolts hold down each cylinder head and the same bolts serve to secure the valve rocker gear. A steel threaded sleeve, screwed and caulked into the cylinder block, locates each bolt.

Core plugs are threaded and have squared recesses for the insertion of a tool for fitting or removal. Jointing material is used with the plugs.

Four lifting eyes are provided, one on the top front corner of each side and two on the rear wall.

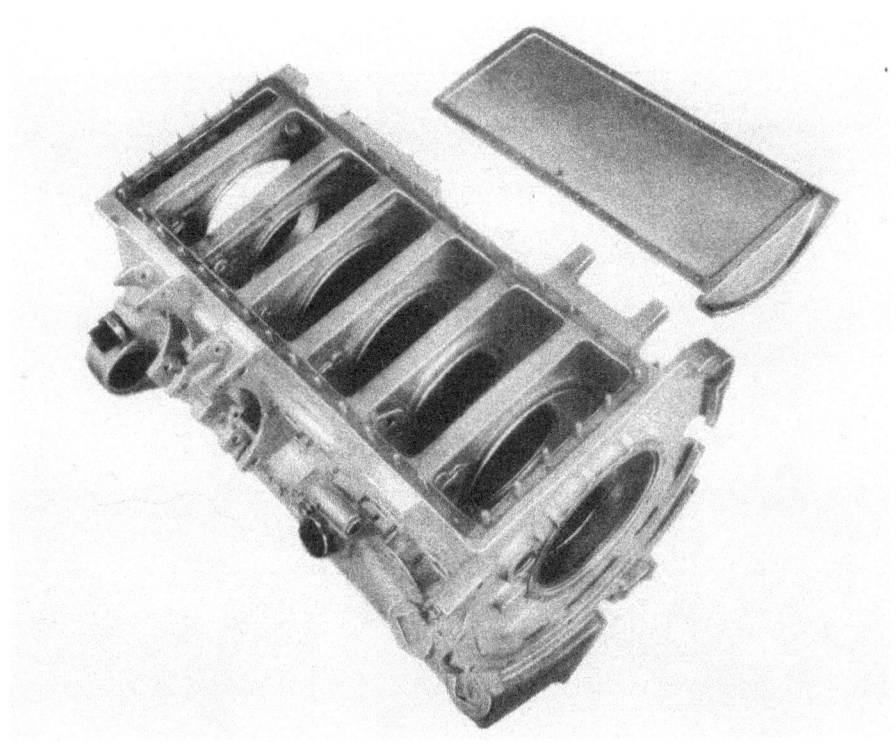

Underside view of crankcase

DATA AND DIMENSIONS

Overall height	685mm
" length	1100mm
Angle between banks	60°
Centre line of crankcase to block face	420mm
Centres of cylinders	142mm
Distance of sump plate from centre line of crankshaft	190mm
No. of cylinder head studs	14
Diameter of studs	14mm

Cylinder Liners

Depth of liners	267mm
Thickness of liners	4mm
Internal diameter	125mm
External diameter	133mm
Diameter over flange	142mm
Depth of water passages	202mm

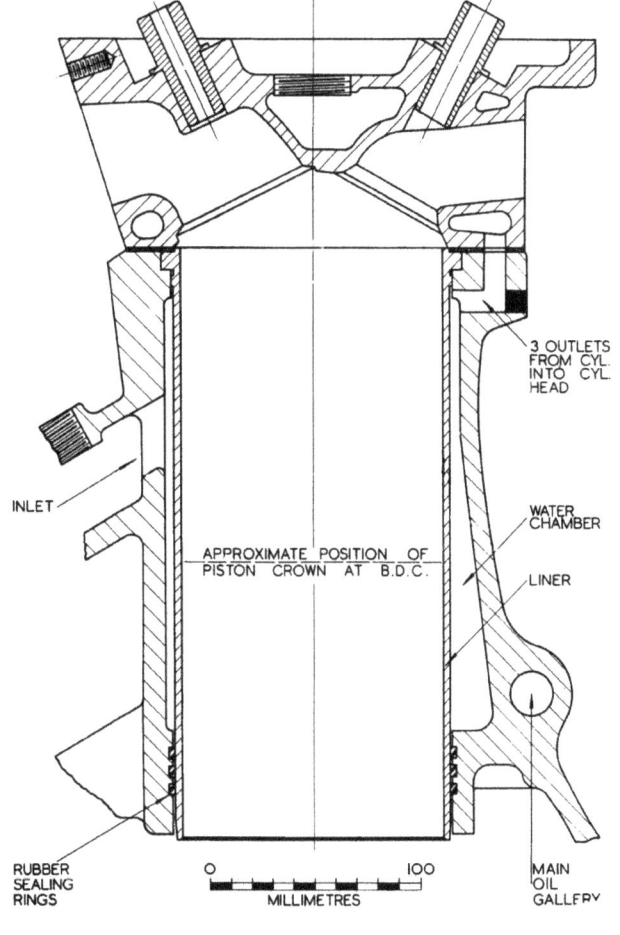

Section of cylinder liner

ENGINE MOUNTING

[Editor's note: This photograph is aimed down into Tiger 131's empty engine compartment. It must have been taken after Tiger 131's engine failed in March 1944, possibly after the previous report (September). The snorkel has been removed: it should be feeding the duct that rises from the floor towards the rear. The wider duct on the rear plate is for feeding air into the engine when under water.]

The engine is flexibly mounted at either end by rubber rings which locate on flanges concentric with the crankshaft. The rings are carried between two pressed steel sections and the whole is bonded together to form a composite flexible structure. At the forward end, the circular housing rests in a cut-away section in the bulkhead and is secured to it by a ring of twelve bolts.

At the rear the framework rests upon two pillars. These pillars are welded to the belly plates of the tank and are strutted.

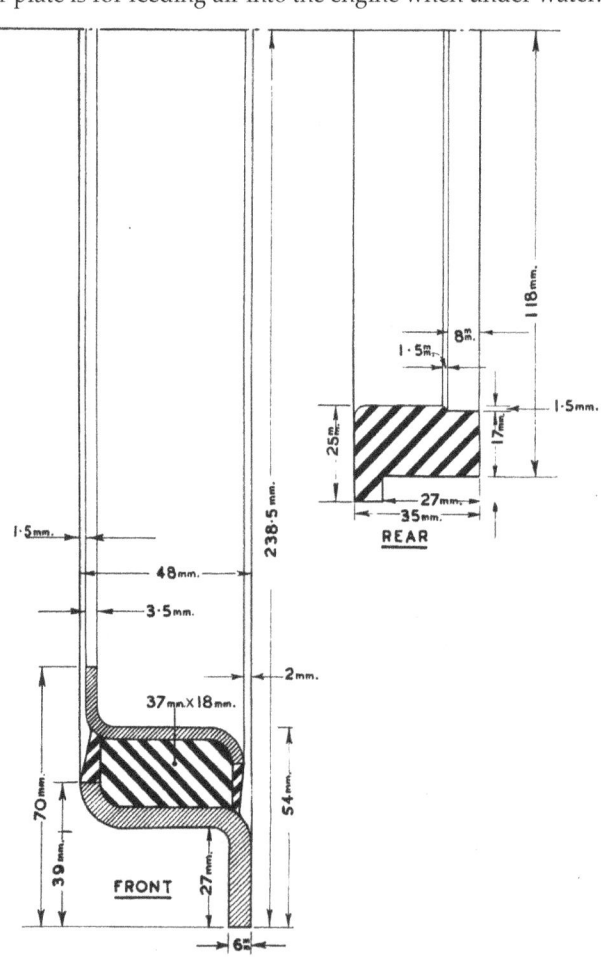

Scrap section of rubber mounting

CYLINDER HEADS

Cylinder heads with camshaft and rocker gear removed

A single cast iron cylinder head is used on each bank of six cylinders. Hemispherical combustion chambers are machined in the head and each valve is inclined at an angle of 60° to the head face. The valves seat directly on the head metal and each is provided with a single port, the inlets being to the inside of each bank and the exhausts to the outside. A single 14mm. plug is situated in each combustion chamber. The bore of the plug hole lies parallel to the inlet valve and breaks into the side of the combustion chamber on the longitudinal centre line.

The sections of the casting are fairly heavy and the machining operations comparatively few and simple. Ample water passages are cored round the valve seats and ports and round the plug bosses. A metal and asbestos gasket is used and as the cylinder liners stand 1.5mm. above the cylinder top face, a high localised pressure is obtained around each cylinder joint. Cooling water passes into the head through holes in the head face below the valve ports. A single water outlet is situated at the timing case end of the head at the side of the rectangular hole accommodating the camshaft driving gear. Each head is secured by 14 bolts.

The top face of the head is milled flat to receive the pedestal bearings for the camshaft and rocker gear, and the cast aluminium valve cover. A tubular extension, on the inside of the valve cover, forms a joint round each plug hole in the head and communicates with a trough in the top of the cover which accommodates the ignition leads. This trough is provided with a separate cast aluminium cover which is removed for access to the plugs.

DATA AND DIMENSIONS

Inlet port dimensions	65mm x 50mm
Exhaust port dimensions	70mm x 37mm
Volume of combustion chamber	211 c.c.
Proportion of combustion chamber volume to total clearance volume	70.5%
Depth of head	93mm.

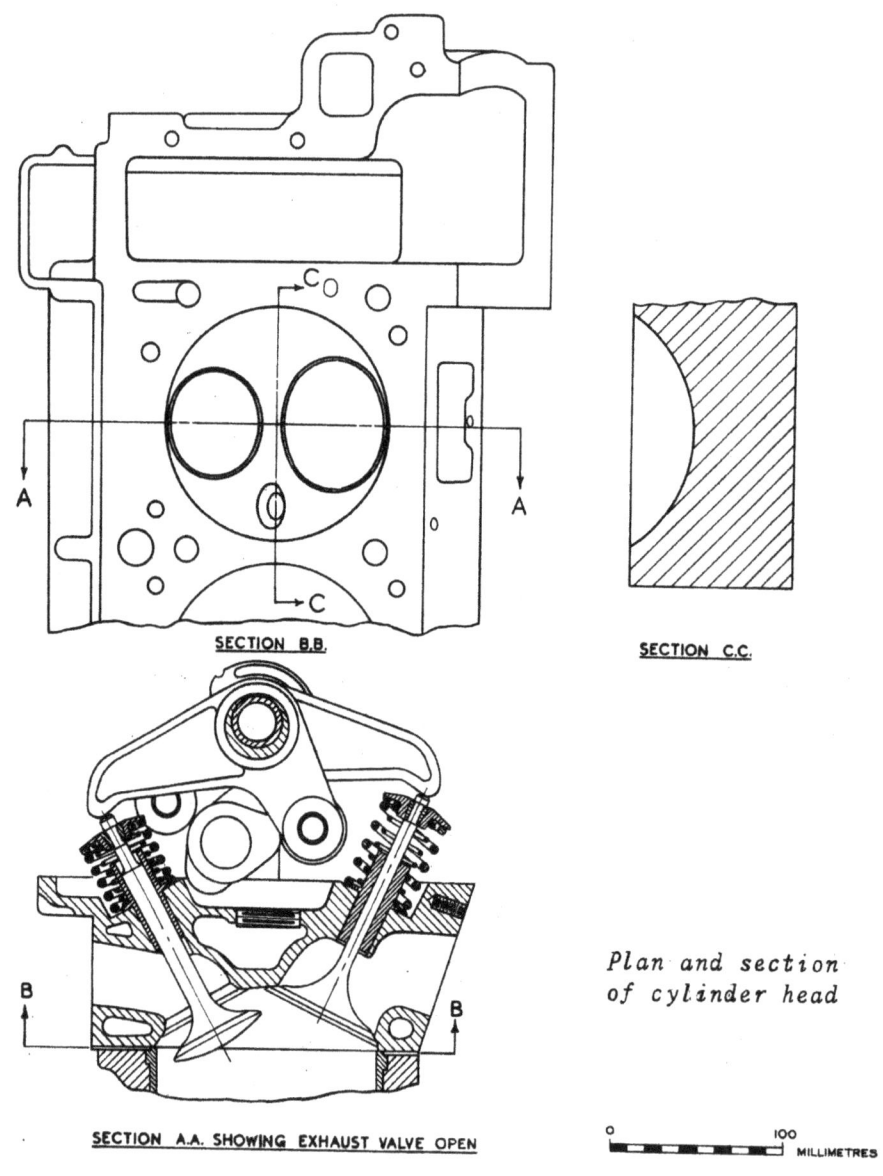

Plan and section of cylinder head

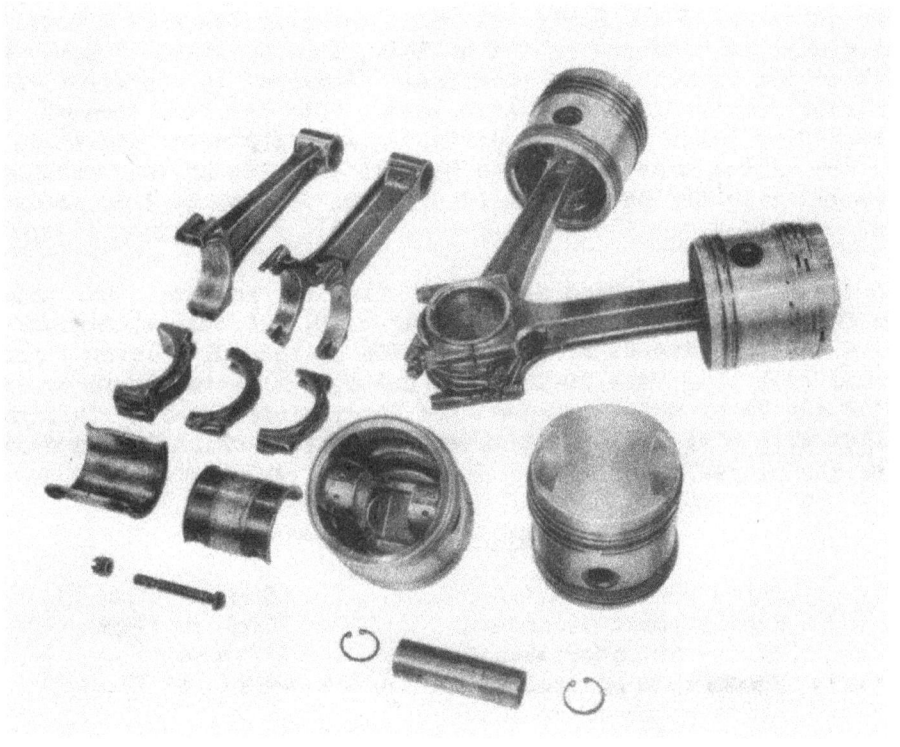

Pistons and connecting rod assembly

PISTONS.

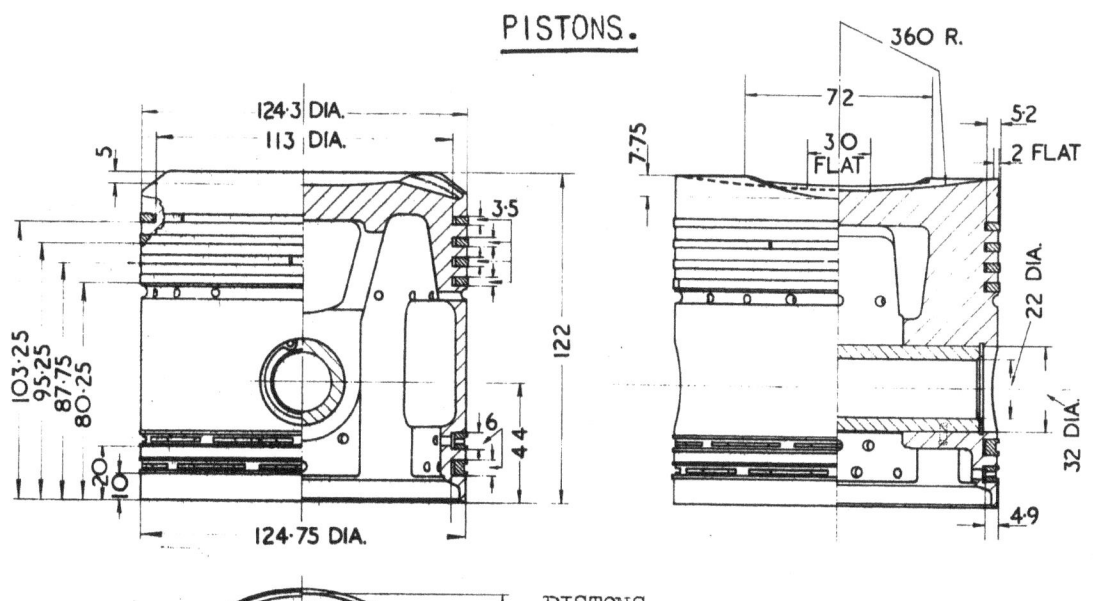

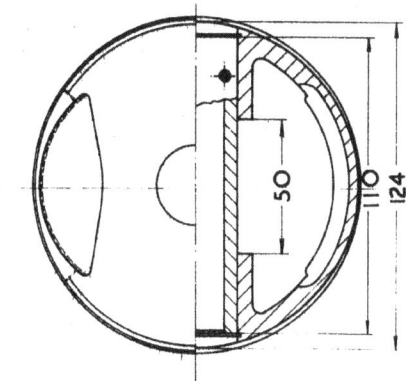

PISTONS

The pistons are hot-pressings of aluminium alloy and carry four butted compression rings. Two butted scraper rings of slotted type are fitted below the gudgeon pin. The crown of the piston is concave to a depth of 5mm. at the centre, and is relieved each side to a depth of 9.5mm. for valve clearance. A section of the skirt at gudgeon pin level is turned elliptically.

A groove 5mm. wide immediately below the 4th compression ring has 14 oil return holes, 3½mm. diameter. The holes are evenly spaced in groups of 7 each side of the gudgeon pin bosses. Each scraper ring groove has ten 5mm. holes.

The gudgeon pin bosses are supported from the crown by two lateral webs. Two 5mm. holes are drilled in each boss for lubrication.

The gudgeon pins are fully floating, parallel bored and located by circlips.

DATA AND DIMENSIONS

Piston

Overall length	122mm.
Diameter	124.5mm.
Centre of gudgeon pin to crown (highest point)	78mm.
Width of ring groove (compression)	3.5mm.
" " " (scraper)	6.0mm.
Width of lands	4.0mm.
Distance from top of ring to crown (highest point)	15.25mm.

Gudgeon Pin

Outside diameter	32.0mm.
Inside diameter	22.0mm.

Weights

Piston (bare)	3.219 lbs
Four compression rings	.418 "
Two scraper rings	.246 "
Gudgeon pin (with circlips)	.812 "

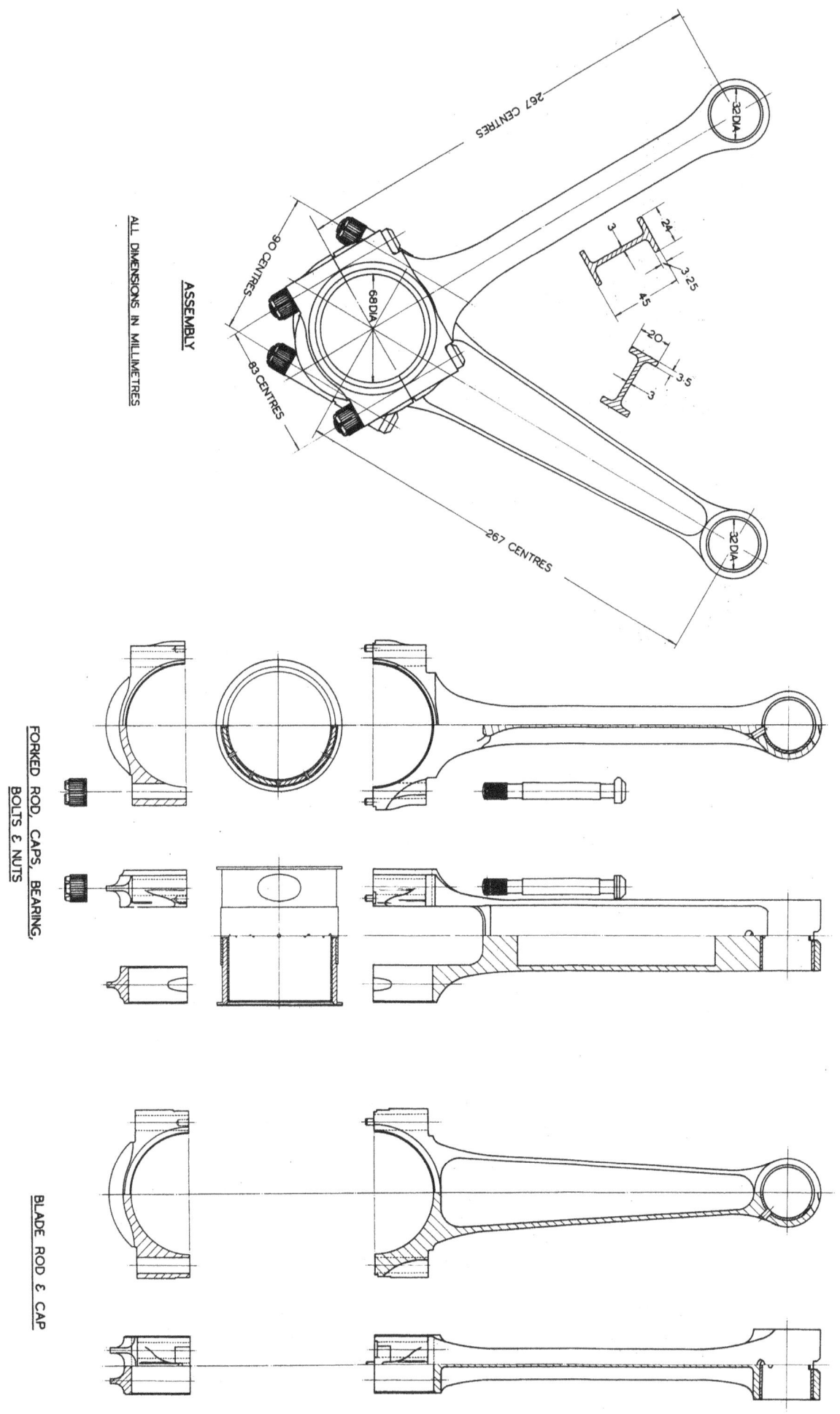

CONNECTING RODS

CONNECTING ROD ASSEMBLY

A forked and blade rod arrangement is employed. The stamped steel rods are of "H" section, machined all over. A high degree of surface finish is apparent on the more highly stressed areas. An unusual feature is that the "H" section of the forked rod is at right angles to that of the blade rod, i.e. the web is parallel to the crankshaft axis.

Four big end bolts are provided for each rod. The heads are shaped to prevent turning and their undersides bevelled to clear the con rod radius. The castellated nuts are of serrated barrel type.

The steel big end bush, which is copper lead lined, is in two halves and is dowelled into one of the forked caps. The blade rod bears centrally upon a copper lead lined surface on the outside of the bush and lubrication is by 12 radially drilled holes. The big end caps of each rod are located by two dowels.

A phosphor bronze bush is used in the small end. A rectangular slot in the bush registers with a similar slot machined in the top of the rod for lubrication. In addition, two holes are drilled through the rod and bush for the same purpose.

DATA AND DIMENSIONS

Connecting Rods

Centres   267 mm.

	Blade Rod	Forked Rod
Flange width	20mm	24mm.
Web thickness	3mm	3mm.
Flange thickness	3.25mm	3.5mm.
Diameter of bolts	10 mm.	

Big End Bush

Width over flange	87mm.
Effective bearing width	81.5mm.
Inside diameter	68mm.
Outside diameter	77mm.
Outside diameter over blade rod bearing.	78mm.
Outside diameter over flanges	82mm.
Width of blade rod bearing	35.5mm.
Diameter of oil holes	2mm.

Small End Bearing

Outside diameter	35mm.
Inside diameter	32mm.
Length, effective	44mm.

Weights

Weight of forked rod (less big end bearings)	4lbs	6½oz
Weight of blade rod	3lbs	11½oz
Weight of big end bearings (worn)	1lb.	8¾oz

CRANKSHAFT

Circular web crankshaft.

The six throw forged crankshaft has circular webs, is machined all over and supported in seven large diameter roller bearings. The circular webs form the inner races for the main bearings. This bearing arrangement results in a very short crankshaft. The crank pins and bearing surfaces of the webs are hardened.

Each web has seven drillings and balance of the shaft is effected by bolting weights through these holes, with the exception of No. 4 web which has a semi-circular weight secured each side by three bolts passing through the drillings. One of the drillings in each web is concentric with a crankpin and an oil seal is formed by conically seated caps secured by a single bolt. Where the drillings are not blanked by balance weights they are left clear with the exception of those on No. 1 web which have light metal dished caps pressed into them.

A band is fitted over the diameter and flush with the side of No. 1 web and is secured in position in six places by tack welding. This band butts against the main bearing rollers and takes care of end thrust in one direction. A plate bolted to the outside of the crankshaft takes the thrust in the reverse direction. The end thrust is very light, as the clutch thrust is not taken by the crankshaft, the main clutch being incorporated in the gearbox. It is noteworthy that in every case the welds have failed.

Oil control at the front bearing is by a somewhat elaborate assembly comprised of light metal dished pressings. This feature has all the appearances of a "one off" job.

On the face of the front web are six tapped holes to receive the flywheel studs.

The free end of the crankshaft incorporates a flange carrying a frictional type torsional vibration damper. It consists of two flywheels, two fibre friction discs, two presser plates and eighteen springs.

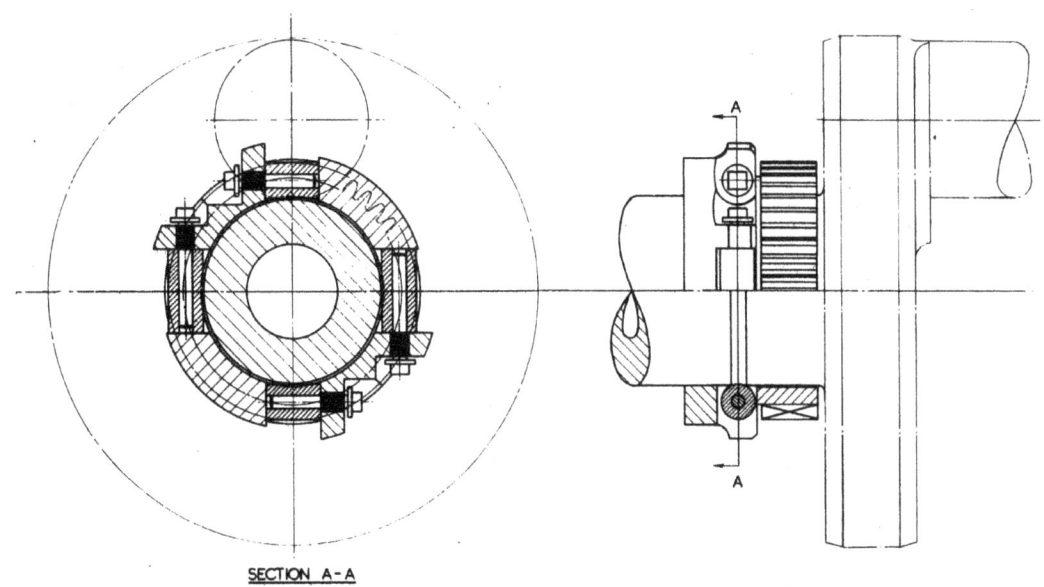

SECTION A-A

Timing adjustment

The master timing pinion is located on the shaft by lugs locked together by radial bolts passing through distance pieces.

Oil is delivered to the crankshaft by an oil muff at the rear end and circulates through the radially drilled webs and hollow crankpins. Three radial holes are drilled in each crankpin, the outer one of which has an internally protruding copper tube to act as a sludge trap.

DATA AND DIMENSIONS

Overall length of crankshaft	1029 mm.
Weight	194.5 lbs.

Pins

Outside diameter	68 mm
Inside diameter	40 mm
Length of pin	88 mm
Radius crank pin to web	3.18 mm
Oil holes diameter	5 mm
Diameter copper tubing inserted in one hole	3.5 mm
Projection copper tubing internally in crank pin	8 mm

Webs

Diameter	215 mm
Width Nos. 1 - 6	40 mm
No. 7	33 mm
Diameter of drillings in webs	40 mm
" " oilway through webs	20 mm
" " circular balance weights	68 mm

Oil Muff

Diameter of oil holes	10 mm

Flywheel Studs

Number	6
Diameter	12 mm
P.C. Diameter	164 mm

Damper Studs

Number	8
Diameter	12 mm
P.C. Diameter	120 mm

Roller Main Bearings

Number	7
Outside diameter of race	270 mm
Inside diameter of race	215 mm
Width	40 mm
No. of rollers	34
Diameter of rollers	6 mm. approx.
Length of rollers	22 mm
Annular groove on circumference of race	3 mm
Diameter of 3 radial holes in above groove	3 mm

Roller main bearing

VALVES AND VALVE GEAR

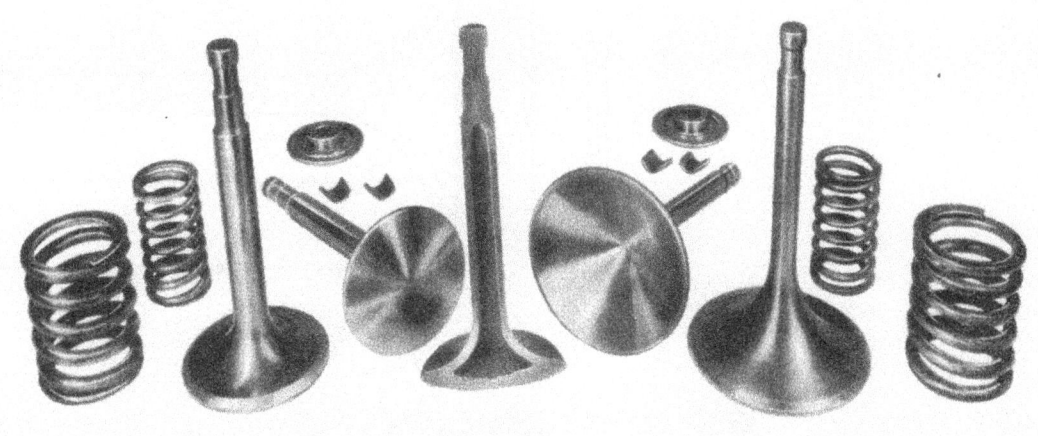

Valve assemblies showing sectioned exhaust.

A single gear driven camshaft to each bank operates one inlet and one exhaust valve per cylinder through rocker arms with roller followers. The inlet valves are of tulip form of unusually large diameter whilst the exhausts have sodium cooled heads and stems. The valves are filled through the head, the filling holes being closed by welding. Double valve springs are fitted in each case; the springs appear to be ground and are lacquered. By contrast with the high degree of finish and light construction found elsewhere on the valve gear, the rocker arms are heavy machined steel forgings. The valve guides are cast iron.

The camshaft, which is slightly off-set from the centre line of the cylinder head, is supported in seven bearings in pedestals dowelled into the cylinder head. The bearings are split, the two halves being dowelled and secured by two screws. The bearing surface is white metal run on direct. A thrust bearing is formed in the rear pedestal by machined faces, white metalled, running against the flange of the camshaft driving gear and a machined step on the first cam.

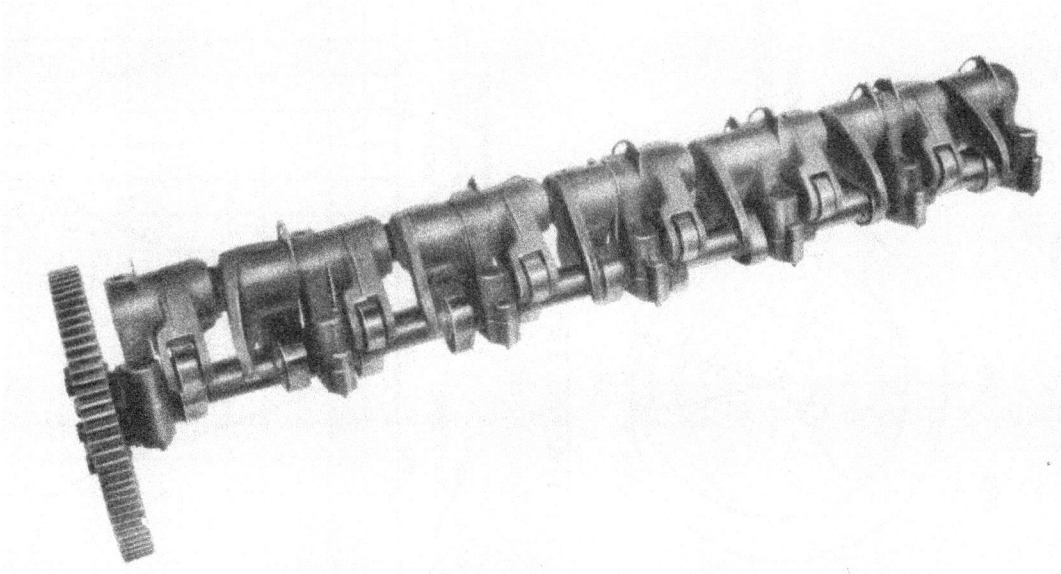

Rocker and camshaft assemblies

The rocker shaft is supported on the centre line of the head in the same seven pedestals which carry the camshaft, and is bored throughout its length and blanked off at the ends by metal plugs. Radial drillings communicate with the rocker arm bushes.

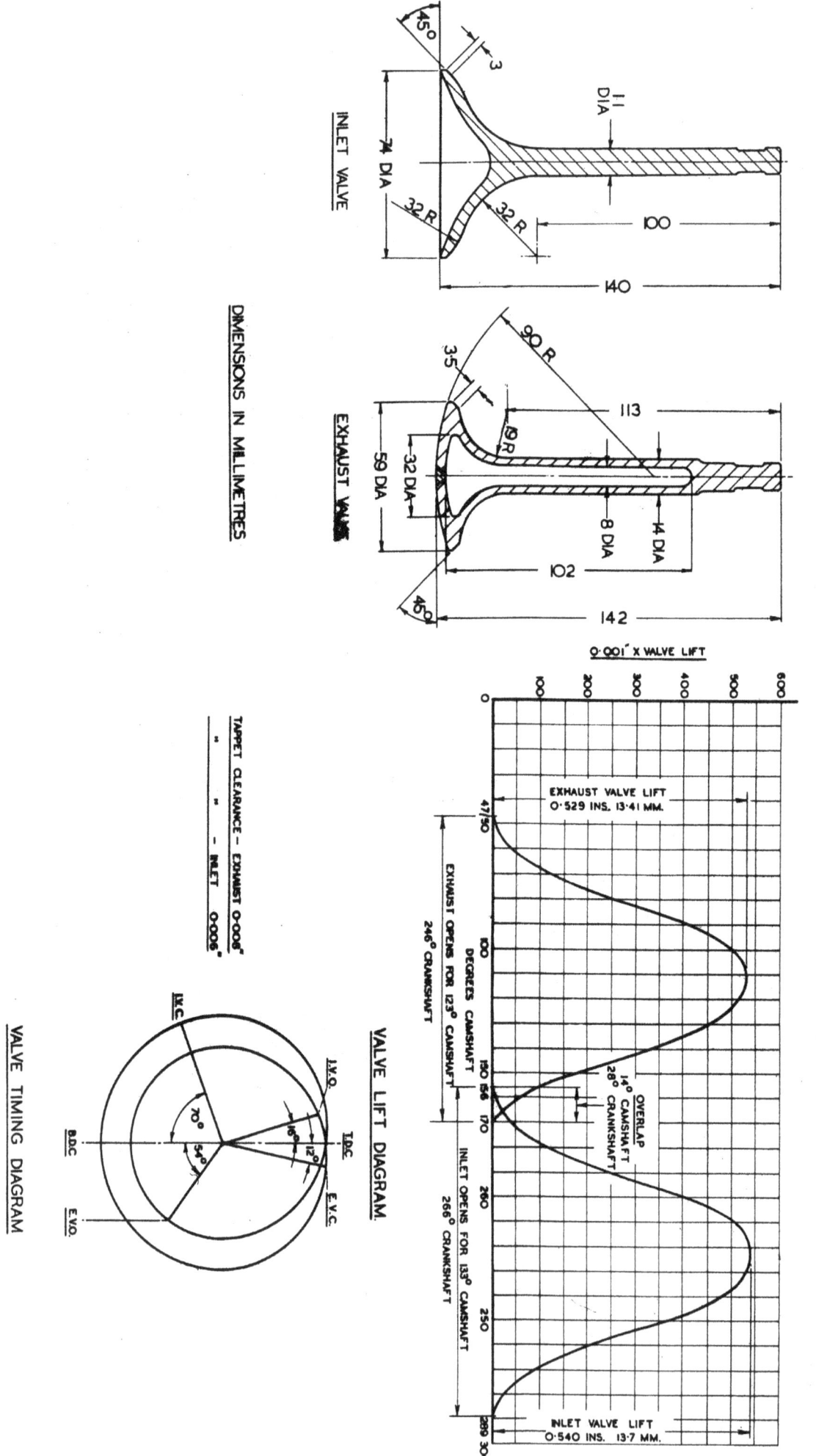

The rocker arm is slotted to receive the pedestal securing bolts, which thereby serve as cotters to prevent the shaft rotating in its bearings. Seven of the cylinder head holding down bolts each serve also as one of the pedestal fixing bolts.

The rockers are mounted on eccentric bronze bushes which are a light push fit in the rockers and on the shaft and which have a slotted flange on one side. Tappet adjustment is obtained by rotation of the bush and is locked by a bolt passing through the flange of the bush into the pedestal.

Rocker, pedestal and eccentric bush

DATA AND DIMENSIONS

Camshaft

Length of shaft	892.5 mm
Diameter of shaft	31.0 mm
No. of bearings	7
Diameter of bearings	32.0 mm
Width of six bearings	33.0 mm
Width of front end thrust bearing	35.0 mm

Cams

Base circle diameter of cam	46.0 mm
Width of cam	17.0 mm
Lift of cam	8.5 mm

Rocker Arms

Diameter of housing for bush	35.0 mm
Width " " " "	51.0 mm
Diameter of roller	38.0 mm
Width of roller	14.0 mm
Effective leverage of rocker	1 : 1.57

Eccentric Bronze Bush

Outside diameter	35.0 mm
Inside diameter	30.0 mm
Maximum eccentricity	3.0 mm
Effective bearing surface on outside diameter	49.0 mm
Diameter of oil holes in bush	4.0 mm

Rocker Shaft

Length of shaft	875.0 mm
Outside diameter of shaft	30.0 mm
Inside diameter of shaft	20.0 mm
Diameter of oil holes	4.0 mm

Valves

	Inlet	Exhaust
No. per cylinder	1	1
Diameter of head	74.0 mm	59.0 mm
Stem diameter	11.0 mm	14.0 mm
Length of valve	141.0 mm	142.0 mm
Angle of seat	45°	45°
Minimum area through valve	38 cm^2	23 cm^2
Valve lift	13.7 mm	13.4 mm
Mean gas velocity through valve at 3,000 R.P.M.	238 ft/sec.	334 ft/sec.

Weights

	Inlet	Exhaust
Valve	.551 lbs	.551 lbs
Inside and outside springs	.370 lbs	.384 lbs
Cap and cotters	.099 lbs	.099 lbs
Rocker arm and roller	2.094 lbs	2.094 lbs

Springs (Inside)

	Inlet	Exhaust
Free length	55.37 mm	54.86 mm
Wire diameter	3.5 mm	3.5 mm
Mean coil diameter	25.0 mm	25.0 mm
No. of active coils	5.5	5.5
Rate	109 lb/in.	108 lb/in.

Springs (Outside)

	Inlet	Exhaust
Free length	58.42 mm	58.67 mm
Wire diameter	5.5 mm	5.5 mm
Mean coil diameter	4.0 mm	4.0 mm
No. of active coils	4	4
Rate	234 lb/in.	228 lb/in.

Valve Guides

Overall length	57 mm
Inside diameter	13 mm
Outside diameter	19 mm
Length (in block)	30 mm
Diameter of flange	30 mm
Width of flange	2 mm
Length projecting in port	25 mm

TIMING AND AUXILIARY DRIVE GEAR

All the gears are housed in the timing case, which is part of the main crankcase casting.

The drive is taken from the master timing pinion on the crankshaft to a large triple intermediate gear supported from the crankcase by two taper roller bearings on a hollow shaft. The outer diameter of this gear drives the camshafts, also through an idler gear, the oil and petrol pump shaft. The magneto for each bank is driven via an idler from the camshaft gear. A two speed fan drive is provided for by movement of a selector rod which engages gears either with the outer diameter of the intermediate gear, or with a second gear cut on a smaller diameter. Also driven from this smaller gear, through an idler, is the pinion on the dynamo. The smallest diameter gear on the intermediate timing wheel drives the governor and water pump situated centrally between the cylinder banks and mounted respectively at each end of the engine. All the gears are steel of straight cut pattern. The magneto for each bank, together with its idler gear, is carried on the valve cover, consequently removal of the cover upsets the ignition timing. Scribe marks on the wheels facilitate replacement. The various pinions are generally supported on ball races.

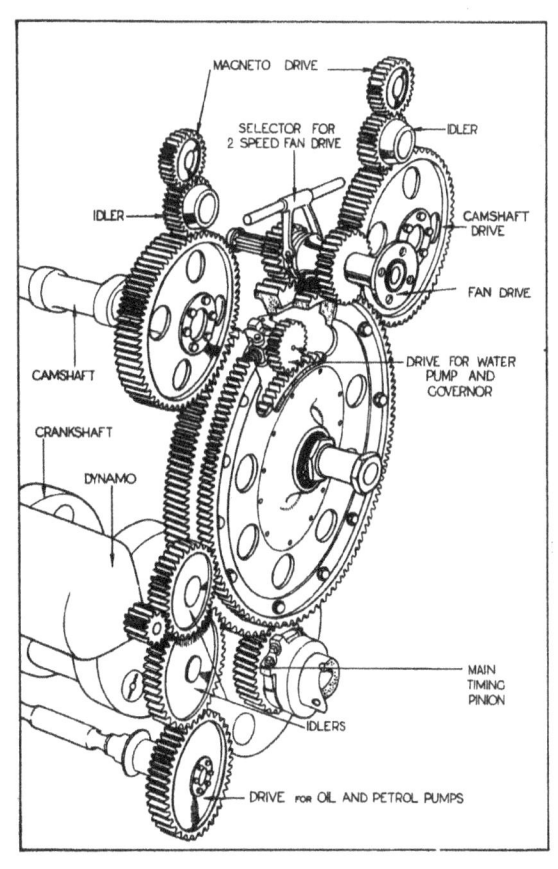

Timing gears and auxiliary drives

DATA AND DIMENSIONS

Gear	No. of teeth	P.C. Diam.	Face Width	Module
Main timing pinion	42	103mm	24mm	2.4mm
Oil pump	52	129mm	15mm	2.5mm
Intermediate oil pump gear	59	146mm	15mm	2.5mm
Intermediate dynamo drive	43	106.5mm	15mm	2.5mm
Camshaft	84	214mm	22mm	2.5mm
Intermediate Mag idler	30	72.5mm	15mm	2.4mm
Magneto	28	70mm	15mm	2.5mm
Governor & water pump drive	24	59mm	15mm	2.5mm
Fan drive (1)	39	96.5mm	15mm	2.5mm
(2)	28	70mm	25mm	2.5mm
Intermediate gear (Main)				
(1) Large gear	182	456mm	25mm	2.5mm
(2) Middle gear	173	429mm	15mm	2.5mm
(3) Small gear	104	259mm	13mm	2.5mm

SPEED X ENGINE R.P.M.

Camshaft	.5	Magnetos	1.5	Fuel pumps	.8077
Oil pumps	.8077	Governor	1.75	Water pump	1.75

LUBRICATION SYSTEM.

General Description and Circulation

The lubrication system is of the dry sump type employing one pressure and two scavenge pumps. An external filter and an oil cooler are mounted on the left side of the engine, whilst the oil tank is bolted to the right hand side.

External pipe lines have been reduced to the minimum and the crankcase has extensive oilways both in the walls and the webs. Crankcase ventilation is via the timing case, and gauze protected breathers are fitted to the valve covers adjacent to the magneto mountings.

The accompanying diagram shows the circuit. Oil is drawn from the tank by the pressure pump mounted on No.2 web through a drilling in No.4 web and is pumped to a three-way junction box. External pipes convey the oil through the cooler, back to the junction box and to the filter. A spring loaded valve incorporated in the junction box isolates the cooler when the oil is cold.

The filter is bolted to a machined boss and the oil passes through a drilling in this boss to an internal gallery which runs the whole length of the crankcase and across No.6 main bearing web. A pressure relief valve is fitted in this boss. Piped to the main gallery is a muff on the rear end of the hollow crankshaft for the lubrication of main and big end bearings.

Two drillings from the main oil gallery, into which reducer nipples are fitted, lead to the block face of each cylinder bank. Oil then passes up around cylinder head fixing bolts, via the pedestals into the hollow rocker shaft. From the rocker shafts oil is distributed by holes, drillings and the pedestal fixing bolts to the valve rockers, roller followers and camshaft bearings. Excess oil then drains back down the timing case, and also through a hole at the opposite end of each block.

Oil Pumps

The three gear type oil pumps, mounted on the main bearing webs, are driven in tandem by splined shafts from the timing gears.

All the pumps are similar in design but the pressure pump is of slightly smaller capacity than either of the scavenge pumps.

The cast iron pump bodies enclose twin helical steel gears with integral spindles, which, in the case of the pressure pump only, are carried in bronze bushes.

The driving gears are splined to receive the driving shaft.

Oil pumps and drive shaft

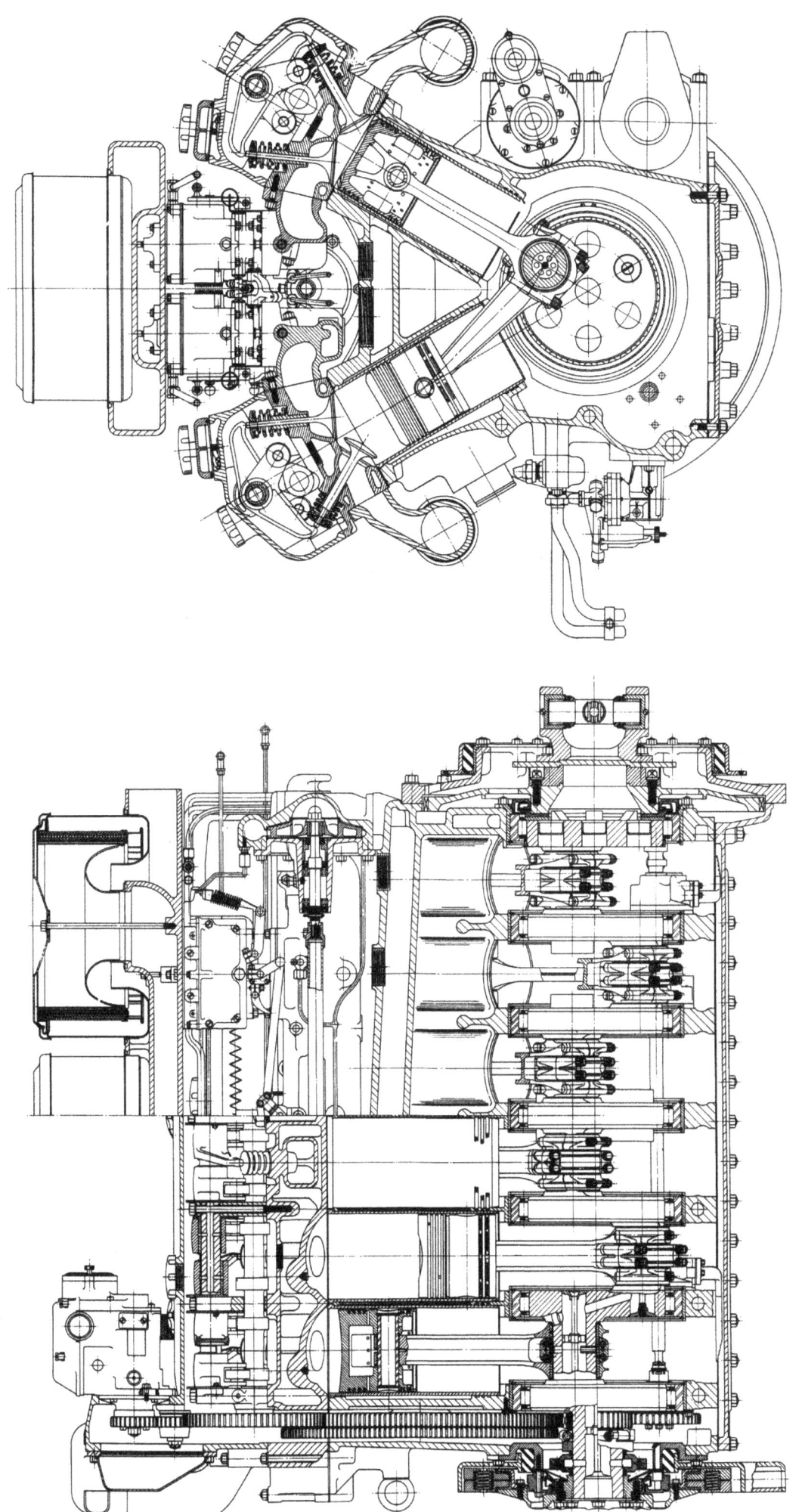

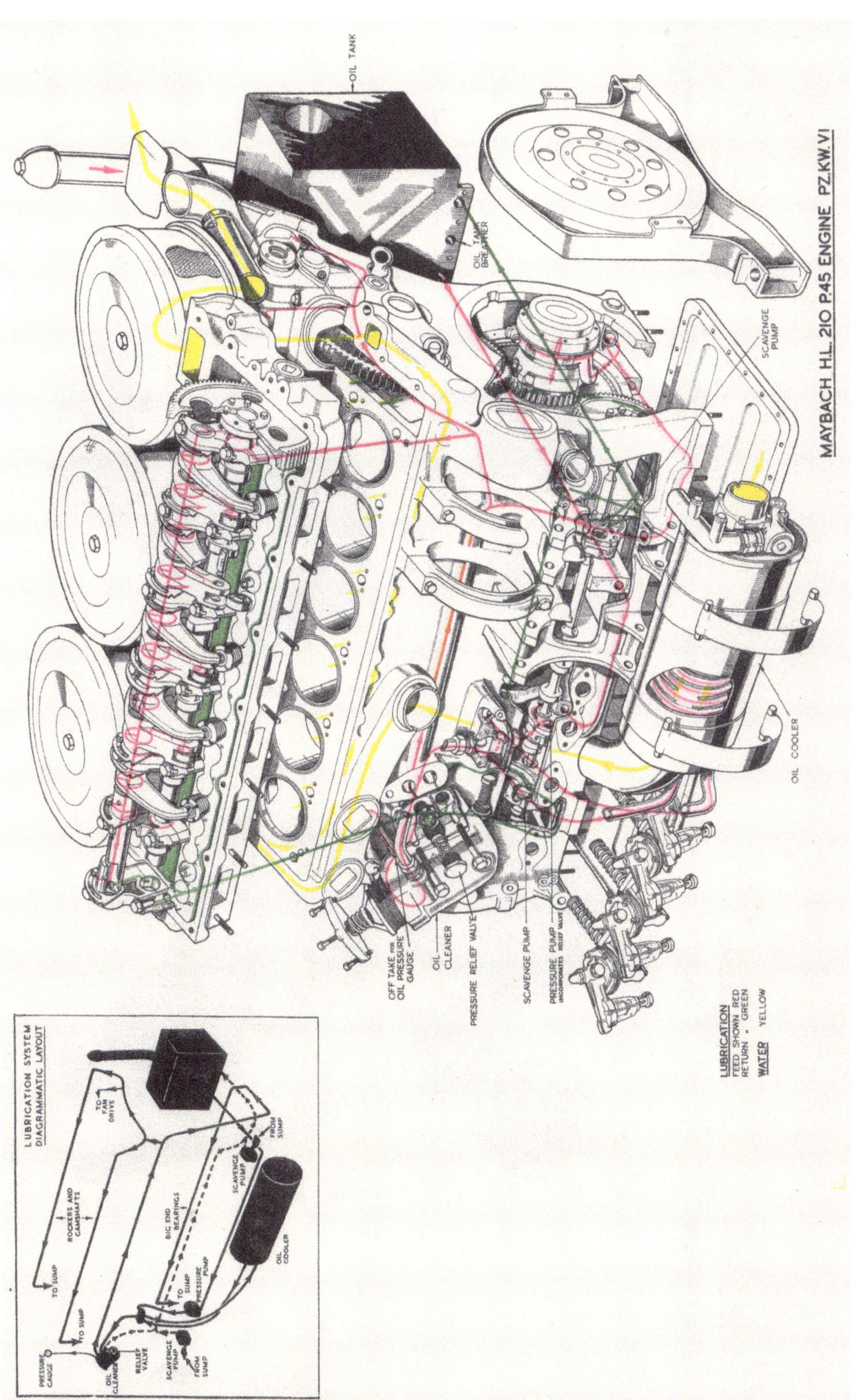

A non-adjustable ball and spring relief valve is fitted on the delivery side of the pressure pump. Pick-ups incorporating coarse perforated steel filters scavenge oil from either end of the flat sump.

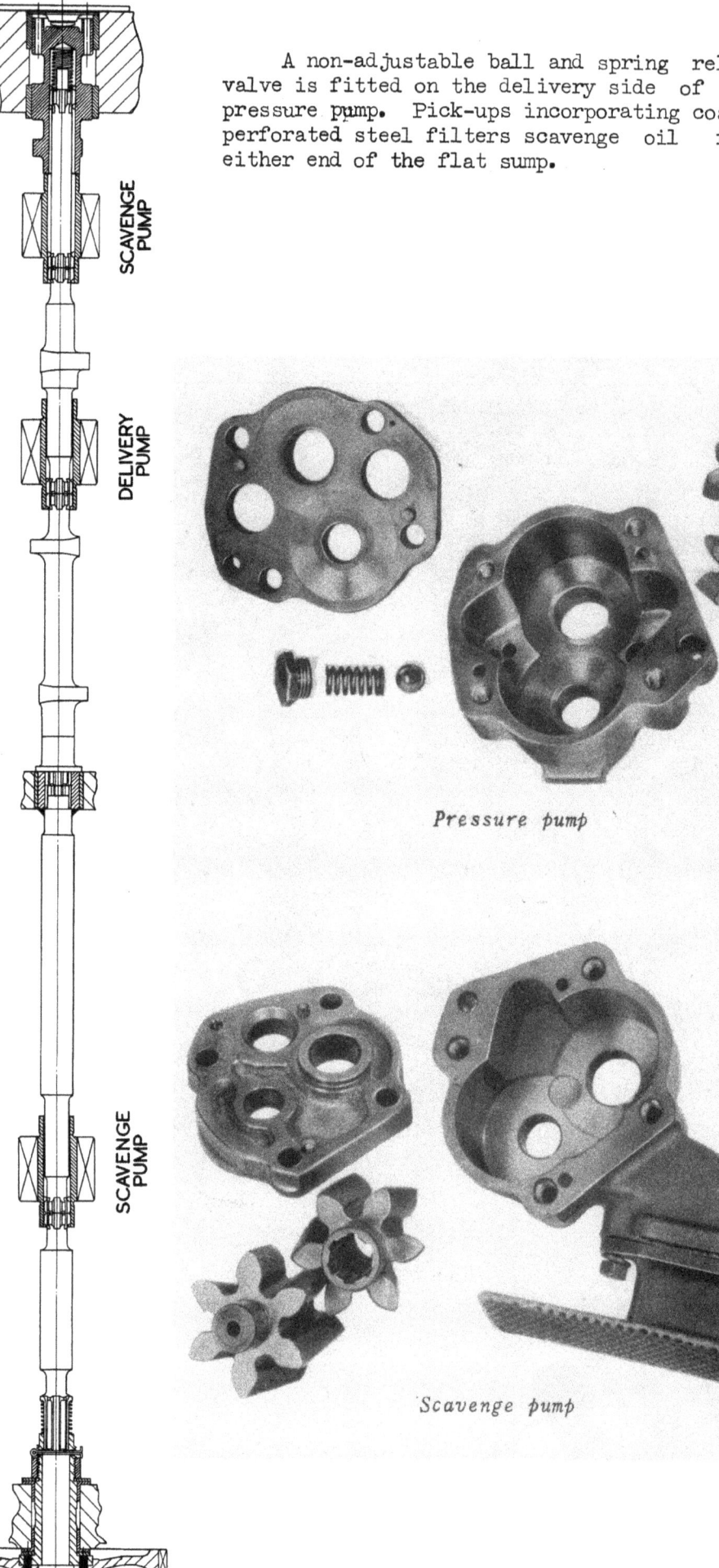

Pressure pump

Scavenge pump

Oil pump articulated drive shaft

Oil Tank

The oil tank which has a capacity of approximately 4 gallons is bolted directly on the crankcase. Three short elbow pipes leading from the bottom of the tank are welded to a machined flange which is bolted to a corresponding machined surface on the crankcase. The two outer elbow pipes register with drillings through Nos. 4 and 5 main bearing webs and serve as delivery and return lines respectively. The central elbow is extended inside the tank to form a standpipe and a breather to the crankcase. It would therefore be possible to flood the sump by careless overfilling of the tank.

A dipstick is contained in the long filler tube, the cap of which has a fine thread and a "bolt head" top.

Lengthwise in the tank is a cylindrical hole through which pass the input shaft and engagement rod of the inertia starter.

Oil Cooler

The oil cooler consists of a close coil contained in a cylindrical sheet metal jacket, through which water is circulated. It is installed together with the filter on the pressure side of the system. In cold climates it is enemy practice to introduce hot water from an outside source, and under these conditions the installation would serve to warm up the cold lubricant.

Filter

The oil filter has an element of gauze discs separated with spacer plates. Feed is from the outside of the element to the centre. If the filter becomes choked, the whole element moves against a spring and allows the oil to by-pass. A pipe for the oil gauge is taken from the outlet side of the filter.

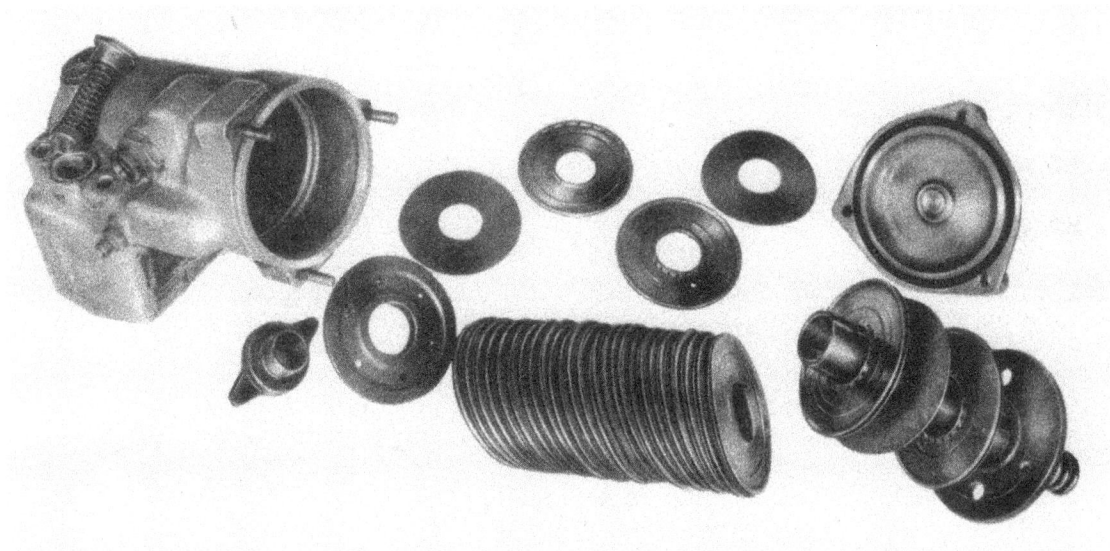

Oil filter

DATA AND DIMENSIONS

Approximate capacity of system   6.2 gallons.

	Pressure Pump	Scavenge Pump
No.	1	2
No. of teeth on gear	7	6
Outside diameter of gear	47 mm.	47 mm.
Root diameter of gear	26 mm.	$22\frac{1}{2}$ mm.
Face width of gear	45 mm.	38 mm.
Clearance between teeth	.33 mm.	.30 mm.
Theoretical delivery at 100% efficiency at 1000 pump RPM	11.3 gals/min	14.37 gals/min (One pump)
Theoretical delivery at 100% efficiency at 3000 engine RPM (2423.1 pump RPM)	27.38 gals/min	69.638 gals/min (both pumps)
Ratio one pressure to two scavenge pumps		1 : 2.54

Filter

No. of spacer plates	29
No. of gauze discs	30
Total effective area of gauze	2050 sq. cm.

ENGINE COOLING SYSTEM

The system, which is sealed, comprises two radiators, and two pairs of fans, and the water is circulated by a centrifugal pump.

The cooling system incorporates several unusual features which fulfil the requirements of submerged running, and these will be described in detail in a separate section. The following description is therefore confined to the engine only.

Water enters the cylinder block via the oil cooler on the left side and returns to the radiators through a single pipe at the rear of each cylinder head. From the oil cooler the water enters a passage cored round the left side to the front of the block, thence via the pump, into a further passage cored between the banks. This passage communicates with the top of the cylinders through small ports, one to each cylinder; these ports are situated to one side of their respective cylinders, thus imparting a swirl to the water on entry. All the cylinders of each bank are interconnected by cored holes at the bottom. A small hole in the rear cylinder of the left bank communicates with a coring which circulates water round the rear wall of the block which forms the casing for the timing gears. Water enters the cylinder heads through holes below the valve ports.

Water Pump

The centrifugal pump is mounted on the forward top end of the crankcase between the cylinder banks.

It is connected to the corings through curved machined faces.

The body of the pump and the impeller are of cast iron. The latter is keyed on a shaft supported in two taper roller bearings. Seals are fitted at either end and lubricant is introduced into the space between the seals through a nipple in the housing.

DATA AND DIMENSIONS

No. of vanes	9
Tip diameter of vanes	146 mm.
Heel diameter of vanes	70 mm.
Width of vane at tip	8 mm.
Width of vane at heel	15 mm.
Inclination of vanes to tangent at tip	30°
Inclination of vanes to tangent at heel	110°

WATER PUMP.

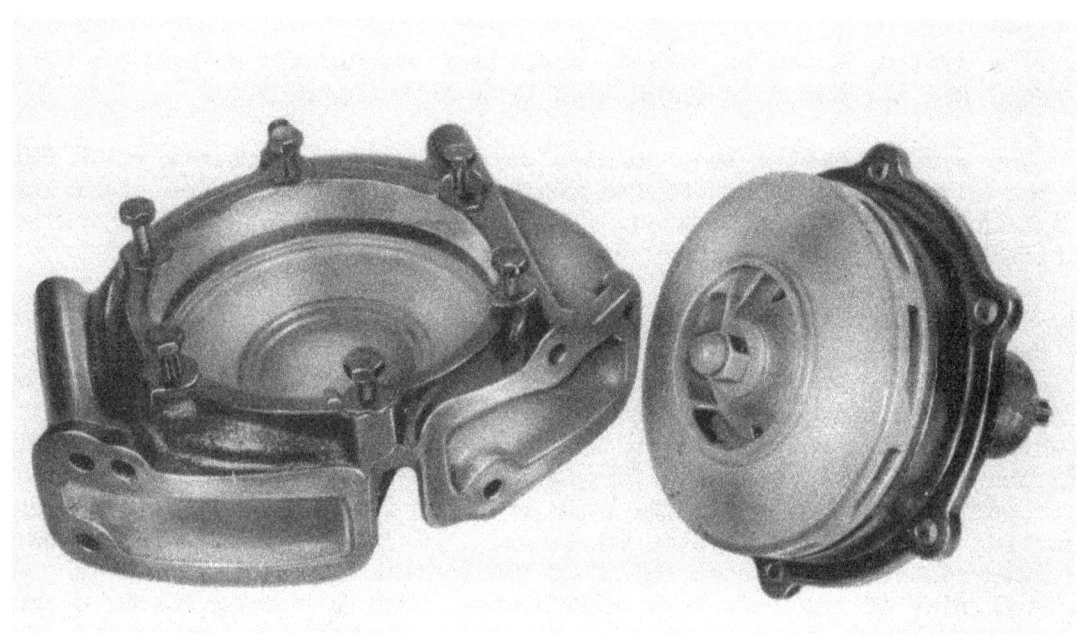

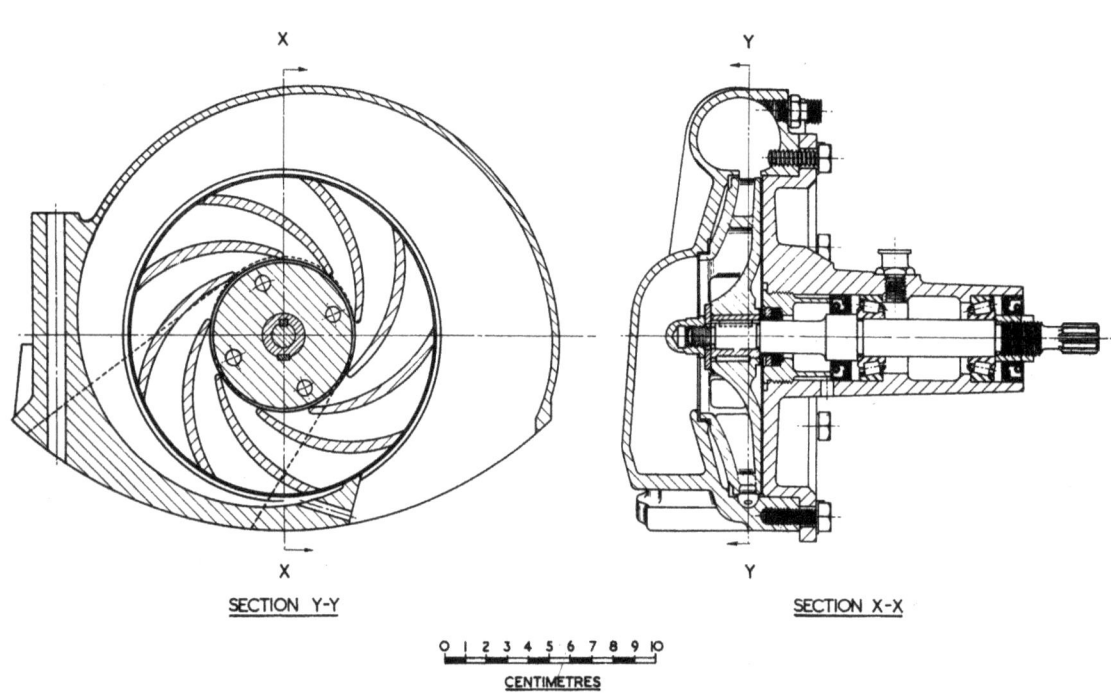

SECTION Y-Y SECTION X-X

0 1 2 3 4 5 6 7 8 9 10
CENTIMETRES

RESTRICTED

The information given in this document is not to be communicated, either directly or indirectly, to the Press or to any person not authorized to receive it.

REPORT ON
Pz Kw VI
(Tiger)
Model H

PART IV

POWER PLANT

SECTION V

ELECTRICAL EQUIPMENT (ENGINE)
BOSCH DYNAMO. TYPE GUL 1000/12/1000 LS 26

Military College of Science
SCHOOL OF TANK TECHNOLOGY
Chobham Lane   Chertsey

April 1944

[Blank page, as per original report]

PART IV

POWER PLANT

SECTION V

ELECTRICAL EQUIPMENT (ENGINE)
BOSCH DYNAMO. TYPE GUL 1000/12/1000 LS26

INTRODUCTION

The dynamo was tested and examined by Messrs. C.A.V. Ltd. who provided the subject matter for this report.

The performance of the machine was found to be good. Its main dimensions are comparable with the C.A.V. Model D8C dynamo although its output is higher and its working temperature lower. With regard to the performance, however, comparison is not justified, as the Bosch dynamo has obviously been designed as a 12 volt machine whereas the D8C was primarily designed for 24 volts.

The commutation of the machine at full load is very good over the working speed range. The reactance voltage, calculated from the usual formula is reasonable for a non-interpole machine, viz., 1.9 volts at 2000 R.P.M x 100 amps.

The light construction and efficient working of the fan are points of interest, particularly so in this installation, as the air in the engine compartment is relatively stagnant, the radiators and fans being housed in separate compartments.

The method of joining the field coils before taping, and the brush box construction are interesting design features.

The ball races are of French manufacture. In view of the date of manufacture, it is noteworthy that the construction of the machine shows no attempt at economy in the use of copper.

Major J.D. Barnes, R.T.R.
D.M. Pearce, B.A. (Cantab)

April, 1944.

GENERAL DESCRIPTION

The dynamo is strapped to the side of the crankcase and is gear driven at engine speed in an anticlockwise direction. It is a 12 volt machine with a maximum output of 1300 watts (maker's rating). The maximum charging rate is stated to be 100 amps. The date of manufacture is 1942.

The dynamo is ventilated by a radial flow fan, which draws air over the commutator through a flexible pipe which opens into the fighting compartment.

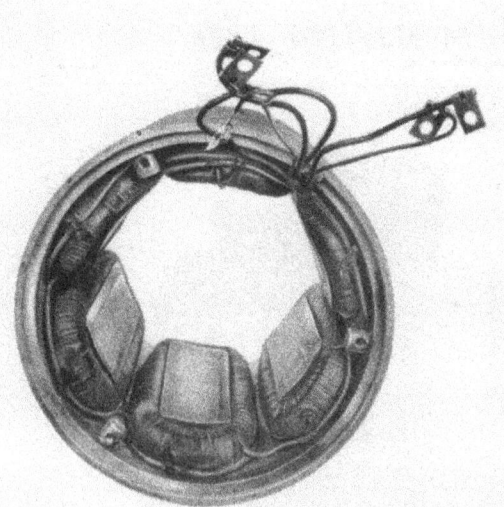
Yoke and Field System

View with End Cover and Fan Removed

Armature

Commutator End Shield

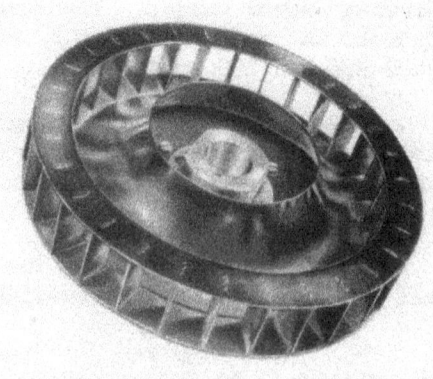
Ventilating Fan

CONSTRUCTIONAL DETAILS AND DIMENSIONS

            Overall length of Machine .. ..   480 mm.
            Weight.. ... ...   114 lbs.

Yoke

            Outside Diameter ... ...   203 mm.
            Thickness... ... ...   10 mm.
            Length, excluding brush gear ... ...   218 mm.

Field System

The yoke carries six poles secured by set screws. The field is split, each field consisting of three coils in series. Two parallel field resistances are wound on two of the field coils. The poles are slightly skewed, and no interpoles are fitted. It was noted that the ends of the field inter-connectors were soldered close to the coils before the coils were taped - this gives the effect of a one piece field inter-connector.

            Pole face . ...   145mm. long (gross)
            Pole chord ... ...   43mm.
            Width of winging .. ..   8mm.
            Pole core, width .. ..   25.7mm.
              "   "   depth .. ..   23mm.
            Resistance of field ... ...   5.5 ohms per field
            Parallel field resistance . ...   16 ohms per
                                                              resistance

Armature & Commutator

The armature windings are of single turn, single coil, strip, wave wound. The slots are slightly skewed in an opposite direction to the poles.

The commutator is of rivetted construction with mica inter-bar insulation.

            Length of core ... ...   143 mm.
            Diameter of core .. ..   135 mm.
            No. of slots...   49
            Width of slot . ...   2 mm.
              "   " tooth ... ...   7 mm.
            Approximate dimensions of strip winding ... ...   6mm. x 2.5 mm.
            Commutator length (excluding risers) .. ..   65mm.
              "   "   (overall) ... ...   75mm.
              "   Diameter ... ...   100mm.
            No. of commutator bars   49

End Shields

Both end shields are of aluminium. The driving end shield is not fitted with a lubricator and the ball race is held in by an aluminium clamping plate. This plate carries the armature earthing brushes, which are situated between the armature and the bearing and bears on a copper slip ring.

The commutator end shield carries the terminal box. The ball race is housed in a brass liner and is held in by a steel clamping plate. Earthing brushes are fitted between the shield and the fan.

            Driving End ball race - O.D. .. ..   80 mm.
            Commutator End " " - O.D. .. ..   62 mm.

Brush Gear

The brush box is of rivetted brass construction. Two sets of four brushes are fitted, the brushes being of the usual German construction. Clock type brush springs are employed.

    Brush size ... ...25 x 8 mm.
    Spring pressure .. ..3.25 lb.

Fan

The radial flow ventilating fan is keyed to the armature shaft. It is constructed of light sheet steel welded together.

    Fan Diameter (mean) .. ..180 mm.
    Fan width ... ... 33 mm.
    No. of blades. 30
    Blade dimensions . ... 33 x 18 mm.

TEST RESULTS

The machine was placed on the test bench and the cutting in and maximum load speeds determined. These were :-

    Cutting in speed . ... 720 r.p.m.
    Maximum load speed ... ... 870 r.p.m. at 100 amps 13.5 volts

The dynamo was then given heat runs at 1,000, 2,000, and 3,000 r.p.m.; on full load, these gave the following results :-

Speed.	Amb. Temp.	Rise in field after ½ hour	Rise in field after 1 hour	Final Temp. (after 1 hr.) Field	Comm.
1000	23°C.	22.5°C.	40°C.	63°C.	83°C.
2000	19°C.	20.5°C.	36°C.	55°C.	77°C.
3000	25°C.	22°C.	35°C.	60°C.	78°C.

The machine was then run at full load and 2,000 r.p.m. when a steady temperature in the field of 69.5°C was reached in 2.1/2 hours, the corresponding commutator temperature being 84°C (ambient temperature 25°C).

The performance of the fan was then tested, and the delivery was found to vary directly with the speed within the working range.

    Speed   Delivery

    1000 R.P.M ... ...   10.5 cub.ft/min.
    2000 R.P.M ... ...   21.6 cub.ft/min.
    3000 R.P.M ... ...   33.0 cub.ft/min.

Efficiency tests were then carried out and the following curves plotted :-

    Speed - Efficiency curve at constant load 1200 W   Fig.1
    Load - Efficiency curve at constant voltage 1000 r.p.m. Fig.2

The following tables were extracted from these results :-

Output Watts	H.P. Input	Efficiency
600 (Half load)	1.3 H.P.	62.5%
1200 ($\frac{1}{1}$ load)	2.42 H.P.	67%
1800 ($\frac{3}{2}$ load)	3.82 H.P.	63.5%

Speed	H.P. Input	Efficiency	
1,000 r.p.m.	2.42 H.P.	67%)	At max.
2,000 r.p.m.	2.55 H.P.	63%)	load of
3,000 r.p.m.	2.86 H.P.	56%)	100 amps.

The iron, windage and friction losses were then separated for 1,000 r.p.m. by the following method :-

    The machine was separately excited, and the field current varied from 0 to 5 amps., the corresponding values of watts input and O.C. volts being noted. Since the speed is constant the windage and friction losses will remain constant and correspond to the watts input at zero excitation.

A curve showing variation of watts input and O.C. volts with excitation is plotted at Fig.3

The armature and field resistance were found to be .0075 ohm and 4 ohms (total, including parallel field).

From these figures and foregoing results the following analysis of losses at 1200 watts output and 1000 r.p.m. was extracted :-

    Efficiency at F.L. 67% Output 1200 watts.
    ∴ Total losses = 580 watts

Armature copper loss	75 watts
Field copper loss...	64 watts
Brush contact loss	200 watts
Iron losses.	96 watts
Brush friction, windage and other friction losses	120 watts
Unaccounted loss	<u>25</u> watts
	<u>580</u> watts

The brush contact losses were estimated from figures obtained with EGO brushes.

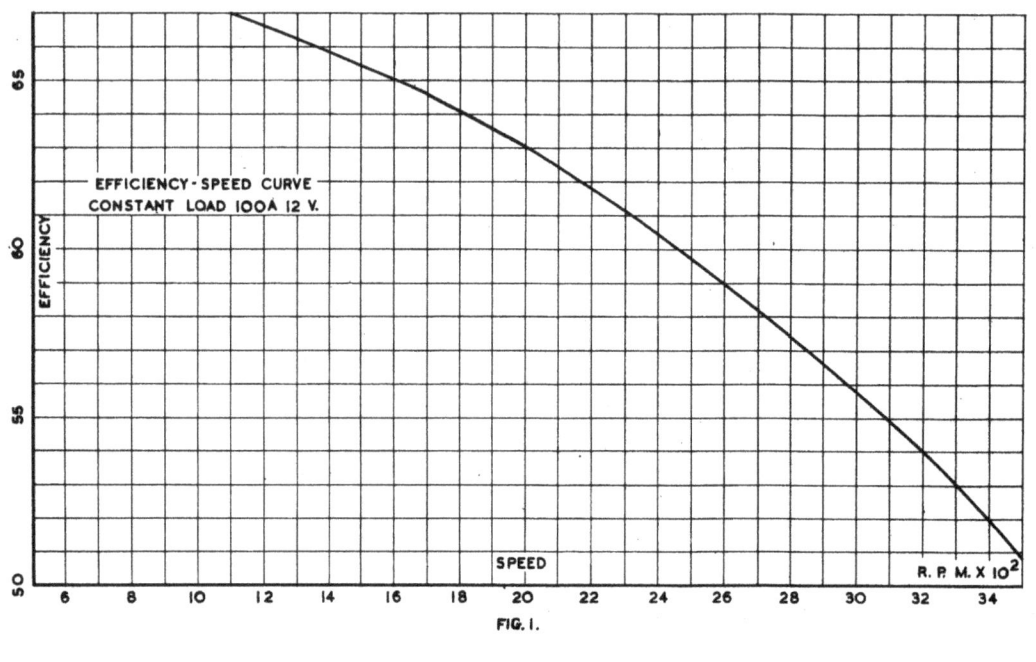

FIG. 1.

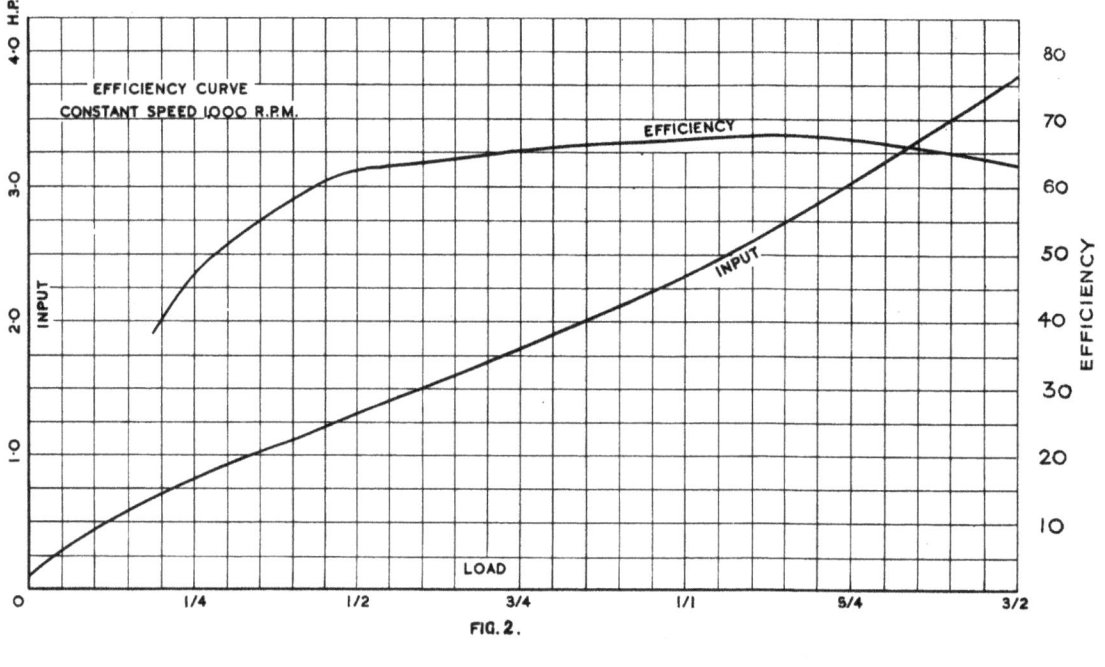

FIG. 2.

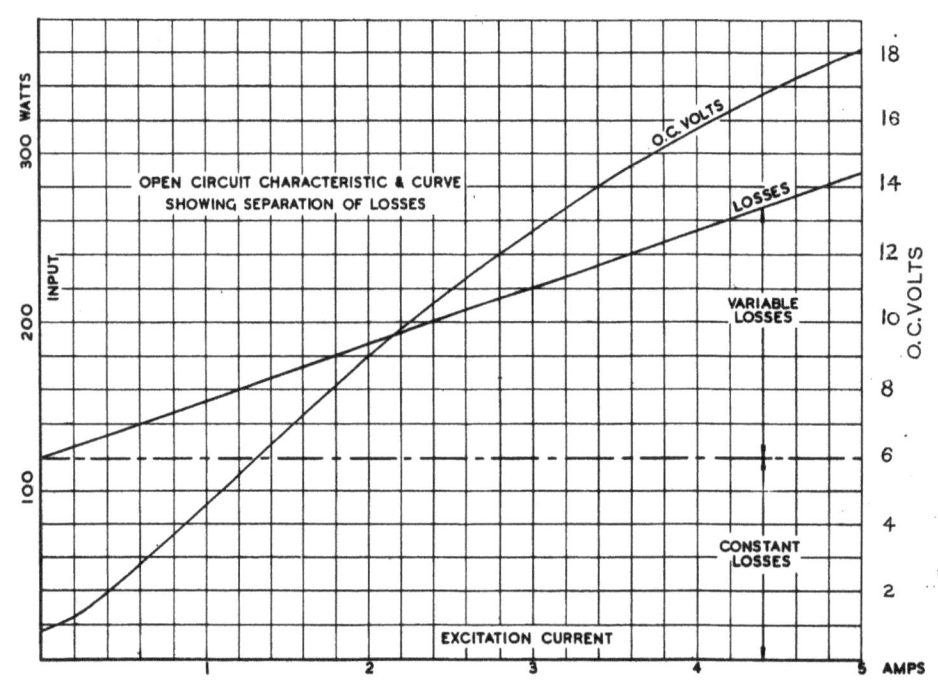

FIG. 3

> **RESTRICTED**
>
> The information given in this document is not to be communicated, either directly or indirectly, to the Press or to any person not authorized to receive it.

REPORT ON
Pz Kw VI
(Tiger)
Model H

PART IV

POWER PLANT

SECTION VI

BOSCH INERTIA STARTER
(TYPE AL/ZMJ)

[Editor's note: This is the first of the automotive reports to be delivered, according to the date below. It might have been the first of all the reports to be delivered. This might suggest that the inertia starter was important. In reality, as the introduction overleaf confirms, this component was practically identical to any other inertia starter seen in German tanks. A superficial reading of the following report might suggest that the inertia starter was the only way to start up Tiger's engine, but in fact it was a back-up in case the electric starter were to fail. No report on the electric starter was produced.]

Military College of Science
SCHOOL OF TANK TECHNOLOGY
Chobham Lane Chertsey

January 1944

PART IV

POWER PLANT

SECTION VI.

BOSCH INERTIA STARTER
(Type AL/ZMJ)

INTRODUCTION

The Bosch Inertia Starter is fitted as standard equipment on all German tank engines with the exception of that in the Pz.Kw. I now virtually obsolete.

The starter is hand operated only, and is mounted on the engine in a similar manner to an orthodox electric starter and engages with the flywheel ring gear. It may only be operated from outside the tank through the tail plate. The hand crank drives through two sprockets and a roller chain to a shaft provided with a universal joint and attached to the starter input shaft.

The type AL/ZMJ fitted to this tank differs from the type AL/ZMA found on the smaller German tanks (Pz.Kw. II, III and IV) only in detail design. In the main it is very similar, and certain parts are interchangeable. The chief differences are found in the input gear train and the clutch engaging mechanism. It is interesting to note that the capacity of the two types - as measured by the total energy stored in the flywheel - is approximately the same, whereas the engine capacity of the Pz.Kw. VI (approximately 21 litres) is very nearly double that of the Pz.Kw. III and IV (approximately 12 litres). The geared reduction from the starter flywheel to the engine crankshaft is, however, very much greater in this case, and the engine is therefore turned over at rather more than half the speed.

The limitations of size imposed by its location necessitate a small flywheel running at a high speed and consequently the precision of design and workmanship must be of a high order. The use of a separate output gear train from the flywheel to the starting pinion appears to be an unnecessary complication, as, with a little ingenuity, a section of the input train could have been used as the output.

Messrs. Rotax and C.A.V. Ltd., have examined one of these starters and we are indebted to them for the "Run-down" Time Curve.

March, 1944

Major J.D. Barnes, R.T.R.
D.M. Pearce, B.A. (Cantab.)

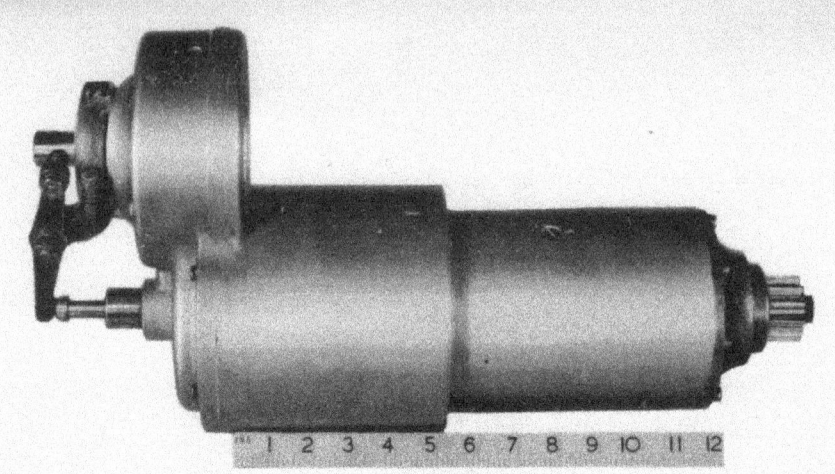

COMPLETE STARTER

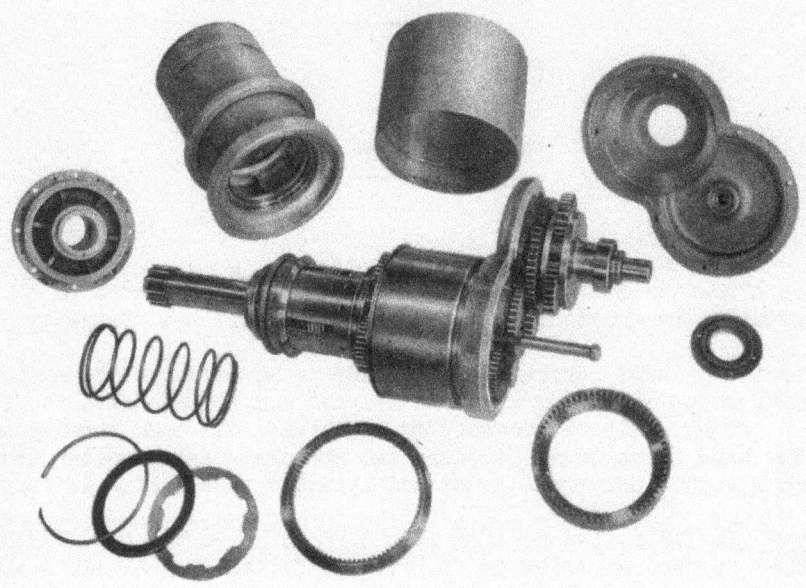

STARTER WITH CASINGS REMOVED

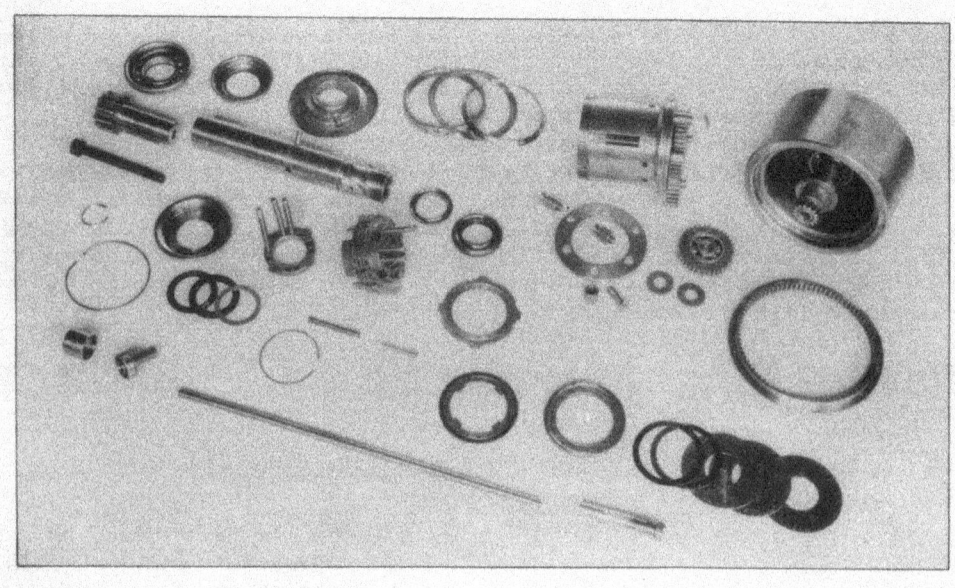

EXPLODED VIEW WITH CLUTCH, ~~REMOVED~~ OUTPUT GEARS AND FLYWHEEL

[Editor's note: The two thick horizontal lines above were used to redact the word "REMOVED". The redaction is the same in all copies of this report.]

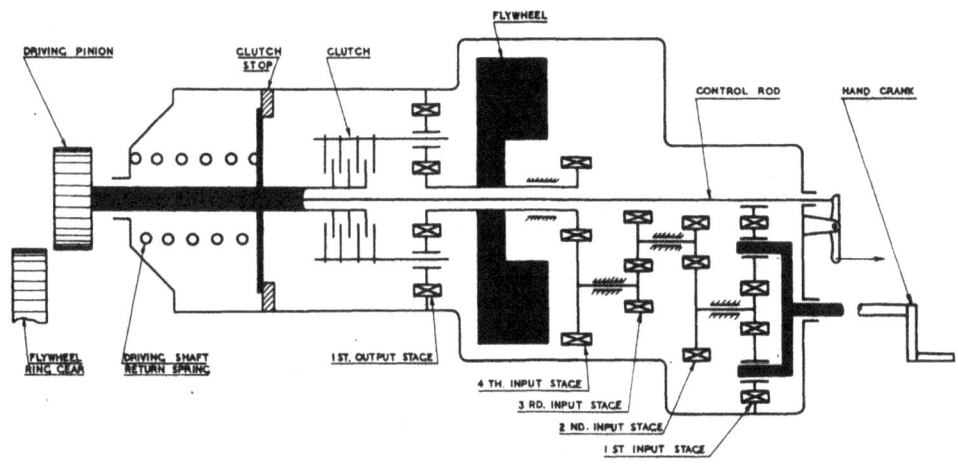

Diagramatic Layout

PRINCIPLE OF OPERATION

The mechanism is basically a simple form of hand operated inertia starter consisting of a step-up input gear train from the handcrank to the flywheel and a reduction output gear train from the flywheel to the engine crankshaft via a starting pinion which axially engages with the flywheel ring gear. Incorporated in the reduction gear train is a clutch which is engaged manually when the flywheel is rotating at the required speed and which slips during the period when the engine is being accelerated.

From the diagram it will be seen that the first input stage consists of a simple epicyclic train, the planet carrier being the input, the annulus fixed and the sun wheel the output. The second, third and fourth stages each consist of a pair of spur gears, the output of one being integral with the input of the following stage.

The output gear train is quite separate from that of the input, being on the opposite side of the flywheel. The first stage consists of an epicyclic train, the sun wheel, which is attached to the flywheel, is the input, the annulus fixed, and the planet carrier forms the output. The output drives through the clutch the external driving pinion which engages with the flywheel ring gear, the pair forming the second and final output stage. Thus the final stage of the output gear train is outside the starter itself.

The multiplate clutch is engaged by a manually operated control rod which at the same time engages the driving pinion with the flywheel ring gear. The clutch is self energised when a torque is transmitted in one direction and acts as a free wheel when the torque is reversed.

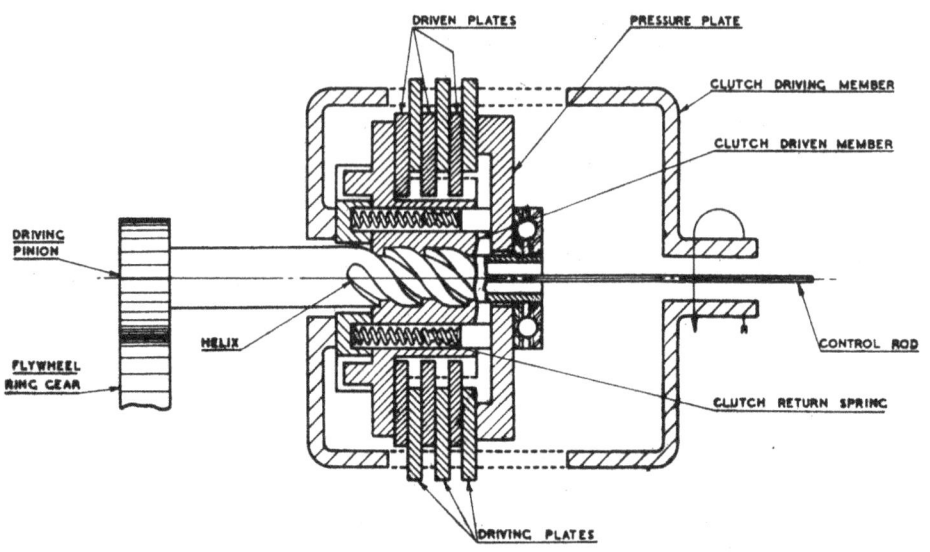

Diagramatic Layout showing clutch operation

The driving member of the clutch is a cylindrical cage slotted to receive the external serrations of the driving plates. These plates are free to slide axially in the slots. The driven member is in the form of a circular sleeve located concentrically within the driving member and grooved to receive the internal serrations of the driven plates. The outer edge of this member (as assembled) is provided with a flange against which the outer clutch plate abuts when the clutch is engaged. The member is free to slide on helical splines on the driving pinion shaft, the inner end of which is provided with a thrust race to limit the movement. A pressure plate disc is interposed between the thrust race and the driven member.

The direction of the helical splines is such that when a torque is transmitted through the clutch, in the right direction for starting the engine, the driven member tends to screw itself in on the shaft thus wedging the clutch plates between the flange and the pressure plate. As soon as the torque is reversed, i.e. when the engine fires, the action is reversed, and the clutch is automatically disengaged.

Light springs normally hold the driven member away from the pressure plate. When the driving pinion shaft is moved out to engage the pinion with the flywheel ring gear, the driven member of the clutch is pressed against a circular plate attached to the outer end of the driving member. This compresses the springs and closes the plates until sufficient torque is transmitted to the driven member to bring about the self wedging action. It will be seen therefore, that, provided the driving pinion shaft is moved far enough to start the clutch engagement, the slipping torque of the clutch is quite independant of force on the control rod but depends upon :-

1. The dimensions of the clutch.
2. The angle of the helical splines.

It will further be seen that the clutch is not engaged until the driving pinion is meshing with the flywheel ring gear.

The control rod passes through the axis of the flywheel and forces the driving pinion shaft outwards to engage with the flywheel ring gear. When the pressure on the control rod is released, a coil spring around the shaft returns it to its normal disengaged position. In this position a flange on the shaft is held against a stationary brake ring, thereby preventing the driving pinion from rotating through the drag in the clutch whilst the flywheel is being speeded up.

METHOD OF CONSTRUCTION

In external appearance the starter resembles an orthodox type of electric axial starter. The cylindrical casing is strapped against the side of the crankcase and a sliding driving pinion engages the flywheel ring gear. A considerable geared reduction is therefore obtained outside the starter itself. This, together with the high speed of flywheel rotation (9,000 - 10,000 R.P.M.) permits of a very compact and light design. In common with other Bosch products the workmanship is of a very high standard, and it is evidently a costly piece of mechanism to manufacture.

CASINGS.

The housing may be split into four main casings; a cylindrical aluminium casting housing the clutch, a steel sleeve surrounding the flywheel, an aluminium casting housing the shafts of the flywheel and third and fourth input gear stages, and a cast aluminium cover for the first two input stages.

The clutch casing is provided with a cast iron end plate which houses a white metal bush supporting the driving pinion shaft, and a synthetic rubber oil seal. This bearing is lubricated from a grease nipple and a felt ring surrounds the bush. The casing is provided with a flange at one end which fits into the steel flywheel casing and is held up against a shoulder in the latter by a ring nut. Between this flange and the shoulder on the flywheel casing is the annulus for the first output gear stage which is held by dowels and set screws on the flange. Pressed into the casing are the two outer races of the ball bearings supporting the cylindrical clutch driving member.

The flywheel casing consists of a length of steel tubing threaded internally at one end to take the ring nut, and provided with an internal flange at the other. Fitting inside this casing and held against the internal flange is the aluminium casting which carries the ball races for the flywheel shaft and for the two shafts carrying the third and fourth trains of spur gears. An external flange on the casting is held between the internal flange of the flywheel casing and the cast aluminium cover for the first two input stages. Long screws threaded into the flywheel casing secure these three components.

The cover for the first two input stages has an extension at one side to accommodate the first epicyclic train, the annulus of which is pressed into the cover and secured by set screws and dowels. The extension of this cover is provided with a felt oil seal through which the starting handle shaft passes. The control rod protrudes through a hole in the centre of the cover.

The aluminium casings appear to be gravity die castings.

GEAR TRAINS AND FLYWHEEL

Straight toothed spur gears are employed throughout. With the exception of the two annuli, which are soft, the gears are hardened but the tooth profiles are not ground. The pinions are made progressively lighter and the tooth face width and module decrease from the low speed to the high speed stages in the gear trains as the transmitted torque decreases.

All the pinions are supported on orthodox caged ball races with the exception of the sunwheel output of the first input stage and, integral with it, the driving pinion of the second input stage; these run on a bronze bush on an extension of the input shaft. In some cases the ball races are housed directly in the aluminium casings, in others steel housings are shrunk in.

Both epicyclic trains are of similar construction. In each case the carrier is in the form of a disc drilled to receive the three planet wheel shafts. Shoulders are turned at each end of the shafts which are held against the disc by a flat ring drilled to receive the other ends of the shafts.

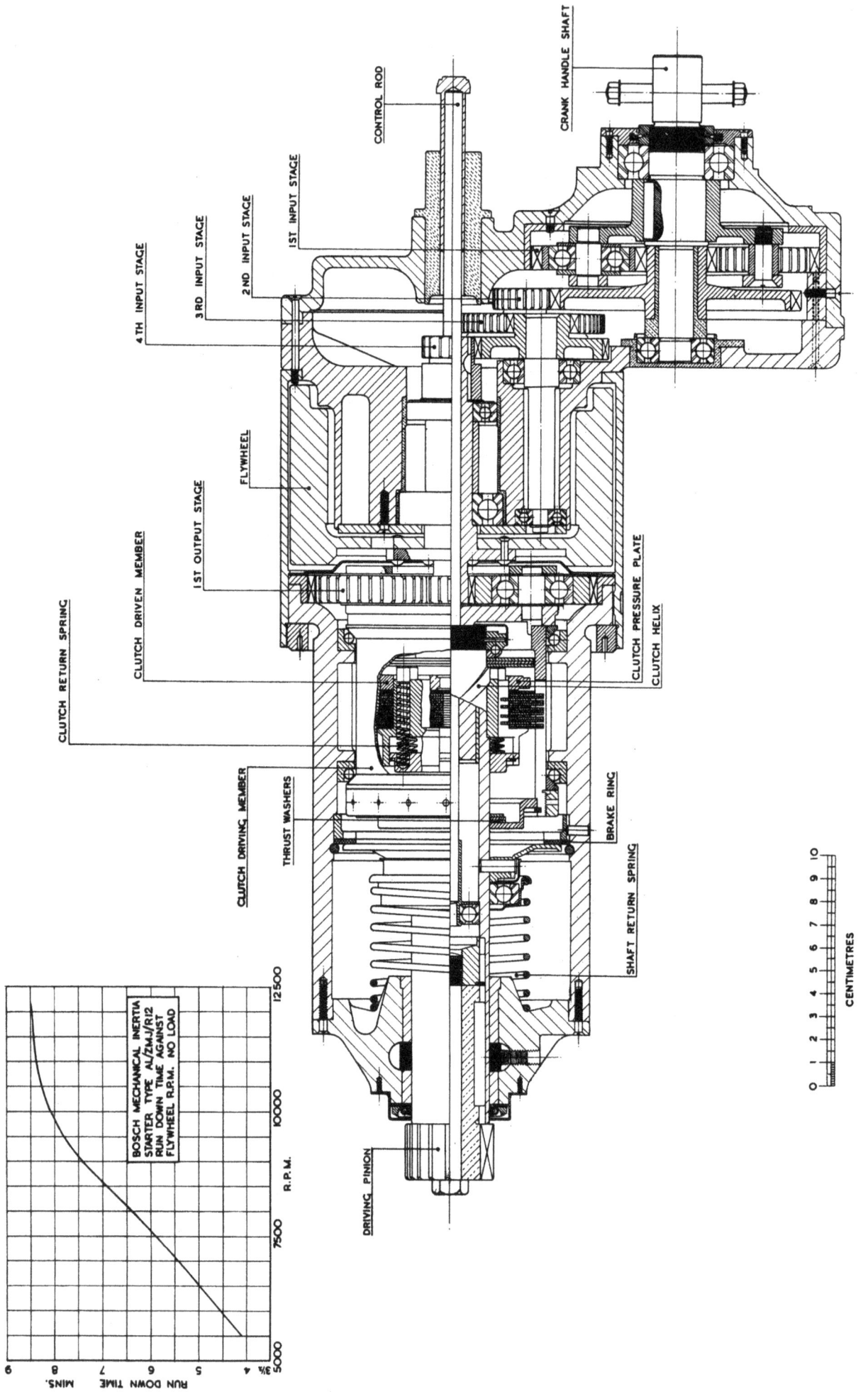

This ring is bolted to the disc by three set screws and distance pieces situated midway between the planet wheels and on the same P.C.D. Each planet wheel is pressed over a ball race, the pinion metal being nipped over the radius on the outer race in six places on each side to secure it.

The flywheel shaft is integral with the sunwheel of the first output stage, and is provided with a flange to which the flywheel is rivetted and dowelled. The steel flywheel, which is machined all over, has a wide rim on one side which surrounds the aluminium casting carrying the shafts of the flywheel and of the third and fourth input stages.

GEAR DATA

INPUT TRAIN		NO. OF TEETH	FACE WIDTH (mm.)	MODULE
1st stage	(Planet	23	12	2
	(Annulus	63	12	2
	(Sun	15	12	2
2nd stage	(Driver	55	9	2
	(Driven	12	9	2
3rd stage	(Driver	34	8	2
	(Driven	13	8	2
4th stage	(Driver	38	8	1.5
	(Driven	15	9	1.5
OUTPUT TRAIN				
1st stage	(Sun	12	13	1.5
	(Annulus	84	12	1.5
	(Planet	36	12	1.5

CLUTCH

The clutch driving member consists of a steel cylinder secured to the planet carrier of the first output stage by set screws and dowels. Fitting over this sleeve are two hardened steel conical section rings which form the inner races of two large crowded ball bearings supporting the sleeve and planet carrier. A ring nut on the outer end of the sleeve adjusts the clearance in the races.

Four slots are machined in the sleeve to receive the bronze driving plates which are arranged in pairs alternately between single steel driven plates. Eight chordal slits are cut in the outer diameter of each driving plate. The small tabs formed by these slits are turned alternately outwards and inwards so that the planes of their surfaces lie at a small angle to the plane of the surface of the rest of the plate. The purpose of this is presumably to cushion the take up and free the plates when the clutch is disengaged.

The driven member is of hardened steel, slotted to receive the driven plates and provided with three internal helical splines. Eight holes are drilled axially around the bore to receive the springs which normally keep the clutch out of engagement. These springs are provided with hardened steel pads at their inner ends.

The inner end of the driving pinion shaft is threaded to receive the clutch ball thrust race. Between this race and the innermost clutch plate is the pressure plate, two shim washers and three large washers. The outer end of the driven member is extended in the form of a sleeve with four axial slots. Fitting into this sleeve and sliding on the shaft is a steel ring serrated on its outer diameter to engage with the four slots. Eight holes are drilled a short way into the inner face of this ring to receive the clutch spring pads.

On the outer side of the ring and fitting over the shaft is a bronze, a steel and a fibre thrust washer. The outermost thrust washer bears against the circular plate attached to the outer end of the driving member and thus compresses the clutch springs when the shaft is moved outwards. The circular plate is located against a shoulder in the end of the clutch driving member and is secured by a circlip.

The driving pinion shaft is supported at its inner end on a spigot on the output planet carrier and a bronze bush is pressed into the bore of the shaft. The outer end of the shaft is supported in the white metal bush previously referred to. A steel flange is secured to the driving pinion shaft by three pins. A combined radial and end thrust ball race is held against the outer face of this flange by a coil spring, the other end of which seats on the inner face of the cast iron end plate. This spring holds the flange against a fibre ring secured by a circlip in the bore of the clutch casing.

The steel control rod passes through the casing for the first input stages, through the hollow flywheel shaft and presses against a small ball race located by a circlip in the bore of the driving pinion shaft. The driving pinion is of bronze and is keyed internally to the end of the shaft.

DATA

Make	Bosch
Type	AL/ZMJ/R.12
Weight of Complete Starter	52 lb.
Overall Length	490 mm.
Maximum Diameter	157 mm.

GEAR RATIOS

Geared reduction from Flywheel to Handcrank

1st input stage	5.2 : 1
2nd " "	4.58 : 1
3rd " "	2.62 : 1
4th " "	2.53 : 1
Total	157.9 : 1

Geared reduction from Flywheel to Crankshaft
1st output stage (Flywheel to Starter Pinion)	8 : 1
2nd " " (Starter Pinion to Crankshaft)	16 : 1
Total	128 : 1

Estimated normal R.P.M. of Handcrank (before engagement)	60
" " " " Flywheel	9474
" " " " Starter Pinion	1184
" peak " " Crankshaft (neglecting clutch slip)	74
" " " " " (clutch slipping)	60

FLYWHEEL

Weight	10.25 lb.
Outside Diameter	145 mm.
Calculated Moment of Inertia	0.0127 ft.lb.sec^2
Energy stored at 9474 R.P.M.	6270 ft.lb.

CLUTCH

Number of Driving Plates	5 pairs
" " Driven Plates	5
Mean diameter frictional surface	59 mm.
Total frictional Area	100 cm^2
Helix Angle	45°
Slipping Torque	82 lb.ft.
Maximum Torque capable of being transmitted to crankshaft	1376 lb.ft.

> **RESTRICTED**
>
> The information given in this document is not to be communicated, either directly or indirectly, to the Press or to any person not authorized to receive it.

REPORT ON
PzKw VI
(Tiger)
Model H

PART IX

SPECIAL DEVICES AND EQUIPMENT

SECTION I

AUTOMATIC FIRE EXTINGUISHER

Military College of Science
SCHOOL OF TANK TECHNOLOGY
Chobham Lane Chertsey

January 1944

PART IX

SPECIAL DEVICES AND EQUIPMENT

SECTION I

AUTOMATIC FIRE EXTINGUISHER

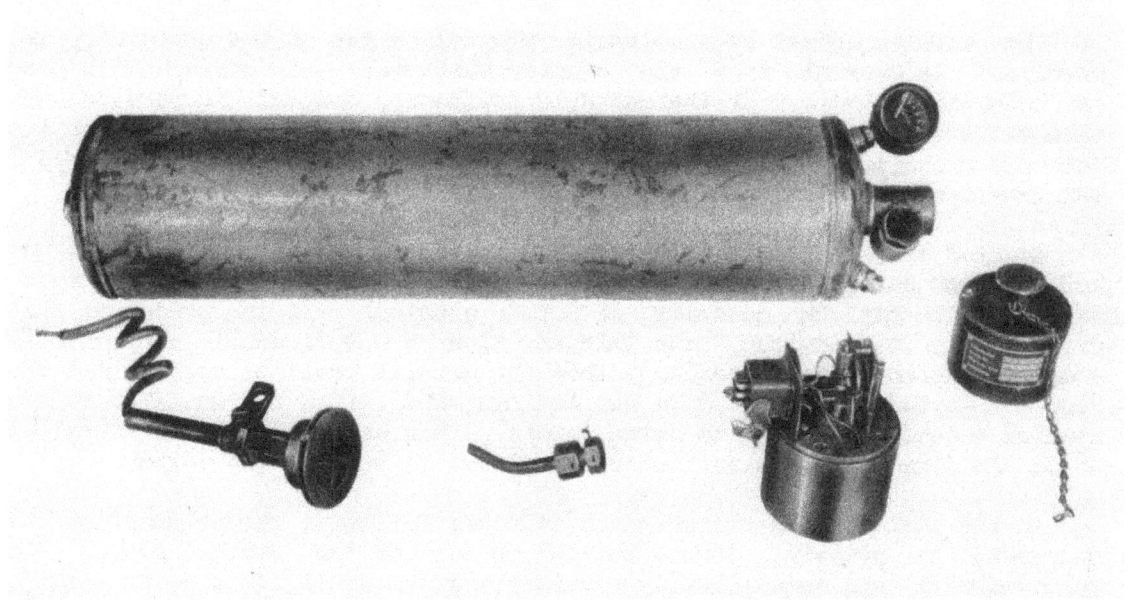

C.T.C. Container, Time Switch and Solenoid, Spray Nozzle and Thermostatic Switch.

INTRODUCTION

The automatic fire-fighting equipment fitted to this vehicle appears to be an innovation since it has not been noted on any other German A.F.V. Normal practice is to carry only portable hand extinguishers.

The origin of the equipment is obscure, and it has probably been improvised from a variety of parts, as the spray nozzles are almost certainly aero-engine equipment and correspond with those seen on enemy aircraft.

The thermostatic switches are not, as far as can be ascertained, used in any form of aircraft. They are, however, of a very common bimetallic disc type such as could be used for a variety of purposes wherein closing an electric circuit gives an alarm or starts an electric mechanism.

The solenoid and time switch mechanism have probably been adapted mainly from standard industrial components; the escapement mechanism in particular has evidently not been made specifically for this job, and may be part of a time fuze for a shell or bomb.

The Pyrene Co., Ltd., have examined the apparatus and we acknowledge their assistance in preparing this report.

January, 1944

Major J.D. Barnes, R.T.R.
D.M. Pearce, B.A., Cantab.

PRINCIPAL OF OPERATION

A cylindrical container holding approximately 5 litres of carbon tetrachloride is carried vertically on the engine bulkhead in the fighting compartment. When full, the container is under an air pressure of 6 Kg/cm^2 imposed by a handpump; the pressure is not maintained constant but is renewed after use.

A spring loaded valve in the neck of the container communicates via a pipe to a distributor manifold leading to four spray nozzles, two of which are directed on the carburettors, one on the petrol pumps and one on the underside of the crankcase.

The valve is opened by a solenoid mounted on top of the container, and energised by current from the starter batteries. In series with the solenoid circuit are four thermostatic switches, coupled in parallel and each situated close to a spray nozzle. The thermostatic switches close the solenoid circuit when subjected to a temperature above approximately 95°C and thus open the valve on the C.T.C. container.

Mounted over the solenoid is a time switch which ensures that once the solenoid is energised, it remains so for at least seven seconds, thus limiting the minimum quantity of C.T.C. ejected. It is presumed that without this time switch, the initial flow of C.T.C. would sufficiently cool the thermostatic switch(es), that the circuit would be opened, and the flow terminated before the fire was extinguished. If a thermostatic switch remains closed for more than seven seconds, the solenoid remains energised until the temperature is sufficiently reduced to re-open the switch.

In the event of the thermostatic switches failing, the solenoid may be energised by pressing down a button on top of the switch gear. The solenoid will then automatically remain energised until after seven seconds the time switch is tripped. In the event of a complete breakdown of the electrical system, the button may be pressed hard down to engage with the end of the solenoid rod, and thus open the valve manually.

The driver has no control over the extinguisher mechanism, but is warned by a red light, coupled in parallel with the solenoid, situated just below his vision slit. The light carries the warning "Fire in engine - immediately throttle down to idling speed."

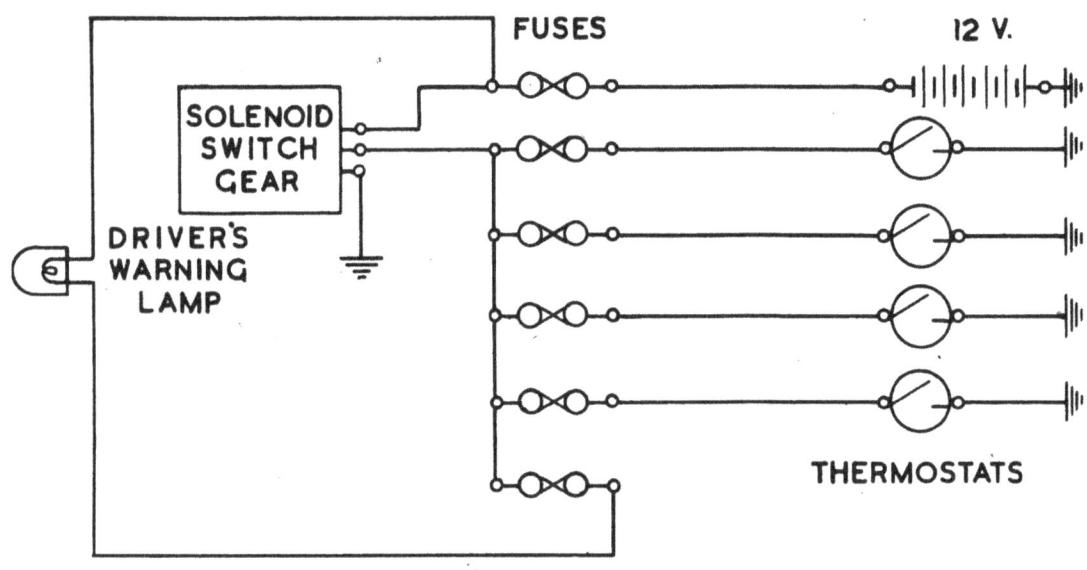

Electrical Circuit

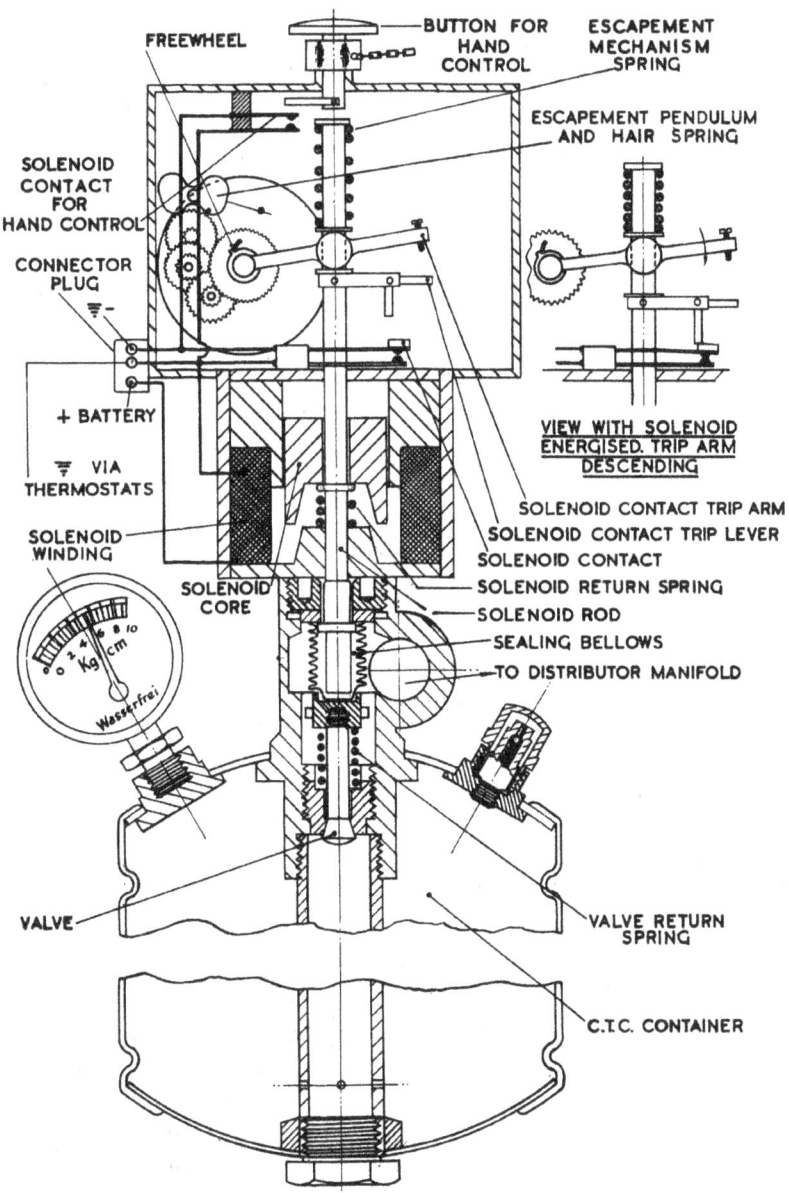

*Diagram of Solenoid,
Valve and Time Switch.*

METHOD OF CONSTRUCTION

In general the method of construction of the components follows orthodox lines and calls for no particular comment.

The container is similar to an ordinary hand fire extinguisher and is made of sheet steel welded together and tin or zinc plated. It is provided with a pressure gauge, a small ball-valve and connection for a hand pump and the main valve.

The main valve is of mushroom type and is spring-loaded. It opens into a pipe which extends to the base of the container, thus ensuring that liquid only is forced through the valve. On top of the valve stem is a small copper bellows which takes the place of a stuffing box and above the bellows is a short push rod.

On top of the main valve is mounted the solenoid, the windings of which are housed in a steel tube which forms part of the armature. The solenoid core is attached to a rod which extends down on to the push rod and up into the casing for the time switch gear.

The time switch consists of a pair of contacts which are held closed when the solenoid is energised by a small bell-crank on an arm attached to the solenoid rod. The downward movement of the solenoid rod compresses a coil spring which forces down a lever. This lever, at the end of its downward travel, presses on the free arm of the bell crank and trips the switch. The lever is attached at its fulcrum to an escapement mechanism which limits its downward speed, and allows the contacts to remain closed for about seven seconds.

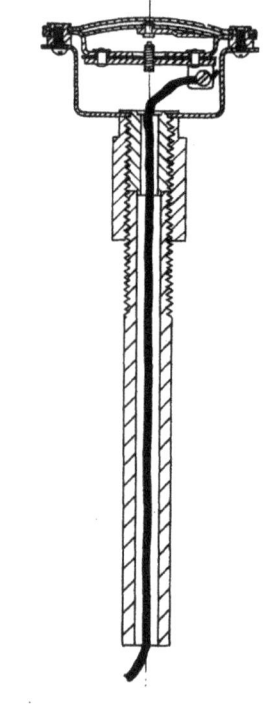

The escapement mechanism is constructed on similar lines to a watch and consists of four stages of gears from the lever spindle to an escapement wheel, rotary pendulum, and straight hair spring. The speed of the escapement wheel is adjusted by sliding the hair spring anchorage in or out and thus altering the rate. A free wheel is incorporated on the lever spindle so that the lever can return freely to its top position when the solenoid is de-energised. The free wheel consists of a coil spring, passing over a shaft, which when turned in one direction tends to tighten and grip the shaft, but in the other direction tends to unscrew and ride over the shaft.

The whole time switch mechanism is enclosed in a light pressed steel cover which incorporates the manually operated button and contact switch. A standard three pole plug socket is provided at one side.

Thermostatic Switch

The thermostatic switches are of the bimetal disc type. The disc appears to be made of steel and brass. It is slightly dished and a contact is attached to the centre. The disc is earthed and at a temperature of approximately 95°C the centre of the disc snaps over and makes contact with an insulated contact, which is connected with the solenoid. The disc and contact are housed in a two piece circular steel pressing attached to a length of steel conduit which protects the solenoid lead.

In common with modern German aircraft practice the spray nozzles are made of bronze lacquered aluminium. A tapered nipple is brazed on the end of the copper feed pipe and the nozzle is held on with a union nut. The nozzle is provided with an orifice of 1.5 mm. diameter behind which is a small swirl chamber. Behind the swirl chamber is screwed a small brass plug with two diagonal grooves across the threads; these grooves impart a rotational motion to the liquid before it reaches the swirl chamber.

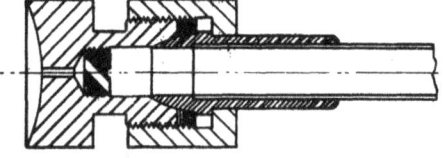

The solenoid circuit, each thermostatic switch circuit, and the driver's warning lamp circuit are protected by standard Bosch fuzes.

Spray Nozzle

> **RESTRICTED**
>
> The information given in this document is not to be communicated, either directly or indirectly, to the Press or to any person not authorized to receive it.

REPORT ON
PzKw VI
(Tiger)
Model H

PART IX

SPECIAL DEVICES AND EQUIPMENT

SECTION II

VENTILATION

Military College of Science
SCHOOL OF TANK TECHNOLOGY
Chobham Lane   Chertsey

September 1944

PART IX

SPECIAL DEVICES AND EQUIPMENT

SECTION 11

VENTILATION

REFERENCES

It appears likely that the enemy have made additions and modifications to the ventilating installation from time to time.

M.I.10 Technical Summary No. 116 dated 8th November 1943, Section 14, makes reference to a method of warming the fighting compartment by air directed from the left hand radiator outlet louvre. This was not fitted to the tank examined.

A further report by M.I.10, dated 11th August, 1943 - (para. 26, under "Preparations for Submersion" makes reference to an apparatus for dealing with carbon-monoxide). An order published by the enemy has forbidden submersion, and it seems likely, therefore, that subsequent vehicles have been substantially modified.

J. D. BARNES, Major, R.T.R.

D. M. PEARCE, B.A. (Cantab.)

SEPTEMBER 1944.

G. BOYD, Lieut., R.A.C.

NORMAL RUNNING

For normal running air is drawn through two mushroom vents, one situated in the hinged engine cover plate, and one in the front top plate between the driver's and hull gunner's access hatches. This latter ventilator provides an air flow over the transmission, and rectangular section ducts conduct the air to the upper end of a cowling surrounding the gearbox. Both mushroom ventilators are screwed down to close when submerged.

An electric fan is mounted in the turret roof above the loader, and expels the fumes resulting from the firing of the turret armament.

Air supply for carburation is passed through two pre-cleaners mounted on the tail plate of the tank, and is taken to the pre-cleaners by two flexible metallic hoses mounted on the top of the engine cover plate, their open ends being provided with gauze protectors. From the cleaners air is supplied via flexible metallic hoses to a manifold bolted on the engine cover.

Circulation of air inside the tank is induced by a Sirocco fan, driven at engine speed, secured through flanges by eight bolts to the engine flywheel. The fan is contained within a volute housing bolted to the forward bulkhead of the engine compartment. The induction branch of the volute housing connects to a trunk situated on the floor of the vehicle. One end of the trunk terminates at the rear of the vehicle beneath the engine, and is open-ended. The other end leads forward into the cowling surrounding the gearbox in the driver's compartment.

Sirocco fan

A manually operated sliding valve is fitted in the trunk, immediately below the induction branch, which controls quantity and direction of air flow. For normal running the valve is moved fully forward and the fan then draws its major supply of air from the bottom of the engine compartment; the valve is so designed that a small current of air is simultaneously drawn over the gearbox. The air is delivered from the volute housing via two independent exits through two jackets surrounding the exhaust manifolds, and thence into two chambers situated on the inside of the tail plate. Pipes with butterfly valves conduct the air from these chambers through the side plates to the down-stream side of the radiators. Two further pipes with butterfly valves also communicate from the engine compartment to the radiator compartments and thus the cooling fans draw air from the top of the engine compartment as well as through the radiator matrices.

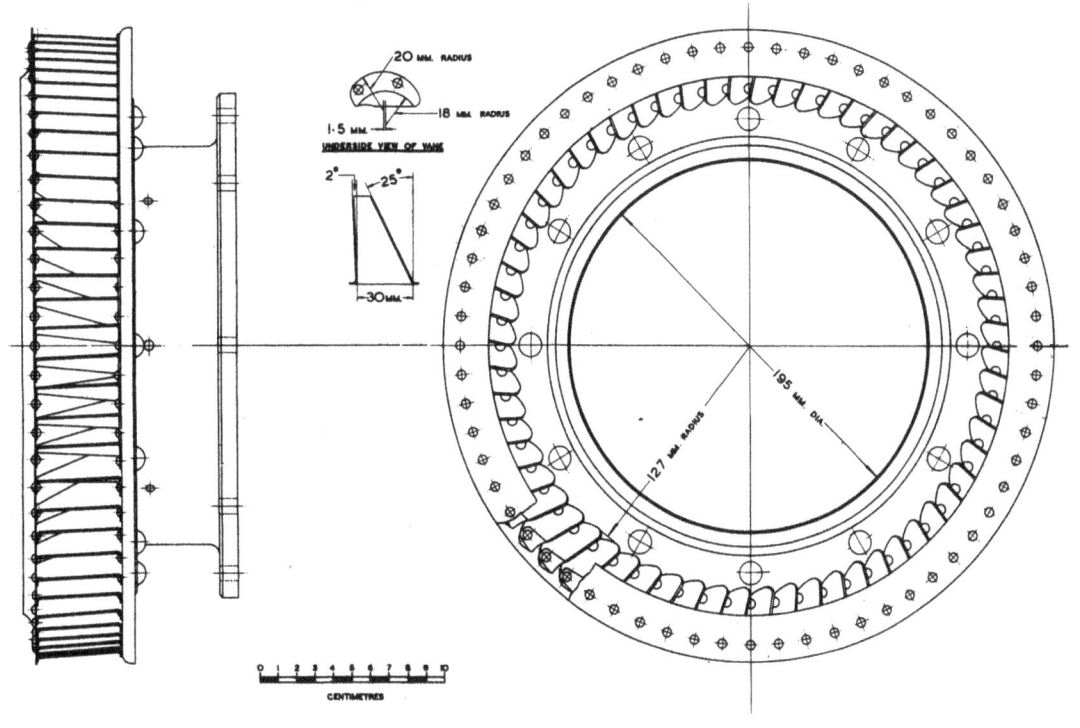

Sirocco Fan

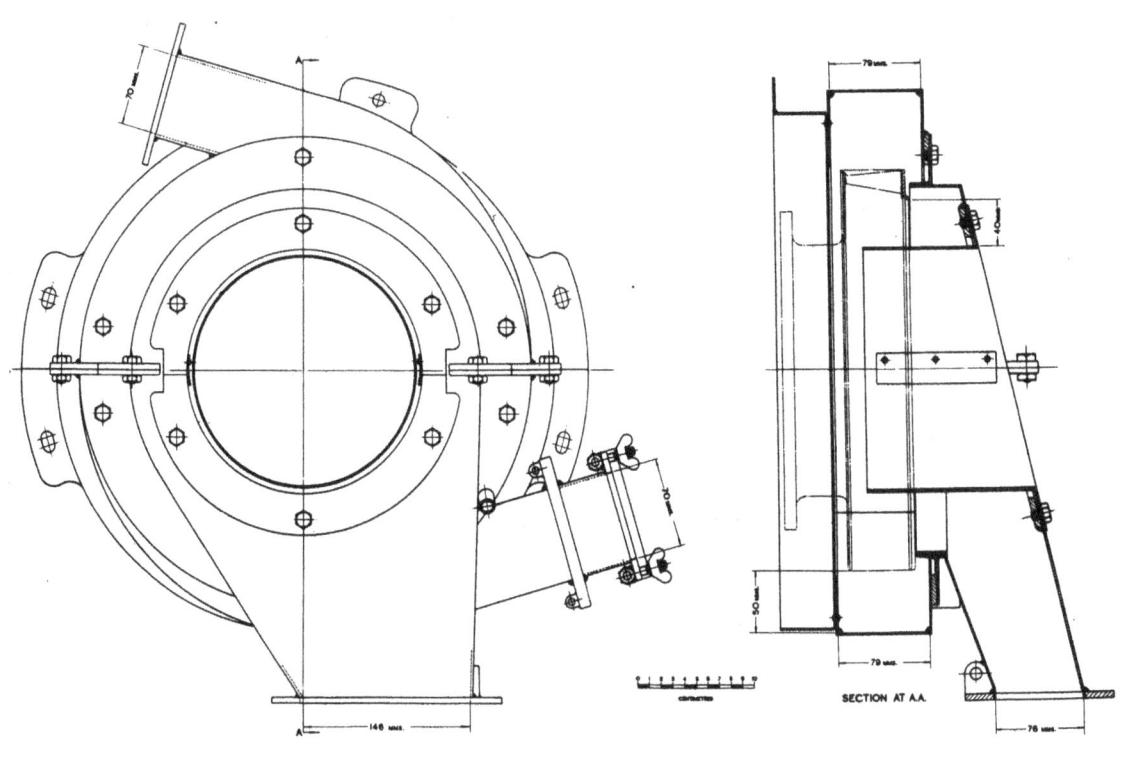

Volute Housing

SUBMERGED RUNNING

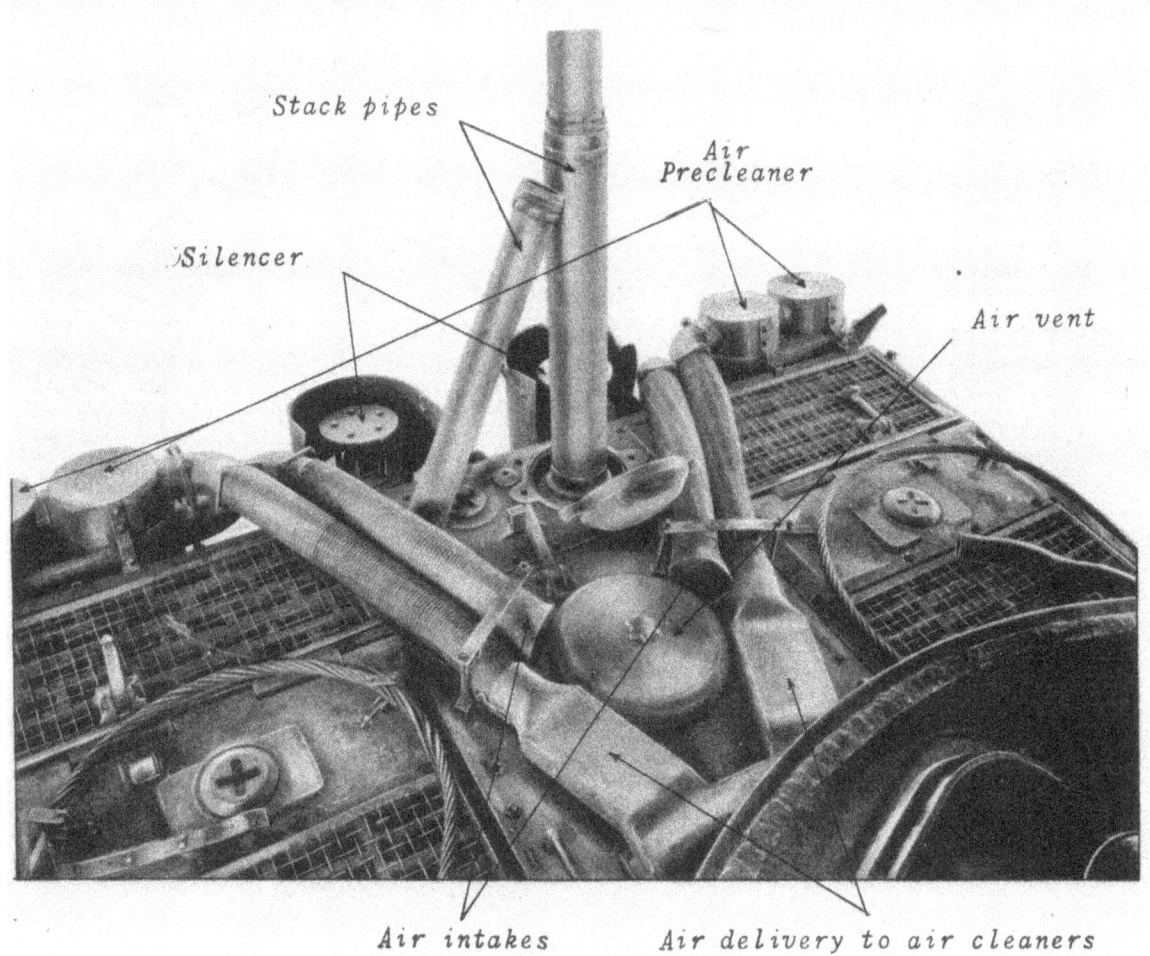

The fact that the Pz. Kpfw. VI has been designed for complete submersion to a depth of approx. 15 feet has necessitated very special arrangements for ventilation and the supply of air to the engine under these conditions.

To prepare the system for under water running, all the butterfly valves referred to above are closed by remote controls mounted on each side of the rear bulkhead of the fighting compartment. The sliding valve in the induction trunk of the air circulating fan is moved to the rear and thus air is taken entirely from the front of the vehicle through the gearbox cowling, and delivered as before through the exhaust jackets to the air chambers at the rear. As the butterfly valves are now closed it cannot pass into the radiator compartments as before. The two chambers are interconnected by a trunk fitted with a pipe incorporating a butterfly valve, now open, and thus the air is discharged into the top of the engine compartment. Air replacement for the crew and engine is effected through a stack pipe which is erected at the rear of the tank. The pipe is in telescopic sections and, when not in use, the three upper sections are stowed in the lower, which is permanently fixed to the inside of the tail plate in the engine compartment. Spigotted loosely into the lower section is a pipe connecting to a rectangular section trunk on the floor of the vehicle. This trunk has an open end terminating beneath the turret floor.

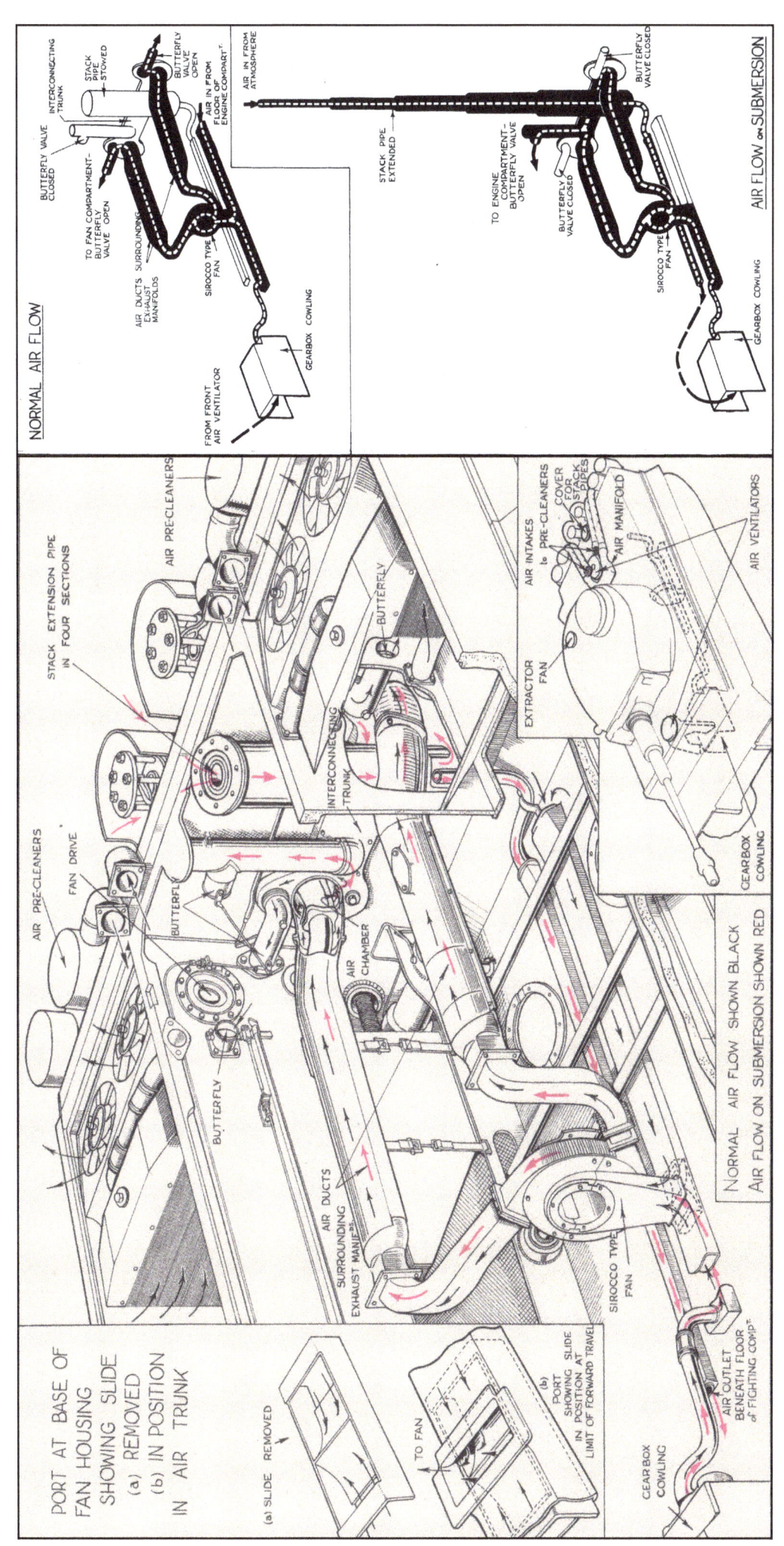

www.ingramcontent.com/pod-product-compliance
Lightning Source LLC
Chambersburg PA
CBHW042021090526
44592CB00022B/2847